WRITERS REPUBLIC

WHERE PAINT GOES

THE ART THAT AFFECTED MY LIFE AND THE LIFE THAT AFFECTED MY ART

LARRY LEWIS

WRITERS REPUBLIC L.L.C.
515 Summit Ave. Unit R1
Union City, NJ 07087, USA

Website: *www.writersrepublic.com*
Hotline: *1-877-656-6838*
Email: *info@writersrepublic.com*

Ordering Information:
Quantity sales. Special discounts are available on quantity purchases by corporations, associations, and others. For details, contact the publisher at the address above.

Library of Congress Control Number: 2021930614
ISBN-13:   978-1-63728-116-1   [Paperback Edition]
                     978-1-63728-117-8   [Digital Edition]

Rev. date: 01/08/2021

Thank you to the folks who have had a memorably good effect on my existence.

(not listed in order of importance)

William Allan

John Singer Sargent

Winslow Homer

Marshall McLuhan

John Muir

Martin Luther King Jr.

Shel Silverstein

Ansel Adams

Kathy Pacheco

Bill Birnbach

John Huggins

Brad Holland

Frank Frazetta

Ruth Grant Lewis

Angel

Hein

Gary Lewis

Pete Chichester

Steve Borges

Herardo

Lawrence Alma-Tadema

Jean Day

Richard Schwerin

Disclaimer

The names of some characters in this story
have been changed to protect
both the innocent and the guilty.

Prologue

I paint, I sculpt, I have designed and constructed lots of stuff. Writing was never in my playbook, and I can now admit that committing myself to this project was a bit overwhelming. I know little to nothing about grammar, I spell "fenetically" (phonetically), and I have read to completion a total of maybe eight to ten books in my lifetime. I'm not saying I'm stupid just challenged when it comes to the written word.

My life, I figure, is just like yours: lived out over time.

"OK, so why write a book?"

I believe that art imitates life as well as life imitates art.

That being said, since I was recognized as, and possibly even nudged in the direction of being, a little advanced artistically from a very young age, perhaps my artistic endeavors had an effect on my life choices and/or how I have approached life in general. Has this in turn affected the art I produce? The following is an account of how I remember my life to present: How the art I have made has affected my life, and how the life I have lived has in turn affected my art.

Just Getting Started

I have vague memories of my earliest days. Playing in the sandbox with my next-door neighbor, riding down the hill on a tricycle you know, regular stuff. Prior to my arrival in the family, my father served in the Navy aboard a supply ship attached to the Pacific Fleet during World War II. After his discharge, he secured a job as a union house painter. Wishing to address his spiritual needs, he attended a Baptist seminary, after which he enrolled in a Christian university located in the Midwest US to study theology in preparation for becoming a minister. My two older brothers are a product of that time. After his graduation from university, my father was offered the pastorship of a church in California's Bay Area. Not much time passed before he became disillusioned with the requirements set forth by the convention governing his ministries, and so he returned to being a union painter. This was around 1953, the same year that I came into play. Even though he had left the ministry, he had not lost his faith. Till his death, he still subscribed to the dogma and doctrine of his faith.

I lived a relatively normal and boring life as a child. I was brought up in a very religiously moral environment by a loving and supportive family. I was recognized as a "creative person" at an early age, and from what I recall, was always addressed as such. Even though I was raised in such wholesome surroundings, I always felt out of place, not ever quite fitting the mold. At one time, I believe when I was seven or eight years old, I thought I might go into the ministry to follow in my father's footsteps. This was as short-lived as many other aspirations of my youth: mortician, architect, archeologist, anthropologist, marine biologist, illustrator, cartoonist. I was drawn to all of these noble ventures, but there was always something missing in the formula for the journey. At that point, I merely forged ahead in my youthful life without a clue.

My childhood was well insulated from the "real world." Church and school were the avenues available to me for outside input. Due to my parents' religious convictions, home was much like church. I was six and seven years younger that my two older brothers, they being only one year apart. The two of them spent time together and were involved in social activities together. It seemed I was always a tagalong. So much of the family energy went toward servicing my brothers' combined needs that the only reason I was included was because I was too young to leave home alone. Do not get me wrong I was not in any way traumatized by this situation. It just seemed to be challenging for me to make my own path in my brothers' shadows.

One memory sticks out in my mind from when I was about five or six years old just starting school. My family had a black and white television at the time, and "B" grade science fiction movies were becoming quite popular. More than likely, it was with my older brothers on a Saturday afternoon that I was witness to a movie that featured a giant tarantula. I do not remember the title or plot of the film. What I do remember is what happened as a result of watching the movie. With no real demands on me at the time, the biggest thing in my existence was "play." We lived in a subdivision located on the outskirts of the town where I was born. There was lots of open space and rolling hills. One afternoon after watching this movie, I was exploring the hills just beyond the confines of the neighborhood. I looked out over the horizon and could, in complete detail, envision the giant tarantula coming over the top of the hill. Unable to rid myself of this horrific vision, I ran home in terror. It was not until much later that I realized this was my first experience with creative visualization and imagination. "Whew, buckle up!"

My imagination rapidly developed in early elementary school, but at the time, I did not have the skill to set anything to paper. I was lousy at coloring. I looked at other students' work and saw that the kids who colored with a light touch and stayed inside the lines received the best grades and got the most recognition. Therefore, that is what I did. Not being satisfied with this easily acquired menial skill, I began to draw. I wanted to create the images that were meant to be colored. For some reason, I was constantly drawing battle scenes so much so that it disturbed my teacher, and a conference was called with my parents. The outcome of the meeting was that I was told by all involved to stop creating the disturbing images, and if I wanted to draw, I should illustrate nice or pretty things. I saw this as an act of suppression. My response was to continue drawing my ideas of choice, only not openly. I would draw nice and pretty things to show to my teacher and parents while I continued to create bloody battle scenes for my closest of friends and for myself, which I would throw away after sharing with my confidantes. I guess it might seem to some folks that I have some behavioral issues.

My attention gravitated to my developing drawing skills. Reading was a hard concept for me to grasp. Math was impossible for me unless I could visualize it. Others began to notice my artistic ability. Subsequently, all the attention and energy given by important parties was directed toward my creative actions and less toward my struggles with learning the basic systems of academic operation. This would become a great challenge for me in the future.

I now had an ability and desire to create images and/or recreate things that I might see by drawing them on paper. Looking back, I must now conclude that this skill was something inherent to me. I was not taught this or given instruction in this action by anyone. Who knows? It could have been a simple behavioral response mechanism, rewarding me for doing good things you know, like training a dog.

While serving my term in the third grade, an opportunity arose: a regional contest set forth to all elementary schools. The task was to create an image of a litter bug. Wow! This was my chance to touch the big time. I thought long and hard, creating what I thought to be the perfect representation for the task. Sometime after the deadline and all the works were collected, a school assembly was called to announce the winners of the prestigious Litter Bug Contest. I was so excited. I knew in my soul that I was a contender. For some reason, I was standing in the back of the multipurpose room near my teacher. On the stage, an adult representative held up a drawing, announcing that it was the overall winner of the contest. It was not mine.

No problem, there was still a chance for recognition. Next, the presentation of the district winner: the representative held up my very own creation. My eyes were wide with excitement. Silently inside I screamed, "Yes!" All this wonderful delight came crashing down when the person on stage called out another person's name as being responsible for this masterpiece. Confusion, fear, and sadness came over me immediately. Even more painful, the name announced was a friend of mine; he promptly went to the stage to receive his undue accolades.

My teacher noticed the tears running down my face and inquired what the trouble was. My response: "That's mine, I did that." The teacher promptly went forward to inform the parties involved that a mistake had transpired. After a brief moment of uncomfortable confusion, the other student was led off the stage and I was called to take my rightful place. The pageant was not at all what I had envisioned. To this day, I am unsure what I took away from that experience. Was it to thoroughly make sure that your name is plastered all over the art you wish to claim as yours? Or, when presenting your artwork to the masses, realize we are imperfect beings, and much more so when gathered together, so "buckle up"?

I continued to draw, gaining more acceptance and responses from family and peers. I was still struggling with basic academics, since the instant recognition I received simply by producing images on paper was far more alluring than a basic education.

My family moved somewhat frequently around the time I was thirteen. One of the moves proved to be quite memorable. We moved from a primarily white, middle class area to an inland, ethnically diverse area. I believe this was done under the auspices of affordable new housing, but whatever the reason, this action was a shock to my system. One day I was running around in a sea of white folks, no consideration for cultural or ethnic diversity. The next day, I was confronted with a multicultural, semi-urban, declining industrial social structure of which I was totally ignorant and in which I was ill-equipped to exist. And, oh boy it was time for puberty to kick in, a wild time in everyone's life. I wished most of all for acceptance. Living in the suburbs, still a bit insulated from the most dramatic factors of my new environment, I was nonetheless confronted with a new urban existence: a new hierarchy of peers, and new forms of community overall. A white skateboard punk thrust into multiculturalism. In those times, it felt like I was navigating through claymore mines every time I walked down the sidewalk. After a few interactions and confrontations, I chose a more passive, camouflaged track.

The racial makeup of the area was representative of the whole world, with homogenous white folks being the minority. Looking back on this experience, I am thankful for this opportunity to expand my horizons. I learned straight up, people are just that: PEOPLE. A short time later, listening to a speech delivered on TV by a pudgy black minister, what I learned on the street would solidify into a belief structure that I still rely on today. Judge people by their actions and the content of their character. This simple ideal has become a true asset in my life.

That being said, this brief time of my life was a bit messy. It being the late 60s, so very much was happening and changing all over the world. I joined a street gang, mainly for survival. As I said earlier, I chose a passive, camouflaged path. Regarding gang membership, I will not elaborate or glorify any actions of this involvement other than to say that it was a hideous/heinous way of life. Although I thought that I got pretty good with unwrapping a butterfly knife and still bear scars from my time there, from what I know now, my involvement, battles, confrontations, and criminal behavior were not only worthless, but just plain wrong.

During this time, I was also drawn to music, and eventually started a band with a few friends. I myself was just learning to play guitar, and none of us were very good at addressing our prescribed musical disciplines; however, we actually played a school function and a city venue, the latter of which turned ugly. Regarding the event that went south, the "mouth" (the band's promoter) promised us additional equipment, which for some reason never materialized. We did what we could with what we had. It was not enough! A large group of volatile youth congregated in a small place the scene got messy quickly. I recall two things from that disastrous night. First: my perfect willingness to purchase and consume a handful of pills offered to me by a stranger the definition of stupid. Second: that my safety was not as secure as I thought it was. I saw a friend of mine surrounded by hostiles, being beaten and kicked. I jumped in and pulled him out by his legs to relative safety and yes, most of the disturbance was racially charged.

I was still in contact with folks who lived in the area we had moved away from, and I was traveling back and forth frequently and it just so happened that it was very easy for me to get ahold of weed. A few times, I returned to my new home with such product, which I then turned over to a couple of influential African American kids with no mark up. Bought it for $12 an ounce and gave it to them for $12 an ounce. Because I was overly fair, ridiculously ignorant of standing capitalistic buy and sell principles, discreet, and obviously financially ignorant, I was accepted and tolerated within the immediate black community. This proved to be very useful in the near future when "race riots" broke out in my school.

One day, about a month later, pretty much a regular school day, the halls were mostly clear of people following several physical confrontations between black and white students. The school was being evacuated and the police were on their way. I was with an acquaintance of mine, and we thought we were the only ones in the hallway. Soon, I saw a gang of black kids advancing toward us; the kid I knew was between the group and me. He was unable to escape, and as I was attempting to exit, I saw this kid brutally beaten. I was next, and it was all happening so fast that I was unable to find an exit before the mob was upon me like locusts on a cornfield.

Just as I was grabbed up, a voice rang out from one of the kids whom I'd had drug dealings with: "Stop." Incredibly, I was passed over. Lots of police, lots of news coverage. It was 1968. A lot of stuff happened in my life that year. Music, sex, violence, drugs, awareness (self and otherwise), an introduction to the art world, realizations about religion, and confusion about most everything.

Biology and US history were the two subjects that actually sparked my interest at school. My history teacher engaged his students by proposing we construct a viable constitution to govern the operation of the class. We all jumped in with grand enthusiasm, creating legislation, governing bodies, and people's rights. Midway through this experiment, the teacher came into class one day, closed the door, and put a cover over the door window all perfectly constitutional, given that he had been elected the president of our small nation and we had created no laws to stop him from taking such actions. The teacher then demanded we all empty our pockets and display any and all of our personal possessions for his inspection. This created an immediate uproar! Beyond just "personal stuff," over half the class was in possession of both weapons and drugs. The teacher then enlightened us that we had not established any standard for search and seizure. According to the laws we had set forth, this action was perfectly legal. After a bit of anxiety, all complied. Blades, cigarettes, pot, pills, pipes, and other various items showed up on the desktops. To the amazement of the class, instead of ratting us out to the proper authorities, he instructed everybody to put all of our stuff away. Then, he went on to express that this was a demonstration of our ability to comprehend our governing body and how it can affect us. My first experience with how government really works or doesn't. Great stuff!

The "hippie" movement was going strong back then, and I fully embraced it, as was manifested in my attire, the music I listened to, my use of mind-altering substances, and finally in my creative endeavors. Still only drawing and cartooning, I was producing works on paper with so-called "psychedelic" lettering as well as cartoons with sociopolitical content. I was mainly doing this for myself to attract attention and acceptance. It seems I was successful in this: I was asked to be the official artist for the school's yearbook. Upon accepting the position, I found myself responsible for the cover art, some inside cartoons, and illustrations for advertising. It was not very challenging, as everyone was easy to please.

Also, during this period, I took on a photo-essay project to use in the yearbook and school paper. Using my brother's SLR camera, I was tasked to roam the school snapping candid, hopefully creative photos of stuff happening on campus. I did this for a little over a month, and after reviewing the images I produced, the instructors and students involved in both publications were pleased with some of the shots and planned on using them in both the yearbook and school paper cool. Alas, after the administration stepped in, some of the images were deemed inappropriate, so the project was scraped. What a waste!

Regardless, I was suddenly the "school artist." Now that I had folks' attention, I thought I might try to cash in on my newfound recognition. I created a whimsical cartoon of the football team accompanied by two flashy unclothed females. Obviously, this was prior to my learning about women's rights I was an adolescent male chauvinist pig. I then made several copies on the copier in the library, which I then offered to a couple of the football players I was acquainted with, for a dollar a pop. The two boys snapped them up without hesitation. I asked if they would be kind enough to advertise to the rest of the team.

Within a few days, I had amassed an impressive $14 along with orders from the basketball and baseball teams for a similar product. It was then I thought to myself, "Why limit my offering to only sports when I could have most every male in the school as clientele?" Rising to the occasion, my next work was of a couple, in a sequence of images that began with the two fully clothed and progressed to the final image where they were in naked and intimate embrace. Again, to the library for copies, this time making only a few at a time. The response was staggering. After a bit more than a week, I was sitting on an extra $47. My imagination went wild, thinking I might enter the ninth grade dripping with wealth.

But soon, all of my thoughts of wealth and riches came to a screeching halt. I had never considered that my works of art might fall into the wrong hands. A few students' parents had become aware of the illicit materials I was producing. An investigation ensued, and when students were interrogated, they sang like damn canaries. All fingers were pointing directly at me. The school principal called a parent conference I could imagine nothing worse. I was charged with soliciting illicit sexual material on campus. My parents, being fine moral folks, were mortified. The outcome of the proceedings was unimpressive at best. My parents were embarrassed, and I was told never to engage in this type of endeavor again. I was informed that I was being watched by the school not much of a deterrent. This was my first experience in the exchange of money for artwork. It was also the first time that I was confronted with the idea of "demographics."

Shortly after this incident, I attempted another project. Equipped with raging hormones and a newfound interest in marketing, I envisioned a seemingly new, innovative way to flex my advertising muscles. Accessing my infinite youthful wisdom, I thought I might take a stab at "*shotgun marketing*," this time targeting the young women of the school. I would sneak into the girls' restrooms at times when I thought I would not be disturbed and scribe upon the stall walls messages like "A GREAT KISSER," including my name and phone number. Other come-ons included "HOT LOVER" and "LARRY'S EASY."

My theory was that my messages, taken with other messages written by girls in the same area, might be presumed as credible information. I expected the outcome to be a possible encounter with the opposite sex. This project turned out to be a bit of a task, as there were several girls' restrooms on campus, with each restroom housing several stalls. The project required a fair amount of time and stealth to avoid detection, the realistic odds of which I did not figure into my evaluation of the process. Toward the completion of the project and upon exiting one restroom, I ran right into the dean of boys. It was an unfortunate event, since I had already been tagged as a sexual deviant. I was dragged directly to the administration, where I was interrogated. Not wishing to be perceived as a pervert, I openly expressed the intention of my actions. In retrospect, I probably should have said I just felt the need to hang out in girls' restrooms. My real intent was far beyond the grasp of the folks I was dealing with. My parents were called in once again and were both very embarrassed once again. The principal of the school *strongly* advised that I retain professional help. In response, my parents suggested that it would be handled through the church, which would hopefully bestow some divine intervention.

I was suspended for the rest of the week. Upon my return to school, I received a mixed welcome. It had gotten around what I had done. I was greeted by some of my male counterparts with a series of high fives and "atta boys," but the general population offered misunderstanding and disgust. Now, many years having passed, I look back on the experience as the investment not being worth the return. Although one girl, inspired by my efforts, did make contact but no, I did not get laid.

As I said earlier, I struggled with academia altogether, but I took an interest in biology, mainly due to the quality of my instructor. Unfortunately, he did not remain my instructor for long. At one point, the teacher had failed and kicked out of class a certain gang member. Shortly thereafter, this student confronted the teacher in the hallway, which ended in a brutal beating and stabbing. In defense, the teacher fought for his life and struck the piece of crap who stabbed him. After his stay in the hospital, the teacher was fired, and the local newspaper provided a negative slant on his actions. The piece of crap kid was expelled for the rest of the year, spent a few months in juvenile hall, and returned to school the following year. This just did not make sense to me. Where was the logic in trading the education of this damaged kid, who in all probability would be nothing more than a burden to society, for the career of a bright young teacher who had already helped hundreds of kids with his tutelage and who, without interruption, in all probability would have gone on to assist hundreds more? It was a travesty.

Our culture seems to pay attention to those folks who scream the loudest, with little regard for integrity, justice, or common sense. Just saying.

As I was being conditioned to be suspicious of authority, I was also becoming more interested in music and gaining attention from the opposite sex. At the time, I was at least smart enough to leave the gang scene. My attempts at the visual arts were still undefined I was mostly doing drawings and cartoons. At this age, my bedroom was my sanctuary, and my father had agreed to let me express myself within its confines. I began by painting high contrast images of my favorite rock heroes on every surface available to me in my tiny environment. This was my first attempt at using paint to express myself.

An opportunity was presented to me when my older brother, while studying art at San Francisco State college, was offered the chance to attend an arts conference in New York with a group of fellow students. An extra space opened up and my brother (I am still unsure to this day why or how) wrangled the spot for me, a fifteen-year-old punk, to tag along. For about a week, we shared a room on the fifty-fourth floor of the New Yorker Hotel. I was granted the privilege of experiencing New York and got to tour the Guggenheim, the Metropolitan Museum of Art, the Museum of Modern Art, and a few galleries in SoHo and Greenwich Village. This was a real eye-opener at fifteen. Unfortunately, I came down with pneumonia and was physically miserable for most of my stay, but it was still a great experience.

Back to California, where I was still flexing my creative muscles in drawing, cartooning, and music. I continued playing the guitar and was becoming more familiar with making music. It seemed as though the timing was right, as this period was rich with change and innovation in the music industry. Living in close proximity to San Francisco, I had musical history happening at my doorstep. On the scene were bands such as Jefferson Airplane, the Grateful Dead, Quicksilver Messenger Service, Big Brother & the Holding Company, the Byrds, the Ike and Tina Tuner Revue, the Doors, the Who, the Sons of Champlin, and Buffalo Springfield. Most of the big names of the time were booked at Winterland, the Avalon in San Francisco, and Pepperland Auditorium in San Rafael, California. Myself being only fifteen at the time and residing in the East Bay (Contra Costa County), thirty to fifty miles from these musical meccas, it was challenging to attend such concerts on a regular basis. Luckily for me, for some unknown reason, after playing at these historic venues in San Francisco, these bands all would come inland to small towns and do gigs in, for example, a gutted grocery store turned auditorium in Concord, CA where I lived. For the most part, I was able to partake of these performances for an admission of around five dollars, although it was a bit of a task just to get to these places because I was not yet old enough to drive.

The first time I attended a concert at the aforementioned grocery store music hall, my father drove me and a friend although he did not know where he was taking us at the time. I knew my parents would not approve, so I had my father drop us off on the street just below the auditorium. This worked out great on the way there, but after the concert, when my father returned to pick us up, it did not go quite as smoothly. After the concert, we exited the building through the main entrance. This is where everyone congregated after the concert to smoke whatever they happened to be smoking and yap about the band or whatever was "happening." As we were leaving, just beyond all the cigarette/pot-smoking, long-haired, wildly dressed folks, I could see my father waiting for us in the car. Not a word was said as my friend and I slipped sheepishly into the back seat, but I could see by the look on my father's face that not all was right with the universe.

After a bit of time passed silently, my father indirectly offered up the question, "What kind of place is that?" I do not remember my exact response, but it was something like, "It's the place to go to hear the newest music." I do not remember the response, only that it was an uncomfortably quiet ride home. After dropping off my friend and returning to the security of our home, I do recall my father, with great intensity, letting me know in no uncertain terms that I was never to go to that place again. To me, this threat simply meant that I must be more creative in my travels. I was able to orchestrate going to that place many more times without the consent or knowledge of my parents.

I especially recall two such occasions. The first was when I went to see the Ike and Tina Turner Review. I was a boy just touching puberty. After a few opening numbers, Ms. Turner hit the stage wearing nothing but this little net dress. I was positioned front and center to the stage this experience was life-changing. I was both bewildered and amazed at the effect this act had on me. The second time was when I had the opportunity to go with a most unlikely companion, considering the friends I usually kept. I was acquainted with this girl at school, Gala, she was not very attractive or very popular, yet for whatever reason, we related to each other. She asked if I wanted to go with her to see Big Brother & the Holding Company on tour for their new album *Cheap Thrills*. Hell yes, I did! She even had transportation via a friend. I made the appropriate arrangements on my end, telling my parents I was staying the night at a friend's house, and we then made our way to the concert. Upon arrival, we could see that the place was packed. Janis Joplin (who was then the lead singer) and the band were gaining notoriety at the time. Once we got inside, Gala asked if I would like to go backstage and meet the band. I was in a state of shock. Gathering my menial senses, I offered a positive reply. My friend led me backstage, where we entered a medium-sized room that was just off the stage. There were quite a few people crowding the space. In all my excitement, I could still make out Janis and the other members of the band. Gala took my hand and guided me through the crowd. All at once, I found myself standing in front of someone I considered to be a goddess of contemporary rock music. Introductions were made; I was so starstruck that everything after that is a blur.

As time drew close for the concert to begin, my friend and I made it out to the front of the stage. The lights went down, the band came out, and the music flowed like water in a fast stream. After a powerful delivery of "Combination of the Two," Janice recognized her friend at center stage Gala standing next to me. When she bent down on the stage to acknowledge her friend, Ms. Joplin also reached over and gave me a kiss on the cheek! Everyone was screaming and clapping; I could barely realize what had happened. Janis rocked the house for the rest of the night. Gala and I caught a ride home, where we orchestrated a few covert maneuvers so that each of us could show up bright and shiny on each of our respective doorsteps the following morning. Over the next few years, I would have other opportunities to meet and rub shoulders with some other music icons, but nothing that would measure up to being kissed by Janis.

I was not the best at deceiving my family. Unlike my older brothers, who were well aware of how to keep their play and exploration within acceptable parameters, I was both too ignorant and too adventurous to know what boundaries were. I continued to explore my new environment to the fullest. I seemed to find myself in trouble more often than not so much so that my mother convinced my father that we should leave the area and return to an environment that offered a few less unsavory distractions for me.

Thirteen Through Sixteen Years of Age

To summarize the extraordinary and sometimes curious, attention-grabbing events of my young life during those crucial years between thirteen and sixteen, I offer the following thoughts. I experienced the contrast of being struck in the face for the first time (which was humbling) and of striking one back (which I found empowering). There was the realization that with a little bit of effort, I could get away with a lot. I had sex for the first time, which I found at the time to be a bit overrated. As for drinking my first beer: I hated it. I smoked my first cigarette, had my first experiences with drugs. My first few choices included pot, hash, reds, yellow jackets, cross tops, bennies, and mescaline. One of the more useful things I learned back then was how to drive a car with a clutch. I also had my heart broken for the first time maybe even for the first three times. Those events also awoke in me a realization that religion and the church were not what I had earlier perceived. I discovered reading was not so bad, and devoured author Marshall McLuhan's *The Medium is the Massage: An Inventory of Effects*; however, at the age of fifteen, I did not have the capacity to comprehend all of its statements. The opportunity to travel surfaced for me back then, to visit and ride the subway in New York City. However, more importantly as pertains to my life as a budding artist, I was able to visit some of the great museums in New York, also visiting several times the De Young Museum in San Francisco, the Crocker Art Museum in Sacramento, the Berkley Museum of Art, and the Oakland Museum of Art.

Returning to an area (Concord, California) I was both familiar and unfamiliar with was once again a shock to the system. I was confronted with new sensibilities, a new hierarchy of acceptance, and old connections in a new environment. I experienced both bliss and frustration. Having no secure footing, I found myself becoming extraverted in an attempt to make myself appear larger or "more" than I truly was. This was a time of conflict. The social environment in rapid flux after my long absence, I found myself on unstable ground. I wished to be accepted while I struggled to set myself apart. As I just said I was a bit conflicted. By way of the arts, I found both acceptance and isolation. I recognized actuating my creative nature to be a formidable tool. Being who I was, I journeyed forth with little consideration for responsibility or consequence. Through my actions in the visual, musical, graphic, and theatrical arts, I found myself elevated to a multilevel realm of involvement. Never having had to embrace this type of influence before, I had no idea the power invested in my actions at the time. I found myself available to all conservative, liberal, radical, quiet, loud, aggressive, meek, creative, intellectual, popular, unpopular, good, and bad. In this way, I was afforded touch with all. Damn, if I had only known how to manipulate the social and political power I held in my hand! The possibilities are staggering.

The late '60s and early '70s were a whirlwind. So much happening in such a brief time. It was hard to keep my footing. I believe this particular time in one's life (puberty) is challenging, at best, for most folks. For me, this phase included realizing my level of importance (or unimportance) regarding social status, acting on emotions without a clue, attempting to address a brave new universe, wrestling with the rites of passage to adulthood, and accepting or rejecting new levels of responsibility. That is a lot of elemental characteristics to develop in just a few short years. Looking back, I am amazed there were not more casualties.

The First Sign of Tremors

The first time I recognized that I had a little "shake" in my right hand, I was about fourteen years old. Not very noticeable, and it had little effect on my attempts at drawing and painting. I was still quite proficient at drawing a straight line and using a brush to cut a straight edge. Over the next few years, the shake remained very slight; however, I noticed it had not only worsened but had expanded to my right lower arm and was showing up in my upper trunk. I finally shared my annoyance with this issue with my parents. My parents, who were both completely enthralled with "modern medicine," jumped into action, rushing me off to the nearest neurosurgeon. After a great many uncomfortable tests and I might suppose just as many dollars a sloppy but acceptable (to my folks) prognosis was offered: I might be having many tiny seizures. This, coupled with the perception of the dimwitted so-called physician that I might have underlying emotional and/or mental issues, was the rationale for the manifestation of the tremors. Because a doctor said it, it was both fact and truth to my folks. I was immediately put on antiseizure medication with talk about antidepressants to be added as well. I was not convinced or pleased with this outcome. I reluctantly acquiesced and took the damn meds which, for your information, had no effect. After a time, I simply stopped taking them, with no change to my symptoms. Fifty years ago, modern medicine had more resemblance to witch doctoring than it did to the practice of the medical arts. Little did I know that this condition would evolve into the debilitative challenge that I continue to deal with today. After a time, I simply stopped taking the prescribed medications, which had no effect on my symptoms. I decided to go about my day-to-day business, ignoring my tremors, for now.

High School: Sixteen to Eighteen Years Old

These years were in essence a balancing act. In addition to moving back to the old hood, I was also compelled to explore the realm of drugs, both legal and not. Sex was becoming commonplace as a way to feel connected and find release from the everyday. Education and literacy were more about trying to fake my way through high school with a fourth-grade reading ability, limited vocabulary, poor spelling skills, and little to no knowledge of mathematics. Oddly enough, I was actually nominated for a scholarship in recognition of my artistic talents only to find that I never had a chance of receiving the award. One of my high school counselors at the time expressed to me that with my limitations, I should realistically consider the military. Hmmm? It was 1970, which was a bit more than halfway through the Vietnam conflict. I did not think that was going to work for me. I did enjoy adventures in cartooning at that time, having great material to work with: Ronald Regan, Richard Nixon, Vietnam, drugs, et cetera.

Just when I thought I had found my niche in life, I had to deal with issues like my art teacher telling me that I would never be a painter. Music particularly getting to know the bands was big for me. A battle between the visual arts and music was raging within me. Being absent from school was also becoming an issue as I became quite creative in finding ways not to be at school. Then there was the fact that even while I was at school, I was not totally there. In addition, as I found myself moving away from the church, a rift began to form between my father and me. Now, I was experiencing a new dimension of having to balance artwork, music, and doing my best not to be involved in school. Right around this time, a fortuitus meeting took place on one of those few days I was actually at school all day. I being a long haired, do anything to avoid academia, roll in music, art and babes' guy, was on lunch break, resting near a tree, intently sketching, creating a new character and totally unaware of anything going on around me. A break in the silence, I hear a voice from above, "what are you doing there?" I looked up to see a clean-cut, handsome young lad, I did not recognize. Being a bit caught off guard, I did my best to respond to his question, we had a brief conversation, after which, he went on his way. Little did I know, this was the beginning of a lifelong friendship, this person would be evident and influential throughout my life, John. Fortunately, I discovered the joy of backpacking. Finding a place for myself in the wilderness was a way for me to once again or maybe for the first time connect with the basic reality and joy of living. The fact that my skills in the arts were still developing did not stop me from attempting to offer them at any given opportunity. At one point, I made contact with a couple of classmates who informed me they were in a band. Earlier on, they had expressed to me that they were in the market for a bass player. With reckless abandon, I offered that I was just the guy they were looking for. The truth was, I had only been playing guitar for a bit over a year and was not very good. Now that I had presented myself as a world-class rock star, I had to come up with the goods. Being not completely ignorant of amplified stringed instrument manufacturers was a start, but having no equipment nor any means of acquiring such equipment, nor having the ability to play a bass, became imminent challenges. I immediately began pressing my father for funding. I offered the premise that funding this project would be a great investment in keeping me out of trouble, bundled with the notion that I would be able to repay the funds with proceeds from the band's earnings. Amazingly, this argument worked! One week after my mad sales pitch, much negotiation, and some dedicated hours becoming acquainted with the new monster of my creation, the moment of truth arrived. On the day of our first rehearsal, I showed up with a big presence, performed marginally, and was immediately accepted into the band. The band stayed together for about eight months, and most of that time was spent practicing. We did play a few gigs, one them paid, but my share of the proceeds was apparently not enough return on the investment that my father made (to hear him tell it). Ultimately, all of us ended up going our own ways to pursue grander interests along with me pursuing the lead singer's girlfriend.

I wished to compose music, become more accomplished at acoustic guitar, and sing. At the time, I thought it made more sense for me to advance my musical skills toward becoming a "crooner" rather than a rock star mainly because I thought ballad singers might get laid more. Amazingly, this is about the same time I reconnected with a comrade from my past via my immersion into the various arts offered in high school education at the time.

Dichotomy: Being compelled to create and express one's self in such a manner to an end of making a thing of significance, while wrestling with the realization that your presence in the universe is about as significant as "a speck on a gnat's ass" (the dictionary of Larry L.).

Music was the bond, and an immediate connection was formed in one meeting. Eric and I had an inherent vocal harmony: shared progressions flew like birds flocking in the sky. It was a truly magical moment. We stared at each other in amazement, agreeing that we had to do something with this. We shared more and more time with each other, attempting to expand our musical horizons. It was no surprise when we formed a group. Much of our time and energy was spent with the idea that we would become recognized as wonderful.

In our exuberance, we failed to realize what was required beyond enthusiasm and modest talent. We had no idea of the importance of the emerging new science of "marketing." Ignoring the importance of branding, trends, demographic alliance, and/or our target market, we were destined to fail. The other required element we were ignorant of was commitment not only to our craft, but also to the concept we had birthed. A third person joined in our musical endeavors, Mike, a gifted improvisational flutist. We played together as a three-piece group for about year, creating our own music: Eric and I) playing guitar and singing, the third playing flute, percussion and third part harmony. We did a few gigs and began to receive a little notoriety.

Toward the end of our flash in the pan, a promoter wanted to book us for a local concert with second billing to the Byrds. I was crazy ecstatic and could hardly wait to share the news with the band. When I first shared the information with Eric, I was shocked by his response. Not only was he *not* excited, but he went on to express that he was leaving the band and moving to Los Angeles with his girlfriend. This was not at all a good time to receive that kind of news. In an instant, I was told that we would not be playing the concert of a lifetime, and that the band no longer existed. Damn!

Yes, I was a wee bit angry, but worse, in my bitterness, I stopped playing and writing music for a while. After I cooled off, I picked up my guitar and began to play and sing once again, but never with serious intention. I played for myself, sometimes at social occasions, and I did play a few weddings. I guess this period was instrumental in my choosing a discipline. At this point, I was just starting to truly embrace the visual arts. Once again, I was being recognized as a creative, being drawn into the industry of communication, specifically graphic arts, journalism, and cartooning. When I signed up for a class in journalism to meet the English requirements for my grade level, I had no intention to further my limited knowledge of English. My desire was a simple wish to take a chance with my emerging abilities regarding visual communication. Because I was established as the resident artist/cartoonist, my journalism instructor took a chance on me and offered me the responsibility of a cartoon strip published twice a month in the high school newspaper. To this day, I still do not know why he was willing to take such a gamble on me. I took on the challenge, creating *"Your Backwards World, Comix for the Blind."* I illustrated a world divided into two equal halves. It was inhabited by metal clad, well-armed creatures that had wheels (where legs and feet would normally be placed); and each creature possessed a human like face. I named the characters "Rads" and "Cons," short for radical and conservative. In the cartoon strip, I offered satire on current social, political, and religious issues.

My work was met with mixed response. I recall one day the instructor was out and we had a substitute filling in. When I arrived in class, I found the substitute studying my cartoons. She asked if I would stay after class for a moment. She was very enthusiastic in expressing how she was impressed with my abilities. She mentioned that she knew a group of professionals who were in the process of creating an illustrated publication. The prospect of this excited me to no end. She offered me a way to make contact with the group; I eagerly accepted and set up a meeting with them. I thought I had struck gold: little did I know I was about to step into the realm of education by experience.

It was about a 150-mile round trip from my comfortable suburb to the tragically hip metropolis point of meeting. My sketchpad full of what I thought to be brilliantly creative concepts accompanied by copies of my cartoon strip was tucked neatly under my arm. I had arrived! Soon after ringing the bell at the address of my *new destiny*, the door flung open. I quivered at the vision confronting me and knew instantly that I *was not in Kansas anymore*. Standing before me, just inside the threshold, was a large, seemingly middle-aged woman with a massive mop of frizzy white hair, sporting a long black lacy gown, complete with a cape. She was holding some sort of smoldering herb in one hand and attempting to move her other hand near my face and head in some ritual manner.

After a moment of handwaving and chanting, she confidently offered, "You're clean. You may enter." Completely bewildered, I obliged, instead of opting for the more sensible route of running for my life. I entered into what I perceived to be a totally hip, upscale hippie pad decked out with all the trimmings. I, wishing to put my best professional foot forward, had been on time which caused me to spend an uncomfortable half-hour or so alone with the "cleansing witch." That being said, at the age of seventeen,

I did indulge and enjoy the offering before me of a little wine and some pretty fair hash. One by one, the other exalted creatives arrived. Finally, after much fanfare and rhetoric, the so-called reason for being there began to emerge. The meeting started with presentations of what each of us was bringing to the party. In the general order of things, I was not one of the first. As the presentations were being offered, themes began to emerge: urban renewal, ecology, organic food, and better education, to name a few. I could not believe my ears. This bunch of weirdos wanted to band together to create an *educational* publication with the intent of addressing and solving *real* issues? Upon presentation of my work, I was considered to be "out there," my concepts too obscure, not in line with offering real solutions. One longhaired gnome was bold enough to come right out and call my work weird.

I returned home more confused than before. My work had been deemed too obscure by what contemporary society was calling the fringe. Although this was hard to swallow and a bit confusing to me, this event might have had something to do with my moving away from journalism and graphics and toward "fine art." I placed a 2' × 3' piece of plywood atop my dresser in my bedroom to act as a drawing board: my first "studio." I began exploring the idea of using quill and ink with light washes of watercolor to construct images of architecture: old buildings, abandoned vehicles, alleyways, barns, and sheds. This seemed to be a logical transition from cartooning to visual art. I really knew nothing of painting beyond my father's work as a union painter although this was not much help to me in embracing the visual arts. I was ignorant of color theory, composition, surface, equipment, and materials. In other words, just about everything. My ignorance posed no deterrent I blasted forward without a clue. I did not show up for school much during this time, but when I did, I made sure I was there for my art classes. Try as I might, over and over again in the realm of practicing "classical visual art," I sucked! My high school art teacher was a staunch and unforgiving English woman for whom, unlike most of my other instructors, I actually had a little respect. Once, after reviewing my work with her full commitment, she expressed to my face, "You will never be a painter!" Although I recall this particular moment, I am unsure if her comment was instrumental in my quest to become just that. Several years later, I met with her and humbly offered examples of what I had accomplished. She reveled in my work and humbly expressed, "I was a needed challenge to you, but possibly a bit arrogant and not very supportive."

Facing my Indifference

I was very busy during my senior year in high school, just not with school. I played music, I had my cartoon strip for the high school paper and graphic work for various organizations within school, and meanwhile, I was producing work for my first art gallery connection. Also, I began producing editorial cartoons and images for a local newspaper, exploring my connection with "the woods," pursuing girls, and having girls pursue me. All this while wrestling with my spiritual convictions and trying to fit in, while trying to set myself apart. Most of these ventures had little or nothing to do with my academic advancement. As I mentioned before, I worked hard at expending the least amount of effort possible to accomplish the standard requirements of high school.

My counselor pulled me from class in the last month of my senior year to inform me of a complex challenge. Even though I had done my best at paying as little attention as possible to academia, I was due to be recognized for my accomplishments at the school with a $200 grant for the arts from the PTA, a $50 gift from the school for my involvement in art-related projects, and a $5000 scholarship from Bank of America to use toward any institute of higher learning for my involvement in the arts. As much as I was surprised, I was also truly thankful, as I had done little to prepare myself for the idea of college.

"Not quite so fast," said my counselor as he then explained a bit of a problem. Apparently, the $250 prizes were a given, but the $5000 award was in question. My counselor added, "The issue at hand is that you have a failing grade in US history." In general, I actually liked history. However, the particular teacher for the US history class that I was about to fail was a World War II vet. As such, he fashioned the course as much as he possibly could around the US involvement in World War II, which held little interest for me, especially with the Vietnam police action hanging over my head. He lost me on about day three of the class. On the other hand, my counselor seemed to think that my future was something worth fighting for and so he set up a conference for the three of us, during which my counselor, acting as my advocate, inquired if it were possible for me to do any form of makeup work to raise my grade from an F to a D.

"NO!" replied the teacher. "He did not make an effort in my class; thus, he should fail the class."

My representing counsel pleaded, "If we cannot find a way to alter this situation, he will not only lose the opportunity to involve himself in higher education, but he also will not graduate and will have to return to school to repeat the class."

The hard-ass bastard responded with, "I am fully aware of that." That was, in his mind, only fair. In remembering this time, I do not know what I did to piss this instructor off, other than not showing up for class a lot and not turning in too many assignments, but the consequences of both our actions managed to alter my future. The slimy thing about this whole experience is that a couple of weeks later when I was no longer eligible for the scholarship, the little man changed my grade to a D so that I would graduate.

I took away two lessons from this experience. First, when challenged with a project, even if it goes south, meet at least the minimum requirements or risk the possibility of losing all. Second, if a single instructor was to have such power over the forward movement of a student, I wished to have no more involvement in the academic experience. This last bit of time before I graduated got very tricky. First, and foremost, I was about to make the galactic jump from the comforts and securities of home and attending school to the "real world." I was in all respects unprepared! My school counselor, who had vigorously represented me so I might entertain the prospect of matriculating to college, was suddenly guiding me in a different direction. With all his wisdom, he expressed that since I had only menial academic skills and no "usable" skills beyond the arts, my only recourse was to consider military service. This recommendation was offered to me in 1971, just a few years prior to the close of the Vietnam conflict. What he was telling me, at that particular moment in time, was that my best option was to hurl myself off a cliff. I did my best impersonation of civility and basically told him to go screw himself. There might have been a few more choice words thrown in to my response. But it wasn't just my guidance counselor. My parents along with many other adults who had been supportive of my creativity and involvement in the arts for the past twelve years had all begun to sing the very different tune of, "You can't make a living with art; you need to cut your hair and get a real job.

In the Woods

Throughout this era of self-exploration, I heard the call of the wild. No! Not the insane lure to indulge in all that youth had to offer at the time, although that was a constant ringing in my ears. It was a different voice an invitation to commune with nature, to experience firsthand what wonders the "woods" had to offer. I am not sure exactly what the draw was. My family would go camping, one older brother liked to fish, both of my brothers had been boy scouts, and I grew up in suburbia nowhere near the wilderness. And then, all at once, it was in my face. Names like John Muir and Collen Fletcher, locales such as the Pacific Coast Trail and Desolation Wilderness, objects like freeze-dried meals, Palco cups, and topo maps these all became a part of my vocabulary. "Backpacking," as it was called, became a new indulgence. I went to the Sierras as often as I could. More often I would take part in this indulgence with one or more of these three folks, John, Steve and or Lynn. The short list of my backpacking partners in crime. Three days, five days, then up to twelve days: it was narcotic. Toward the end, I got involved with cross-country skiing and mountaineering, purposely going into the woods in the late winter and early spring to experience the woods and high country covered in the cold white stuff. Over a short period, I had equipped myself adequately well for my indulgence. Via reading or experience, I familiarized myself with most all the particulars regarding backpacking, snow-packing, and mountaineering skiing.

The last snow-packing trip that I took turned out to be a bit of a disaster. Shortly after I graduated from high school, Steve a fellow snow-packing enthusiast and I planned a short trip into the Desolation Wilderness area, near Lake Tahoe. I believe it was mid-autumn. There was already a lot of snow, and it was pretty cold, but off we went. A weather front had moved through the area the previous night, dropping a fair amount of new snow on top of a substantial existing snowpack. This offered up a challenge as the highway we needed to use was now closed, leaving us with no access to our intended destination. Plan B? Out with the maps to consider alternatives! We decided on an area about twenty miles below our original site the first of a few poor decisions made during this particular trip. Completely wrapped in the ripstop nylon with down filling of cold weather gear sleeping bags, hooded parkas, mittens, down pants, and booties packs fully loaded, we began skiing up the trail. After several hours of trudging upward in three feet of fresh powder, we found ourselves atop a small ridge at 9,000 feet ASL (above sea level) with a spectacular 360-degree view of the surrounding geography. It seemed to be a great place to make first camp. By now, it was late afternoon with darkness coming soon. We had originally thought of constructing an igloo, but with so much powder, the idea was shelved. Instead, we built a "snow cave," digging a rectangular pit in the snow, placing pine branches over the top, and then piling more snow atop the branches. We then angled in an entrance at one end. The enclosure was wide enough to house both of us with a little room between us for a camp stove. Melting snow for water, we prepared our evening "freeze-dried" feast and had a cozy lie-down dinner. After we ate, we just yakked until it was time to sleep.

I woke early and was eager to get out and ski around the area. I geared up expedition boots, down pants, down vest, down coat with hood, down mittens, wool facemask; I was set for the cold. The sun was not up yet; it was -20 °F and the wind was blowing at a good clip. I am unsure of the actual temperature considering windchill; I do recall being colder than I had ever been before. Steve, "the smart one," was still fully encased in his down mummy sleeping bag. The visuals were more beautiful than I could imagine, the High Sierras blanketed with white and the sun on the rise. Skiing out for about thirty minutes, I began to feel a remnant from the previous evening, featuring our freeze-dried extravaganza. I needed to remove my wool mask and loosen my hood so I would not puke on them.

In order to accomplish that task, I had to remove my mittens. I thought I was being mindful of the time that I was exposed to the cold. I was not wishing to expose bare skin to that kind of cold for too long. Oops! After attending to necessary business, I realized my nose, lips, and all my fingers were completely numb and white. Looking at my hands, they began to turn blue. Not a good thing.

I managed to cover my exposed body parts and make my way back to camp, where "Smart Boy" was still in bed. I crawled into the cave and asked Steve to heat up some water. While I was waiting, I lay face down with my hands under my body. As my hands began to thaw, the pain started. It was as if hundreds of mad bees were attacking my fingers. After a few hours, having regained some feeling other than pain in my extremities and making a visual assessment of my hands, we both agreed that I was affected by some degree of frostbite. We talked it out and decided it best to return to civilization. We left the hills for home, my knuckles, nose, and lips peeling, bleeding, and displaying a few darkened spots. The trek out wasn't as hard as coming in, but it was still a good two or three hours of skiing to get back to the car, then a four-hour trip home. Upon our return I went to the emergency room at a nearby hospital, where I was treated for second-degree frostbite. To this day, when the temperature drops below 60 °F and my hands are exposed for even a short amount of time, my fingers begin to turn white and grow numb. Needless to say, after enduring this experience, I did not spend much more time snow-packing.

Back to the art stuff. Against my parents' wishes, I was determined to break into the arts industry. A close friend of mine, Steve, the same friend I went snow-packing with was also inclined to work in the arts, and we decided we were going to "go for the gold." Both of us were loaded with lofty ideals and youthful energy. After a small amount of uninformed research (no internet at this time), we believed that we had identified a location where we might make a living while we constructed a platform from which to become recognized as important artists our Mecca: Monterey, California. Steve and I assembled what we thought were the required tools. First and foremost, we needed funding. We pooled together the riches we had amassed over the last few months, which added up to the impressive sum of about two hundred dollars. We had a car that would at least get us there. We selected a few discriminating examples of our work to offer up as proof of our brilliance. Finally, we had our attitudes: We were the next force to be reckoned with in the history of the arts.

Our journey began with great enthusiasm. Upon our arrival, we scored a map of all the galleries located in the area. We set ourselves to task introducing ourselves at one gallery after another. After a few exhausting hours, we began to recognize a trend: the galleries were completely impervious to unsolicited offerings. This realization put a damper on our whole project, and we began to simply collect information in order to salvage our efforts. Hours passed as our brutal education continued. It was not so much that we were being rejected as it was that no one was interested in what we had to offer. What a heartless industry! After a couple of days of abuse, Steve and I returned home with our tails between our legs and thoughts of the alternative: "Cut your hair and get a real job." It still saddens me today that the art industry is set up to discourage emerging artists when it could promote and encourage them.

My Art: *"An intuitive journey that I survey and map along the way*

In this period of uncertainty, I hooked up with a girl I knew from school, Linda, who was a couple of years older than me. I guess when one is confused, they are likely to make erratic choices? Choices like hooking up with a girl you normally would not choose to hang out with and, in an attempt to accept guidance from my elders, I also agreed to get a "real" job. I took on an apprenticeship as a union house painter, working out of the same shop as my father, although this career move would be short-lived. In my younger years, I had worked with and listened to my father concerning residential, commercial, and industrial painting, and I had actually become pretty skilled at the trade in the process. It made no sense to me that I would have to endure a three-year apprenticeship making $3.21 an hour. Nor did I see any sense in having to work a forty-hour week while attending between eight and sixteen hours of evening classes every week at the local junior college, this being a requirement of the union for an apprentice. An additional kicker was that out of my nothing paycheck, I still had to pay union dues. All of this while being confronted on a daily basis with the fact that I was indeed as qualified or more qualified than most of the journeyman painters I worked with journeyman painters who were all making $25 an hour plus benefits. This was just a wee bit frustrating! This existence screamed to me, "You do not belong here!" I lasted less than six months. When an opportunity arose to work with my older brother in visual presentation, I jumped on it like a starving animal. Before I knew it, I had stepped into the "World of Display."

But back to hooking up with Linda. I was still living at home with my parents, but I wished very much to flee the nest. I knew this girl from school; we did not run with the same crowd and had never paid much attention to each other. However, she bailed me out of a jam, and the next thing I know, I think I'm in love. The relationship was firming up; we were seeing each other pretty much every day. She had already moved out on her own and was sharing an apartment with a friend. I began to verbalize to my friends the importance of my budding relationship. I was a bit surprised at their votes of no confidence, and even more surprised when the Linda's mother took me aside to express her concerns. She offered, "I like you. You seem like a good boy," and continued by way of warning me that her daughter was not the person she seemed to be. All of this caution became moot when Linda informed me that she was pregnant everything changed in an instant. Provided with this information, the parents who had previously expressed caution were now demanding that marriage was the only option. A difficult gesture at best, as her family was devout Catholic and mine was Southern Baptist. Her father refused to recognize the union unless I converted to Catholicism, and my father was warning that if I were to leave the church to become a Catholic, I would be sinning against God. We were not given much of a choice, were we? To the dismay of all parties, we ran off to Reno, Nevada, and eloped. Go figure? This began seven years of a ridiculously absurd existence during which time I came to realize the girl was not the person I had married: just like her mother had warned me.

There were real conflicting interests in our relationship. I wanted to advance my artistic endeavors, but her only aspiration was to make babies and do little else. During this time, I continued to work in visual presentation while my wife worked in retail food preparation; together we managed to carve out a menial existence living paycheck to paycheck. Under duress, I continued painting. I recall few times of joy or happiness one of those few joys was watching my daughter Lina grow up. While becoming a father had not really been part of my playbook, I would do my best to grow into the role. Lina, was true adventure from the start. In the beginning we shared a magical connection; unfortunately, in time, that connection would be interrupted and not quite so magical. I tried desperately to keep connected with the arts. Via my ignorance, I sought only what was readily available to me: art fairs, award shows, and invitational art exhibits in Northern California. For the most part, I did okay, collecting a box full of ribbons and some cash awards to supplement my regular income that averaged $500-800 a month. I took part in an invitational show in Sacramento, California, where the Crocker Art Museum purchased one of my works for their collection. Not too long after that, I made contact with the de Young Museum of Art in San Francisco. The people there requested a set of slides representative of my work to place in their archives. I did manage to get my work into and maintain relationships with a couple of galleries. I was even afforded the opportunity to present my work at a few one-person exhibitions.

All of my creative peers were immersing themselves in the college experience, of which I was highly envious at the time. I tried to keep close to these folks to build any networking possibilities; however, I found I was simply on my own. When I would get together with my "college art" friends, who were all studying under folks like William Wiley, Bill (William) Allan, Robert Arneson, and other art gods of the time, I could not help but notice that when it came time to "talk shop," all I ever heard was "this is a study on that" or "I'm working on this study" or "I'm almost done with this study." Did no one have completed paintings or sculptures to offer? Yeah, I know they were learning. Later, I would find out that for some, offering one's work as a "study" was a disease contracted in art school. If you offered your work as a "study," you did not have to stand next to it and say "I'm completely responsible for this work." When viewers were critical and ripped you a new one, it was okay because it was not your *work* it was just a "study." I found this behavior to be most cowardly.

"Standing in front of a blank canvas is still one of the most frightening things I can imagine. Looking at a blank canvas is like being confronted by the abyss." –L. Lewis

Attempting to juggle my new family, my work in display, and my desire to create fine art was turning out to be a handful. I was still doing drawings and ink, but more and more I found myself drawn to paint. Not being the most patient of folks, but having already had experience in applying water-based ink with a brush, as well as experiencing adjusting values by means of adding water, it seemed the logical next step would be to explore the use of watercolors.

It seemed as though I possessed an inherent and immediate grasp of the fundamental attributes of this medium. After a few introductory attempts, I zeroed in on a suitable technique that was patterned roughly on treatments I had observed from Andrew Wyeth, N. C. Wyeth, and Winslow Homer. My knowledge of color theory, however, was very limited. I picked up a couple of books on the subject and began to acquaint myself with it. Who knew that later I would be teaching color theory? Working in retail display, I began to be recognized for my abilities in prop design and construction. I advanced from Display Manager to Shop and Property Foreman as I moved from department store to department store, learning as I went. I was working with different materials such as plastics, foams, Mylar, wood, and metals while experimenting with the physical attributes and limits of their application. In this way, I was also becoming familiar with the basics of physical engineering shear strength, tensile strength, stress, load-bearing capability, structural integrity, and weight distribution.

In the mid-1970s while I was a display shop foreman in a department store, I worked with an older creative woman, Mrs. Day.. She was a very different sort of individual, the type of person I had not come in contact with before. A bit older than my parents, she was socially and culturally aware, religious and moral yet open to new thought, creative, and above all, dedicated to living life well. She introduced me to CA *Communication Arts* magazine. This slight gesture opened a connection that would change my life, opening my eyes to a completely new universe. I was familiar with graphic arts, visual presentation, and the raw fundamentals of promotion and marketing, but it was not until now that I finally saw that the connection between all of these industries was "communication." It was an epiphany I just did not know what to do with it. Gradually, I began to connect the dots, first by applying my creativity more toward the graphic arts, with a fair amount of consideration to logos and corporate identity. Suddenly, I felt confident in offering my newfound abilities to folks in exchange for money. More and more, I found myself talking to businesses about branding, image communication, logotype, trademarks, clientele perception, corporate typeface, and corporate colors. I was evolving into something I could not before conceive. I was tying my hair back and throwing on suits. Equipped with a few of what I thought were genius logo mockups, I would go pitch my ideas to executives of both large and small companies. It was a big evolutionary jump from being the long-haired artist-hippie type.

My marriage was showing signs of stress. As I think back, I believe neither one of us truly thought we worked well as a unit. We were both just too stubborn to come out and admit it. A few years into the relationship, we attended my five-year high school reunion, which was an informal event, a picnic in the park. It was okay seeing a few folks from the past, but overall, I had already moved on. As the day went forward, both Linda and I consumed a fair amount of draught. She grew more and more uncomfortable at the sight of me having conversations with people who might have been old girlfriends. This came to a head as she was emptying her beer in my face and expressing what a jerk I was.

She finished off with an ultimatum: "If you don't come home tonight, we're through!" Then she took the car and left me stranded there. The way I saw it, I needed to find a place to stay for the night. I partied for a little longer, then found a ride to an afterparty. After I hung out there for a while, I walked to a nearby park and bedded down for the night under a tree. In the morning, I walked home, where all was forgiven which was unfortunate because it just postponed the inevitable.

Into my Twenties

I am fortunate that I was not drafted, which meant that I did not have the misfortune of dying or being damaged in Vietnam during that troubled time as did many of the young men my age. My leisure activities began to move away from backpacking, which was becoming a luxury I could not afford since I got Linda pregnant and was forced into doing the "right thing." The feeling now was that my energies would be better served getting a handle on being a father, even to the point that I began to curb my use of illegal substances.

I would not be pursuing the "college thing," and I had valid reasons. First, my experiences in high school had completely disillusioned me to academia. Did it make sense to set myself up to face such battles again, especially since I was already working in the industry that my course of study would follow? Second, my parents could not afford to assist me in such an endeavor. I was making decisions that could have an ultimate effect on my future, or the perception thereof. Any ideas I entertained of becoming a professional musician were abandoned. However, there was one thing I did not give up thanks mostly to the availability of books and manuals of *carnal knowledge* during that era, my sexual prowess was expanding in contrast to other areas of my life that were narrowing was beginning to address a higher level of conceptual work in my painting practice. At that time, I made the choice between a focus on "illustration" versus "fine art" as my understanding of "what it means to be an artist" was solidifying in my soul. I also began honing my skills in visual presentation (display), which seemed to me to be a gift that I inherently possessed. Through all of it, the ability to discern the difference between "BS" and a qualified offering was undergoing an attempt at development. Unfortunately, I was not aware at the time that nurturing this skill would be a lifelong process. Linda and I made peace with each other after the dreaded reunion debacle, and the experience prompted us to reevaluate our relationship and recognizing we have the responsibility of rearing our new offspring, Lina. Attempting to juggle supporting my newly acquired family, my work in display, and my desire to create fine art was turning out to be a handful. In all of our wisdom, Linda and I concluded that we needed to move. So, we made a few calls, arranged a place to stay, and moved to Chico, a small college town in northern California with the idea that my wife would take a regular job, and I would paint, do freelance graphic work, watch our daughter, Lina and take care of the domestic responsibilities. A weird concept for the time, but off we went. After a short period of acclimatization to our new locale, we ended up on the outskirts of town in a single-wide mobile home planted on about an acre of land. I had a very small studio where I painted (a lot) and did small freelance graphic jobs, and I managed to tend to a medium size vegetable garden while taking care of our little homestead.

During this time of flux, I managed to maintain a solid relationship with one gallery while stepping up my involvement in invitational art shows, art fairs, and award shows.

This was a few years prior to the availability of computer graphics. I found myself doing mostly logos, logotypes, stationery, and corporate identity packages. These were the days of the Rapidograph pen, hot press illustration board, acetate overlay, transfer type, and marker comps. I worked for a wide range of clients, from local woodworking shops and landscape companies to international food distributors. I was making editorial cartoons and illustrations for the local newspaper while creating concept illustrations for local architects. During this period, I was even contracted to create conceptual drawings to pitch one of the "pier" buildings near the Embarcadero in San Francisco as a suitable location for the offices of the Chinese Consulate. At this point, my paintings were becoming more conceptual and were starting to look more like illustrations so much so that I had to stop for a moment and ask myself "should I be an illustrator or should I be a painter of fine art?" Being an illustrator, I could do pretty much the same thing I was already doing, but I would have to do so within the constraints of a client's desires. The upside of being an illustrator was that they got paid more often for their efforts. Still, in my youthful exuberance, the painter's life seemed more noble or honorable. A perplexing question.

Right about this time, a friend of mine contacted me about a symposium that was going on in Sacramento. Not only were the top illustrators in the nation in attendance but they were also doing portfolio reviews. Holy crap what an opportunity! My friend was already planning to go, so I grabbed my seemingly brilliant but less than perfect portfolio and off we went. We arrived at the convention center right about the time the reviews were wrapping up.

I was ill equipped with knowledge of the illustration industry but no matter; there I stood in front of Mark English, Allen Cober, Bart Forbes, and others. These guys were the "rock star" illustrators of the period. They passed my portfolio around, talking among themselves. Then came the questions: "Where did you study?" "How do you develop your concepts?" "Explain your techniques." I did my best to formulate clever responses, which in retrospect were more than likely sophomoric at best.

I did overhear one of these gods of illustration say to another, "This could be the next guy." Wow. As if that were not enough, Mark English presented his card to me, with the name of his rep and phone number written on the back. He exclaimed that his rep was well established and was not taking on any new clients, but in my case, he would suggest an exception.

He also, with big intent, expressed to me: "You will have to move to New York." If you can remember this time, the internet did not exist yet, the personal computer did not exist yet if you were going to do business in a metropolitan area, you needed to be geographically present. I returned home with more questions than I started with. If this was my chosen direction, then wow, what a break. I began the process of summing up myself, my family situation, and everything else I was involved at the time. I knew that if I was going to achieve any level of success, I would have to give it everything I had. Unfortunately, "everything I had" wasn't exactly available for me to offer. At least not without instituting some drastic changes in my life.

My assessment: My family and I were just barely getting by not what one might call "financially sound." My marriage was unstable and had been dysfunctional for several years. We were attempting to raise a six-year-old daughter. Personally, I had never really wished to reside anywhere east of the Mississippi. Although I was fairly competent in the advertising and graphic design industry, at that moment I was not 100 percent involved. Finally, I was just beginning to feel as if I might belong in Fine Arts.

Even with my limited scope in regard to foresight, considering the idea of relocating to New York to establish myself as an Illustrator gave me visions of apocalyptic disaster. I attempted to weigh out all the possibilities, and in the end, I called Mr. English, thanked him graciously, and respectfully declined his brilliant offer. I do not remember much of the conversation, but I do remember one thing he said: "Better you make that decision there than here."

This was a part of the process of myself evolving into a real artist. My involvement was growing to a point where it was demanding much more time and energy from me. Once again, I was growing and moving forward while my partner wished for little more than to make babies and exist. As things progressed, our differences became much more apparent so very much so that one afternoon, I found myself in the hallway of our house sobbing uncontrollably while trying to put my fist though the wall. My aim not being the best, I managed to make direct contact with a stud, breaking the last knuckle of my right hand a subtle reminder that I did not belong there. That same day, I approached my wife and expressed that I could not do this any longer. She was partially in agreement something had to change. We agreed to separate. I expressed to her that she could keep everything. We started the process and very soon after I left, taking with me all that I could fit in a sandwich bag. I found a run-down hotel on the edge of town where I rented a room for $80 a month and continued to paint while I looked for extra work. These were hard times. I had little money, no phone, and no car. I survived on beans and some fresh fruit and vegetables, and when I could splurge, a six-dollar twelve-pack of Lucky beer. Over the next few months, I got to the point where I could share a studio with a local architect. The place was a small two-room building with a bathroom and shower where I could live and work. It was a good move. I was able to network with the architect's clients and provide them with graphic work. In the late 1970s, the graphics industry bore little resemblance to the industry it has evolved into today. Back then, there were no computers, no digital presence everything was accomplished by hand. If you wanted to see it, it needed to be physically produced. This was a wild time. Not only was my work beginning to blossom, but my life in general was becoming a bit more expansive. Since my early teens, I had developed a keen appreciation of perhaps an obsession with the opposite sex. At the time, casual sexual encounters were quite acceptable and almost as meaningful as shaking hands. Myself being in my mid-twenties, I was virile to the max. I worked hard, and a lot. When I was not working, I desired fun and amorous fulfillment.

Now that I had relocated, I embraced the downtown scene. Even though it was a small college town, Chico, California, offered a plethora of opportunities to interact with the opposite sex. On one occasion, I was up early in the morning to work on developing corporate imagery for a new client. I worked till mid-afternoon, then took a break. Next door to the studio was an old, two-story house where five college girls resided, one of whom was a friend of mine Becky, I guess you might say a "friend with benefits." I went next door, Becky and I had an afternoon romp, after which I returned to the studio and hosed off in preparation for heading out to a local hot spot that offered live music and dancing. After arriving at the club and assessing the crowd, I spied a young lady I had seen there a couple of times before. I went to introduce myself, and before I knew it, we were drinking, yapping, and dancing. After a while, she invited me to her place for a little fun. Off we went; after a few hours of play, I politely excused myself and left to return to the studio. By this time, it was near 2:00 a.m. On my way back to the studio, while stopped at a traffic light, a car with three girls inside pulled up next to me; the driver rolled down the window and inquired if I might like to join them for coffee. Yes, I answered. We found a 24-hour dinner and the four of us crowded into a booth. It was obvious the three were celebrating. Come to find out, one of the group was turning forty, and her girlfriends were teasing her that she had not had sex in five years. It was unanimous, I was the one chosen to bed the birthday girl: "birthday sex." We drove back to the studio, where I apologized for the accommodations; we bedded down on the floor of the studio, engaging one another for the next three hours. Unfortunately, the architect I shared the studio with was coming in at 8:00 a.m. I drove the young lady home, then returned to the studio to start all over again. These casual exchanges with many women did not seem wrong, immoral, or bad to me. It was simply life as it was unfolding.

I connected with one woman, Mary, a nurse, who somehow struck me as a person I should get to know. We seemed to hit it off very well so well that I eventually moved in with her. I was painting a lot and trying to settle from my wandering. But as I spent more time with Mary, I began to see some concerning behavioral trends. In hindsight, it might have served both of us better to get to know one another prior to shacking up. Mary worked hard at her job, and when she was not working, she liked to drink a lot. In addition, I soon learned that I only knew the façade. She was emotionally closed off and only pretended to be involved. I maintained a studio in the house. Mary offered me a certain low level of respect as a working artist, I was a curious novelty to her and her close circle of friends.

Still unable to bring in enough money via painting and graphic work to pull my own weight in the relationship, I subsidized my contribution to the domestic unit by any means I could: house painting with a couple of local contractors at $12 an hour was one thing. Another opportunity came through the two local hospitals: patients' families would hire me for $10 an hour to sit with patients who were critical, terminal, amputees, or otherwise seriously handicapped. It was a real challenge and one of the most emotionally demanding projects of my life. For example: I was hired to sit with an elderly woman for several nights. She had just had both legs amputated at the knee. I sat with her at night when nurse availability was at a minimum. Though heavily medicated, she would wake often; she was never quite sure who I was or what I was doing there. She always complained about her legs hurting. I would do my best to calm her; I tried explaining that her daughter hired me to sit with her at night, but she was too heavily medicated to grasp that concept. It worked better for me not to sit too close to her; to just listen and respond to her in a kind and gentle manner. I sat with about ten different patients, of whom four were terminal and died. It was not something I really wanted to pursue as a career.

One of the more physical projects that I took on during this time period was "bucking hay." I lasted only two weeks. In that brief period, I went through two pairs of leather gloves, lost fifteen pounds, worked with men who could barely form a sentence in any language, found that I could repeatedly lift over half my body weight above my head for ten hours, and received $100 in cash at the end of each day. It was a grueling endeavor I would not recommend. My final task during my tenure was to assist in the construction of a "drying barn." One of my newfound acquaintances had giving my name to a local "herb" grower up in the hills. I drove up and met with the man; after an hour or so of conversation, he presented his offer. It started with $8 an hour in cash until the structure was complete. Included were a few stipulations: I was not to discuss what I was doing with anyone, I was to drive safely up the hill so as not to attract the attention of any law enforcement, and I was to follow his instructions without question. I Immediately liked the guy, and agreed to all of it.

As we worked together, we developed a mutual respect. It was hard work, but it was in the woods and it was with good company a couple of my favorite things. After about a month, the project was nearing an end, and one day we returned to his place after a good day's work. Over a couple of beers he had chilling in the creek, he expressed that he had something else to offer.

He began with, "This is a matter of trust. I propose to you that you watch my crop as it is drying." This was big! He added, "For this I will give you $10,000, a pickup of your choice, and any other vehicles you deem necessary, along with any weaponry you wish."

I looked at him, gathered all my composure, and replied, "This is going to take some thought."

He nodded in agreement and added, "I need an answer by tomorrow." I had not taken any notice of the fact that he had earlier asked me to leave my car at the top of the hill, and he would pick me up and drive me to the site. All was good I had just been told I was trustworthy and had a new job opportunity to boot. On our way to my car, he pulled over in a remote part of the woods. Reaching past me into the glove box, he extracted a .45 caliber semiautomatic handgun and immediately cocked it.

With an intensity I had not seen from him, he pressed the gun to my temple and asked, "How do you feel right now?" Other than the thought I was going to soil myself, I could not think of much else.

All I could get out was, "What?"

He lowered the weapon and carefully replaced it in the glove box, then said, "I need you to give serious consideration to what I am asking of you. I am asking you to protect my investment, and in doing so, you need to be realistic about the possibilities." Damn! It was a lot to digest. I returned home with just a wee bit of pee in my drawers.

After much consideration, I called him the next morning and said "NO." I could not accept his offer. I told him, I would do anything else, but not this if it came down to my life or taking someone else's, I was pretty confident I was not capable of carrying out the required action.

He responded, "OK; we're cool."

I must thank him for his abilities in presentation. In the later months after I had moved on, I heard reports about casualties in a hostile takeover effort. In what I guess was one of the few good decisions I've made in my life, I was back to painting full-time, once again without extra employment. Even though I had solid relationships with two galleries, the sales my work generated were not quite enough to support my survival, much less any financial growth. It was time to recreate myself.

A little earlier, I had made contact with James, a relative of mine who happened to be a successful abstract painter working out of San Francisco. I respectfully thought I might gain knowledge regarding how I could improve my status in the fine art industry. After a few phone conversations, James suggested that it might be good for me to visit his studio, where he could review my portfolio and suggest direction.

Finally, a break! I arrived at his studio in the city, which was a full upper floor of an older industrial building with 24' ceilings, freshly painted white walls, hardwood floors, and large windows looking out over San Francisco. I had arrived. I was standing in the place I had visualized for my future self.

He viewed my work with respect, and after a few hours of discussing the workings of the industry, he posed a delicate question: "How would you feel about dropping your imagery and moving into abstract?" It was a big ask! I had been working for over eight years to hone and develop this skill set. I had respect for abstract work, but had never considered doing it myself. I returned home with my life as an artist in question. After a great deal of deliberation, I concluded that if this was a necessary step toward my work being recognized in a grander arena, then so be it I at least would take a qualified stab at it.

No easy task: not only was I attempting to completely alter my approach to the craft, I would have to consider renegotiating with my current galleries or find new ones. In addition, there was the daunting process of learning how to apply new materials in new ways. Basically, I would be reinventing myself.

Being not well funded at the time, I would need to generate an immediate cash flow in order to purchase new supplies. I figured since I was going to be doing completely different work, it might be good to liquidate my old work. At the time, I had accumulated quite a few pieces around my studio. I sent out the call to galleries, family, collectors, and patrons. Not a huge response. One couple whom I considered patrons at the time did respond, however, and were kind enough to bring along a possible new prospect, excited at the idea of viewing work not available in the galleries that was being offered for pennies on the dollar. They plowed through the work like bulldozers. After the smoke cleared, they had set aside about $2000 worth of paper. At that time, with that amount, I could purchase the needed supplies and get by for another two-and-a-half months.

Now, the new person they brought along with them presented a different challenge. With great attention, he scrutinized each work, each time pointing out a flaw or a small element that was not to his liking. He expressed that he was drawn to my work he just could not find anything in the offering that suited him. Since his friends had just scored a bunch of my pieces at great prices, he was reticent to make any purchases from a gallery at retail. His behavior was an enigma to me. He called and returned to the studio a couple of times over the next few days, taxing my time and energy with nothing in return. Eventually, I called him and expressed I had uncovered a piece I had forgotten about. Over the phone, I described the work, being careful to address all the important elements he had mentioned in our prior contact. "Yes. This is the perfect piece," he expressed his wish to purchase it immediately. I offered that I was on my way out of town and would not be returning until the next day. He set an appointment to meet for that afternoon. I set about creating the work I had just described over the phone, which did not yet exist. When he came by, I had just finished the piece luckily, the paint was dry! The gentleman was very excited to see the work, he laid down the cash, and then left a very happy puppy. This exercise offered me some new insight into the psychographic process of purchasing art.

A Concentration of Life-Changing Events

While exploring the possibilities of creating abstract work, I just could not find it within myself to drop imagery completely especially considering that I was still producing graphic work on a freelance basis. I was a busy boy. Meanwhile, my relationship with Mary was failing. I moved out of her place and onto the floor of a shared studio space, though we remained in contact. From earlier times, I had become a bit of a motorhead. I would never refuse an invitation to wrench on cars, and one day she inquired if I would be interested in changing out the brakes on her International Harvester Travelall. Feeling a bit guilty about the part I played in our failed relationship, I said yes you buy the parts, secure a place where the repairs can be done, and I will do the work. Little did I know this decision would affect my life to this day.

She set up the vehicle at a friend's place. I jacked up the rear of the car to access the wheels, placing jack stands under the axles for safety since I was going to be under the vehicle for an extended amount of time. About halfway through the process, I was working under the vehicle when a resident of the property appeared and alerted me that they needed to retrieve something out of the back seat of the vehicle. My response "Be very careful." Then he opened the door, climbed in, got what he was after, and then climbed out and closed the door. During this process, I saw the car wobble a little. When he closed the door, I saw the car over my head move. Fearing for my life, I began to roll toward the side of the frame. My response was quick enough that I was not flattened under the weight of the 1.75-ton vehicle, but not quite fast enough to avoid the full force of the body striking me on my lower back.

I lay on the ground beside the car in shock. I experienced electrical burning sensations accompanied with stabbing pain running all around my lower back. Everybody gathered around and expressed the need to get me to a hospital.

In my delirium, I insisted, "No. I have no medical insurance and not enough money to consider such a thing. Just let me rest." As the hours passed, my back began to swell and discolor, and I was seeing a good amount of blood in my urine, and so I acquiesced and agreed to go to the hospital. Such an ordeal! Of course, I had to show up at the hospital where my ex-wife worked. Not the best of exchanges. Me incapacitated, my ex standing over me in her self-proclaimed official capacity, expressing with great enthusiasm what an idiot I was it was just intolerable. Sucked to be me!

I had lots of tests, x-rays, and stuff. After what seemed like an eternity of poking and prodding, two surgeons confronted me with their assessment of the situation, expressed with concerned immediacy. In their opinion, I needed to be opened up so they might attempt to repair the mess I had created. By this time, I was pretty high, having been injected with mass quantities of pain meds. I was still aware enough to consider two of the more important elements about the proposition being presented to me.

One was the fifty-fifty chance of complications involved in performing the procedures being offered, the other was that financially, I was barely getting by. The thought of funding major surgery accompanied with a prolonged hospital stay seemed ridiculously unobtainable.

My response: "Hell no!"

One of the two cutters offered with the best intentions, "You might die if you don't agree to surgery!" I was faced with little choice on one hand, I might die due to my injuries; on the other hand, financial suicide. There was the idea that I might die in surgery and/or I would face complications that I was not even aware of yet. I was told I had fractured the lobes on three vertebrae in my lower back, had done some damage to various organs on the same side of the body, and had some internal bleeding. "No cutting!"

The doctors and the cutters reluctantly released me and sent me home with a bucketload of pain meds. I had instructions to stay off my feet and do as little as possible. I retired to the studio and, for a bit over a month, did little more than take drugs and lie on my back. My ability to sustain myself financially had become greatly diminished. With a little help from friends and family, I was able to make it through this dark time. On my last return to the hospital for my final checkup, the doctor expressed to me how lucky I was, adding that he had treated a young logger who came into the emergency ward a few days after I was admitted. The man had been pinned between two logs and sustained injuries very similar to mine. The doctor then sadly reported that the young man had since died from his injuries. In time, it seemed as though I had made a full recovery. However, my lower spine was never the same, and now, over thirty years later, it has become a bit of a challenge. Juggling work and clients over this period was a bit tricky, but juggling the various relationships I had going with different women proved to be a greater challenge and was coming back on me like bad lasagna. Just getting back on my feet and attempting to fit everything back in its place, I was beginning to realize that not everything can be reconstructed once it's been damaged.

My Late Twenties

A recap of this time. I was beginning to learn the importance of "patrons" and "collectors" in the career of an artist. I found there were people out there who stepped beyond the idea of purchasing a piece of work simply because it spoke to them. There were folks out there who wished to relate to all I was doing and were willing to put up funds to support my continuing to do it.

At the time, I was completely amazed by this concept. Leaving my marriage with little more than I could fit in a sandwich bag was both harsh and enlightening. Having to recreate myself with little support and even less financial foundation was definitely an eye-opening experience. It seemed I was depending more and more on graphic work to subsidize my life, which made me wonder "why not just do graphics?" Every time I entertained this thought, there was always a voice deep down inside screaming "you're a goddamn artist, now get on with it!" In an attempt to come to grips with this inner battle, I continued progressing in both fields.

I was still living in a small college town in northern California, so wildness was readily available. For a time, I took up residence near the college, above a bookstore where the entire floor was made available for artist live-in studios. I lived there with two other artists, "Crazy Paul" and "Fast Eddie" both very colorful characters, one having returned from studying in Europe to complete his master's degree in fine art and the other completing his BFA in "making paper." A ridiculously insane time at best. One thing we three art gnomes shared was the Madison Bear Garden located right across the street, a very colorful tavern with booze, food, and entertainment where we all spent a great deal of the time when we were not working.

While occupying this studio/residence space with my two fellow artists, I resided in a relatively small room with enough square footage for a drawing table, a small open closet where I kept my clothes, a small refrigerator, a hotplate, and a designated space where I slept on the floor. I remember a time when my parents paid me a surprise visit. I was painting trout on a Saturday morning when there was a knock at the door of my studio. I opened the door to find my mother and father standing at the threshold. I was a bit surprised and a bit overwhelmed. Immediately, my mother was overtaken by the thirty or so dried trout heads staked to the doorframe. I have to guess that she was also not amused by the empty bottles of bourbon displayed on my window ledges. Maybe it was that I had not rolled my sleeping bag up who knows? As she entered my domicile, she began to cry. My father simply stood in the doorway and glared at me with discontent. After only a few words, my mother left in tears as my father turned to me and uttered with a great deal of disgust, "How could you?" then followed my mother's exodus.

"What?" I thought I was doing pretty well, all things considered. A good deal of events occurred during these few years that would have a lasting effect on my future. Divorcing my wife Linda, was one thing, but doing so changed my contact with my daughter, Lina not such a good thing. Identifying to myself that creating art was one of the most important driving forces in my life was another; incurring a lifelong injury due to poor judgment and learning how simple choices can produce dramatic unintended consequences was a third. Questioning my reason for existing and developing rationale for my "hows" and "whys" regarding the so-called "ultimate relationship with the opposite sex" a whole bunch of stuff to digest.

I was still visiting the clubs at night whenever I could pull together a couple extra bucks. At one place I frequented, I noticed a gentleman who was there by himself every time. One night, I struck up a conversation with him. He explained he was in town from San Francisco to open a retail store. Immediately we began to discuss business, and over the next few weeks, I assisted him with marketing, advertising, and in-store visual presentation. He quickly became a good client and a friend. One evening while hashing out some projects, he announced that he had found a manager for the store and was moving her up from San Francisco; then he asked if I would help get her acclimated.

"No sweat" I was happy to help.

His new manager had arrived in town and the three of us were to meet at the club that evening. I had no preconceived expectations other than to do what he had asked help her get situated in this new environment. I arrived at the club and saw the two sitting at a table. As I got closer, I could see that his manager was quite an attractive young woman, answering to the name of Kathy. I sat down, and after introductions, we went right into business mode. There was something about this person that was affecting me. After the business talk, we began addressing issues of a more personal nature. As the evening progressed, I found myself completely intoxicated with this woman. My client later excused himself, leaving us to our own demise. We talked, danced, and drank till we closed the place down, after which I drove her home, walked her to the door, and we kissed on the cheek.

Just as I was about to leave, I muttered, "Call me when you need me." As I drove back to my studio and reflected on my actions, I was astonished, questioning these unfamiliar feelings. "What an idiot!" There I was at a crucial moment and all I could muster was, "Call me when you need me." That night, all alone in the studio, I wrestled with my thoughts. I had never before been so stirred by such a brief encounter. I was completely taken by this person. The next few days were torturous at best. As per my parting words and in the absence of a phone call, she obviously did not need me.

After three days of me going insane, she called. She told me that she was working on the finishing touches for the store's opening and that her boss had suggested she give me a call for assistance. Not exactly what I wanted to hear, but an opportunity nonetheless. I jumped at the chance. I pooled every ounce of my energy, contacts, and experience into meeting her professional needs. Over the next few days, we worked hand in hand to secure a "grand opening" for the store. After the successful opening, her boss treated us both to a night out. A good time shared to celebrate our labors. Little did I know this night would have an important effect on my life that would persist for the next twenty years. At the conclusion of the celebration, she and I found ourselves once again at her doorstep. This time, I was able to compose myself enough to express my true thoughts. To my surprise, she offered that she was of similar accord.

"DAMN." We ended up spending a magical night together, neither one of us aware of the adventure we were about to embark on.

We immediately became as one, our experiences shared to the same end. After a brief time, we moved in together; it was an amazing time. In the beginning, it was not so easy, financially speaking, but as we pushed each other forward, life began to change. This was all happening at the end of the 1970s, as everyone seemed to be gearing up for the debauchery of the 80s.

My newfound love had grown up in the suburbs just outside San Francisco, yet she appeared to have a more evolved knowledge of worldly things than I. Prior to gracing our small town

with her presence, she had been living with her best friend, whose romantic involvement was with an older bisexual gentleman who worked as a brakeman for the railroad. This elevated sense of responding to one's social environment offered a fair bit of challenge to my limited sensibilities.

As I said before, I had worked in display more formally known as "visual presentation" or "retail visual merchandising." During the earlier years of my involvement in display, I experienced very little contact working with gay men, who I would eventually come to learn had made quite a place for themselves in the industry at large. I recognize that at this time, I was homophobic; for me to share space with an outwardly effeminate man or a man who outwardly expressed his homosexuality was a challenge. I would eventually outgrow my homophobia. This struggle became, I believe, apparent in my artwork. After moving away from abstracts, I revisited my representational work. Normally, I would produce Wyeth-like imagery of storefronts, barns, and older structures. Suddenly introduced into the mix were wild, brightly colored harlequins interacting with ill-fashioned dogs. I'm sure Freud would have had a field day.

In a short time, my partner Kathy and I outgrew our limited environment. It seemed we had exhausted all our attempts to excel on any level. Neither of us could find any upward mobility within our respective careers. We entertained the idea of relocating to a more metropolitan area, and after some research, we decided upon Los Angeles. The rationale was that with her expertise in retail management and mine in fine arts, residing in or near a large city was the logical choice. My older brother and his family were located in the Los Angeles area, and they agreed to host us until we could get settled. It was done: Within a few weeks of our arrival, we had secured employment, she as a recruit for management in a high-end, high-tension, retail fashion store in Century City and myself as a trimmer in display at a well-known department store.

My First Day of Work in the New Metropolis, Los Angeles

Braving rush-hour traffic in Los Angeles, I made my way to within a few blocks of my fancy new job. While stopped at the red light at an intersection within view of the store, I noticed both marked and unmarked police cars showing up in abundance around my location. All at once, there appeared at my window a police officer fully outfitted in military-style gear, brandishing an automatic weapon. He knocked on the window, instructing me to get down. I lay across the seat of my car, not able to see what was going on. Shouts rang out around me "Freeze, don't move, drop your weapon," etc., after which came a few short bursts of gunfire. I lay plastered to the seat of my car for what seemed an eternity, hearing only indistinct conversation. Next, I heard a knock on the window; it was an officer directing me to move my vehicle. I gathered what was left of my wits and moved as directed through the intersection. At that point, I was stopped and questioned, after which I was informed that suspected criminals in possession of stolen goods had been maneuvering the box truck that had been stopped in front of me at the traffic light; in addition, I was informed that one suspect had been injured in the gunfire. I was instructed to go on my way. I drove the remaining distance to my new place of work. Arriving close to an hour late, I proceeded to unveil my adventure to my supervisor and crew. To my amazement, it met with no astonishment, only a few unsupportive words from my manager: "Welcome to LA." This incident surely set the tone for the next seven years.

We stayed with my eldest brother and his family for a couple of months, until such time as we might bankroll our transition to our own digs. During this time, I began to notice Kathy becoming more dependent on me for all her emotional needs. It seemed as though my life was overshadowing hers. It came to enough of a point that we questioned our relationship. We decided to continue together, even with things being a bit bumpy. We ventured out together on our own to a place in the suburbs of LA and committed to making a go of it.

We moved into a cute little old one-bedroom flat with a windowed breakfast area that I would call my studio. It came with no stove or refrigerator. We had the funds to buy one or the other, but not both. We opted for the refrigerator and worked off an electric cooktop. Both of us were stretched to the limits, attempting to find that elusive place in the universe while existing in the brutal reality of life in LA in the 80s. Continuing my work in display, I began painting once again, which had briefly been interrupted by our relocation. Listening to my inner voice, what came out was abstract expressions on paper. I was calling them *LA Portraits*.

Kathy had found a position with a medical tech company that required big commitment for little remuneration. Our new neighbors were racehorse transporters from the UK a bit eccentric. My immediate supervisor was a handful who required periodic rescue from intense bisexual indulgence. I, at a place in my life after over ten years of involvement in the arts, was seriously hoping to witness some form of return on that investment. Despite moving south, I still maintained a relationship with a few galleries up north. Periodically, I would travel back to resupply my purveyors' resources with my works.

My painting was taking a bit of a left turn around this time. Still working exclusively on paper, I was experimenting more and more with abstract expressionism and distancing myself from more traditional work. My *LA Portraits* series featured some pretty wild stuff, with recurring disjointed creature faces, palm trees, cartoonish cars, cartoonish figures along with statements and quotes written on the face of the painting. They were a bit weird even by my standards, but I was truly becoming emotionally involved in this body of work so much so that on my days off, I would go down to Venice Beach to hang with the street folks. It's a very inspiring experience to share a bottle of Ripple wine while exchanging stories with street folks as the sun sets over the Pacific near some of the most expensive real estate in the nation. As you might imagine, this behavior was not the most conducive to regular home life and, after a short time, came to an end. I continued to work on the *LA Portraits* for a while. When offering the work to several galleries, they were always rejected as being "too raw and brutal." Oh well, on to the next.

I was advancing quickly at the department store I worked for, earning recognition for my creative abilities. My direct supervisor, although a bit high maintenance, was also somewhat of a rogue despite commanding a respected position among the managerial ranks across the forty corporate stores. I had landed in the right spot at the right time for my involvement in this particular industry. All at once, I was taken off of dressing mannequins, changing staging areas, and schlepping floral arrangements and was given full control over the shop, which included actually creating and designing these staging areas, signage, and backdrops.

A few years ago, I had been responsible for this very thing, only on a more limited scale. My weapon of choice was now as it was then *foam core,* a panel product made of Styrofoam sandwiched between two layers of paper. Its uses seemed limitless as I created freestanding signage, wall-mounted signage, backdrops large and small, full freestanding props and staging areas, even a full-size gazebo all out of paper and foam. Due to my perceived creative ability to solve immediate visual presentation issues, I was given free rein in my workings. I was even recognized by others than my employers I was becoming known to the competition: May Co., Robertson's, Macy's. All this was thrusting me forward at a rapid rate. My world was expanding so quickly, I felt as if I could not keep up.

While I was in the fast lane, Kathy was showing signs of being left behind. This was a truly difficult time. Our relationship was still relatively new, yet we had already formed very close bonds and were used to meeting life equally, side by side. The discrepancy in our career trajectories was starting to create stress. Kathy was feeling the effects of being overshadowed, and I was ill-equipped to deal with or understand these unintended consequences. On a daily basis, I felt like a spectator watching what was transpiring in my life. My response was to indulge myself in the absurdity of the moment, instead of stepping back and taking time to nurture my troubled relationship.

During this time, I reconnected with my good friend from high school, Steve, you remember, the young man who joined me on the journey to Monterey, California so that we might become renowned artist and the same person that was with me snow packing in the high Sierras where I had issues with frostbite, you know, that guy. Who had moved with his girlfriend to southern California to seek their fortunes a story similar to my own. Good times ensued, and we began to spend a lot of time together as couples, growing very close. I had worked with Steve in display in my earlier years, and so I was eventually able to help secure a position for him on my team. It was a great comfort to have a close friend working by my side in such a bizarre environment.

I continued to paint, but on a lesser scale as my creative energy was being directed to tasks at hand. For a brief moment, there seemed to be a calm in the rush forward. That being said, it was the 80s, and I was working in a flashy industry populated with colorful individuals who were overly ready to embrace the times. Periodically, my supervisor would greet me upon my arrival to the workplace with wild tales of his encounters the night before, accompanied by an offering of a little "Bolivian marching powder" to keep the upcoming day interesting.

The temporary calm soon returned to the wild thrust forward I had become so familiar with. As I mentioned before, there was growing tension between Kathy and me, and even though we both loved each other deeply, she felt left behind. We discussed the topic at length on many occasions only to conclude, in our youthful ignorance, that it might be best if we separated to find our own paths. It was a ridiculously idiotic assumption! Heartbroken, I stayed in LA and she returned to San Francisco. This period produced as much adventure as it did anguish and pain.

Alone in LA

As I mentioned before, periodically I found cocaine being offered to me at work. It was viewed as a nice gesture, sharing. Toward the end of my time working in the store, I noticed it was becoming more and more readily available, largely thanks to one of the head members of the visual team.

I was about to embark on a short journey that would prove to play like a disturbing crime drama from the 80s. During the time I had been working at the store, I had developed a friendship with the supervisor I mentioned. I was aware that this guy lived life in the fast lane. Even though he was little more than a display man, his existence was flamboyant. He spent a good deal of time with folks in Beverly Hills, hung out with celebrities, and seemed to be partying at the hottest clubs in town *all the time*. Surprisingly, one day he asked if I would like to join him in his adventures. I was ecstatic at the invitation. I thought that I might experience in real life the things I had only ever seen on TV. We drove to a huge villa-style dwelling on the lower side of Beverly Hills. Rolls-Royces, Bentleys, Ferraris, etc. surrounded the place. Every vehicle in sight cost more than four times my annual earnings. Welcomed by all, we casually strolled in the front entrance to a place filled with indulgences that I could barely conceive of. Music filled the air; "beautiful people" were everywhere you turned. Food, booze, and drugs were ubiquitous. The level of excess was truly unbelievable. After being there for a while and indulging myself in various worldly pleasures, I began to piece together the foundation of what was going on. Basically, a group of wealthy so-called friends had somehow managed to make direct contact with a cartel in Columbia to purchase and then distribute around half a million dollars' worth of cocaine, and these folks were partying on their perceived profits. It was a fundamentally bad idea that would turn sour in no time.

At the height of all of this, my friend informed the display crew he was taking a few days off to visit Hawaii. A stretch limo arrived to receive him at the end of the workday, all the crew standing at the curb waving goodbye and bidding bon voyage. Just before making his exit, he motioned for me to come to the car. I approached the door of the limo to find my friend reclining with an older gentleman alongside four barely clad beautiful young women. Strategically placed in the center was a small table holding a plate piled high running over with cocaine. He shared a little toot and off he went, returning in a few days to invite me to witness more insanity.

Due to the recognition, I was receiving for design and construction of in-store props and signage, I was offered a position at corporate headquarters as one of two head designers (the official title was Promotional Concept Designer). This was a huge leap for me on many levels. I would be going from in-store visual shop manager, where I had minimal responsibilities beyond showing up five days a week and making visual aids on a limited budget, to being responsible for conception of projects for forty stores involving vendors like Estée Lauder, Levi's, Calvin Klein, etc. Please note that I was also as yet unschooled in the political workings that exist at the corporate level.

After I accepted the position, there was a sixty-day period before I actually made the move. I did not realize how much could possibly happen in so brief a time. Kathy and I had already separated, and I had moved into a small studio in downtown Los Angeles. It might be important to point out that at this point, I was in my late twenties, not unattractive, newly separated, and reverting to old habits of immersing myself in the opposite sex. Prior to my partner and I separating, several women at the store where I was working had made their interest in me known. At that time, the advances were unimportant to me, but in the absence of a romantic commitment, I was open to entertaining them.

One such advance came from Gabriela, the executive secretary to the manager of the store, an attractive Latina. We shared a brief time together drinks, talk, dancing, and light petting. Nothing serious, transpiring over the course of a couple of weeks. All seemed OK, I was attempting to move on from Kathy and I was sharing what seemed to be a harmless relationship with a woman. We really did not seem to share too much in common, and soon I would be moving on to work at corporate. So, I politely explained the situation to her and said it might be best if we stopped seeing each other. To my surprise, she took the news poorly and became very emotional. I came to work one morning soon thereafter to find a message that the store manager wished to meet with me. I quizzed my supervisor to no avail and went to meet with the store manager, completely ignorant of the meeting's purpose. Upon my arrival in his office, I sensed he was not a happy puppy. He inquired if I had been seeing Gabriela his executive secretary. My response was yes. He cryptically expressed he had had prior involvement with the person in question and that he held me in low esteem because I made her cry when I told her I did not think we should continue seeing each other. He also let me know I was to be fired immediately.

I left his office bewildered. Returning to my shop, I was met by my supervisor and team members, eager to hear about the outcome of the meeting. Still in shock, I shared with them what had just happened, ending with my termination. Everyone was just as amazed as I. My immediate supervisor, a great supporter of my work for the store who was also instrumental in my move to corporate, was furious about what I had just shared with him. He instructed me to wait in his office while he spoke with the store manager. About an hour passed before he returned and proudly expressed that I was not to be fired, but I would be leaving for corporate "a little sooner than expected." It was Friday, and I was told to report to corporate on Monday. I had not been scheduled to start there for another five weeks. This was just a taste of what I was about to step into.

I was twenty-eight years old, and although I had a little experience with creating corporate images, I had zero experience with working in a business environment at the corporate level. On Friday, I was a shop manager for the visual department at a retail department store making $7.80 an hour. On Monday, I was one of two concept designers at the company responsible for forty stores, making $19 an hour. What a rush!

I believe the stage was set for a certain amount of adventure. As I said earlier, I was still fresh and uneasy about separating from my partner, my residence was a small studio in downtown LA, and my means of transportation a well-worn ten-year-old Fiat 124 spider. My studio was located just on the edge of what was called "Little Cambodia." Two blocks southwest from the corner of Vermont Ave and Beverly Blvd, my unit was set right at the front door of a sixty-year-old apartment building and cost me $460 per month for about 200 square feet. Old style "small" space. The main room would be completely filled by a full-size bed, so I constructed a platform in the closet to sleep on, hanging my clothes to one end over my feet and using the space under my bed platform for storage. This way, I could keep a drawing table and a chair in the main area. At this point, I was without an anchor. I had no sense of where I was going to or coming from; so, I went blindly forward. At this particular time, I didn't do much painting, as once again I was spending my creative energy at work in design and my free time on life in general. I was spending nine to twelve hours a day, five days a week with my new position at corporate. I was not so comfortable being alone, so on most weekdays after work I would meet someone for drinks/dinner, or I'd hit the clubs to drum up female companionship I came home alone about as often as I managed to find it.

My thrust into the world of design was brutal at best. Arriving at my position a bit earlier than expected, I found there had been no preparation for me. That did not translate to there being nothing for me to do just no place for me to do it. I was set up in a back room on a desk with a small portable drawing board and whatever supplies/tools I could scrounge up. In my first two weeks, I was given just under fifty incomplete projects to brilliantly finalize. Bravely showing up in my cheap suit every morning, I was quickly overwhelmed by attempting to complete an unreasonable workload while simultaneously attending meetings where I had to somehow justify why I had not completed this unreasonable workload. Very corporate, pure insanity.

After a time, I was assigned my own space along with some minimal tools. I was eager to please. "Yes" seemed to be the only word falling from my lips. In looking back on this time and my ignorance of the politics I was dealing with, I realize I was nothing more than a deer in the headlights of an oncoming truck. Day after day, I showed up ready to design my little socks off only to find that at the end of the day, there was no fulfillment or accomplishment, rather the feeling of simply being battered and bruised.

For example: One morning, I showed up for work to find a note on my drawing board from my direct supervisor who wished to see me first thing. Not a big deal. I went to his office to see what was up. He laid out the story for me. A project had been "misplaced" and a representative from Estée Lauder was going to be present later that morning to check on the status of said project. He asked me if I could come up with something to cover our butts. My supervisor assured me this was very informal and that I would be creating something just to let the company know we were working on it even though we had not been.

"Yes." My word of choice. No sweat, I had a couple of hours to throw something together. I ran back to my workstation and began pulling concepts out of my ass. After a couple of hours of frantic work, I had put to paper two OK concepts that I thought might be sufficient for the problem at hand. With the somewhat finished drawings in hand, I went back to my supervisor's office, arriving just prior to the deadline I was given. I found the door closed with a note attached: "Meet me in the auditorium." I was a bit confused, but what the hell. Rushing down to the auditorium, I opened the doors to an ungodly sight. There before my eyes were over fifty folks formally seated in front of a spotlit stage.

I could not believe my eyes. While in the process of instantly soiling myself, my supervisor grabbed my arm in an attempt to steady me, expressing, "It's a little more than I told you, but I know you can pull it off." He also added that in attendance were most all of the Estée Lauder VPs and a few executives from our mother company. I could not have dreamed up this scenario in my worst nightmares. I was about to present a couple of rough concepts I had thrown together in the last few hours to a room full of hardcore, well-known retailers who were under the impression that I had been working on this project for the last three months. I have no words to describe the torture of the next twenty minutes other than "devastating."

After the presentation, I crawled off the stage, and my supervisor met me at the rear of the auditorium to say, "Even though you appeared to have a rough time of it, I think you pulled it off."

My only response, with all the intensity I could muster "If you ever do anything like that to me again, I will end your fucking worthless life!" Estée

Lauder, for reasons beyond my understanding, actually went forward with what I had proposed. After this experience, things there seemed to slowly deteriorate, although this had nothing to do with my little nightmare. I just happened on the scene at a time when a few years of departmental mismanagement were becoming apparent. I continued to design, and even completed a few successful projects. After a few months of craziness, the department turned toxic. Little or no direction, ridiculous deadlines, inconsistent/wrong information-sharing, lying from the administration and throwing folks under the bus to save their own sorry butts it was insane. Finally, my sense of survival kicked in, and I put the word out to the industry: I was available.

A Summary of Life in LA, or, Just a Quick Primer in Debauchery

The seven years I spent living in LA were full of adventure, full of change, full of learning, full of growth, full of excitement, full of new experiences, full of mistakes, and sometimes just full of shit. In the future, after I left Los Angeles, when I was asked if I would consider returning there to live, I always had the same response. First: "There are not enough riches in the world for me to consider returning to live in LA." In the same breath, I would express: "What I experienced there was priceless."

Moving from a somewhat rural area to an internationally recognized metropolitan environment was at best an adjustment. Kind of like getting slapped in the face with a good size log. Being adaptable was a necessity. For example, in my experience thus far I had, with only a few issues, encountered a few gay men. All of a sudden, somewhat enabled by the industry I was working in, I was surrounded by capital-G *Gays* to the point that I was the only straight man in the workplace. This became increasingly challenging over time as I was not gay and did not seem to share the same interests as my coworkers.

Life in a major metropolitan area was not the easiest thing for me to get a hold on. I also believe that Los Angeles was its own animal in comparison to other major cities around the globe San Francisco, New York, London, Paris, Hong Kong, etc. Los Angeles proper has a population highly concentrated within a small geographic area, but Los Angeles as a whole is spread out over many square miles with multiple centers of engagement. One needs mobility to traverse the vastness of the whole scene. Being there, I was discovering firsthand that I could find funding for my efforts in visual design. At the time, I was not finding a similar return on investment in the fine arts. As before, it was a choice between the money and what I deemed important and honorable.

I was becoming a regular at some of the LA hot spots: The Troubadour, Whisky a Go Go, The Roxy, Sloan's, Club China, Nichol's. Seeing some of the hottest musical acts of the time and rubbing shoulders with well-known celebrities. None of it had much effect on my desire to further myself as a painter or a designer. Still attempting to make it on my own and still working as a designer for a corporate retail chain, an opportunity arose. I auditioned at a club just off of Sunset in North Hollywood a venue with a twist. Opening at 8:00 p.m., the club provided male dancers as entertainment for a female-only audience. At around 10:30-11:00, the male dancers stopped and men were admitted to the club. The pay was crap, but the tips were great. I did find it odd that most of the dancers were gay. This gig only lasted for about three months as weird as life was at the time, I found this means of making money too weird even for me.

I immersed myself in the craziness of the LA experience. I recall one night when I went to see the Pretenders at the Whiskey a Go Go in West Hollywood. After the music ended, I was highly energized but was going home alone. It was early in the morning and I was using Wilshire Blvd to get from West Hollywood to my place downtown. At that time of day, there was no one on the road. I'm not quite sure what came over me, but I felt the need for speed. I kept pressing my little Italian convertible to make the next green light. Before I knew it, I was traveling in excess of 115 miles per hour. What insane behavior, but it seemed appropriate at the time.

In my personal life, I was still hitting the club's way too often, using all my energy and funds on indulgence and instant gratification. Disillusioned with the direction of my career path, I sought to explore outside the box. An old coworker and friend shared with me information about an offer he had received to work in the adult film industry." Being the excitable,virile young man, I was at the time, I was intrigued at the possibilities. I joined him and met with a local director and producer. It was textbook! We showed up at the director's studio being greeted by a slightly overweight middle-aged man, cocktail and cigarette in hand, warring a Speedo, bathrobe, and thongs (the director). He and the producer - (pretty much dressed in normal attire) laid it out in simple terms. : $450 for four hours on the set. If you were physically able, that could turn into six or eight hours on set. He added that if you showed well on film and you were OK to work with, you could book one gig every week to start.

I was throwing it all together in my head: $1800 a month for sixteen hours of work, not bad. He elaborated that if you were very good and gained some recognition, you could move up from $450 for four hours to $1800 for the same. That was the extent of his realm; the bigger stars in the industry made much more. Damn! The idea of doing one of my favorite things and possibly getting paid over $7000 a month for two days' work was quite enchanting. I wouldn't even have to quit my day job. This was both a profitable and exciting adventure. Since it was a bit outside the norm, I thought it best to consider the unintended consequences of my involvement. After a few days of rolling it around in my mind, I concluded that the risks were greater than the return. In the moment it was all very fun and exciting, but the future might not offer as much. The idea of my sexual exploits being captured on film for who knows how long and being offered to who knows what audience became the determining factor. Nope. I'm sorry, dear reader, but you cannot see me in *The Painter's Dripping Brush*, or *I Want to Lick Your Hue*. It was back to retail design work.

Meanwhile, the office politics were becoming intolerable. I had received a few offers elsewhere, and after weighing the prospects, I zeroed in on one from a person whom I had worked with before at another retail chain. The job was a step down from my current position, but because the store was in the prominent location of Beverly Hills, I would make more money. This pay bump coupled with the probability of quickly moving up the ladder back to my previous status (with a proportionate pay increase) all seemed to make perfect sense in my head. So, I put the wheels in motion and tendered my resignation. The immediate response was pretty much as

I had anticipated: A little "we saw this coming" along with "what the hell are we going to do without you." I had given a month's notice; in response, I received a ridiculous workload from my direct supervisors.

A few days went by, and I received an invitation to meet with the regional vice president of the corporation an interesting development. I had no idea what he might wish to discuss, as I was simply moving on from a disgusting departmental situation. Upon meeting with the VP, I was totally caught off guard.

After a few cordial exchanges, he asked, "I would like you to be candid with me. Why are you quitting?" I thought for a moment and said to myself what the hell, you're out of here let him have it. I spent the next thirty or so minutes revealing the bizarre atrocities that I had encountered in the time I had held my position. He seemed to listen intently.

After a little more exchange, he offered, "We realize there are issues in your department, and it is important to the company that we address those issues. We have recognized your talent and wish that you stay with the company." He then added that if I would consider staying, he could offer me an increase in salary and the possibility of being considered to head the department or perhaps to relocate to the head offices in Chicago to join the design team responsible for all the department stores in the corporation. Both somewhat attractive offers, though I was in no way prepared for this. I asked if I might have a day or so to consider. Due to the perceived importance of the issues, I was given three days to decide. Once again, my life hung in the balance. How does one consider all of the elements to make such a decision? My experience with retail had thus far proven to be an experiment into how much radiation a human body can take before it melts into goo. Would I rather live in second-rate Chicago than world-class LA? I was still a *creative* and should be making art, not designing for department stores. I returned to the VP with my response, expressing that I was both surprised and honored by the offer. However, I strongly believed it was not in my best interest to relocate back east, and I had a growing mistrust of the corporate environment. I would have to respectfully decline the offer. The VP seemed a bit surprised at my response and urged me to reconsider. No! My mind was made up. I wished to complete the time I stated in my notice and move on.

Meanwhile, Kathy, my ex, had returned to the area. She had been offered her old position and had moved in with a roommate in an upscale condo complex across town. So much in flux!

With all this going on, I guess I got a little run down; I picked up a bug of some sort and had to stay home sick for the day. I was in the laundry room of my apartment building trying to catch up with my chores when one of the folks who lived on my floor rushed in and expressed with a great deal of excitement, "I think someone is breaking into your car!" I dropped everything and ran down the street. Upon nearing where I had parked, I saw a sickening sight: three young men ravaging my vehicle. The convertible top had been ripped open, the car was jacked up on one side with one wheel removed, and the stereo was laying on the trunk. The hood was open with one of the little shits attempting to remove something from the engine compartment, while one of the other pricks was fishing though my tool box, I guess for the appropriate tool needed to remove whatever other item they were after. Besides being sick as a dog, I could not believe this was all transpiring in broad daylight. I screamed at the top of my lungs, stringing together as many bad words as I possibly could on short notice. The punks saw me at a dead run toward them and decided to bail. One grabbed the stereo, one nabbed one of the dual carburetors he was in the process of removing, and the other picked up my open tool box. I'm not quite sure why, but as they fled, they simply dropped everything and disappeared into the landscape.

After several trips, I had salvaged what I could and piled all the debris into my tiny apartment. I then contacted the police only to be informed that I shouldn't bother I should just contact my insurance company. That call did go much better. Next, I called a garage to have what was left of the car picked up. After collecting myself for a moment, I realized I had left my laundry unfinished. A few hours had passed in dealing with the pressing catastrophe. I went down to the laundry room to finish things off only to find all of my clothes had been removed. My first thought was that it had been a fair bit of time that I left my laundry unattended and possibly someone had collected them for safekeeping. I went to the manager's apartment, which was located directly above the laundry room and right across the hall from my apartment, but the manager could offer no information regarding the whereabouts of my laundry.

Returning to my humble abode, something snapped! I was ill, I had been violated twice in as many hours, I was alone and disillusioned with just about everything at the moment. Some type of response was required. I concluded that since I resided in a controlled and somewhat secure environment, someone within my living complex must have decided to make what was mine theirs. Unacceptable! In a crazed reaction, I set about knocking on every door in the building in order to regain my possessions. I began at the unit next to my apartment and systematically continued door to door. After almost completing the first floor, I knocked on the door of one apartment and a younger man answered. With the door open, I could see a couple of my shirts draped over his sofa.

With assertive measure, I said "Give my goddamn clothes back, now!" It took a few seconds for the brain cells to kick into gear, after which the thieving punk disappeared inside, soon returning with what looked to be about two loads of laundry.

He meekly piled the clothes at my feet and muttered, "sorry." I then gathered my stuff and returned to my apartment. A recognizably bad day, though the experience forced me to evaluate my recent history.

For Example: I had gone to a bar in my neighborhood, just exploring. When I entered, I quickly noticed I was the only non-Asian person there. I sat at the bar, and the bartender seemed to ignore me; I politely asked for attention with no response. After a few uncomfortable minutes, an older man came and stood next to me.

He offered, "you do not belong here; it would be best if you were to leave." At first, I just didn't get it. Then it sunk in I was witnessing bigotry. Holy crap here I was, a born and raised "white bread American" in one of the most diverse metropolitan centers in the world and I'm being told I'm not welcome because of my race. I had been around racial tension before, but this was really the first time I had been discriminated against; it was a real eye opener.

Another time, upon returning home from work, I noticed as I was approaching my building that there were many people hanging out of the windows, cheering and yelling. As I drew near the entrance of the building, in the alleyway just below my apartment window were a man and a woman having sex in plain sight out in the alley. Probably a good indicator that this was not the most wholesome environment one might choose to live in.

Late one night, I heard a disturbance outside my window at the main entry of my apartment building. I looked out the window but saw nothing, so I returned to sleep. The next morning when I left my apartment for work, I was confronted with a good deal of blood on the front steps next to my window, accompanied by police and the media.

Another time, I was woken up by FBI agents who told me to lock my door and stay low inside until I was otherwise informed because they were raiding a suspected drug house across the street. No shots were fired, but there were lots of folks with tactical gear and automatic weapons.

OK! So, maybe a change was in order?

My career was in flux. I wasn't putting much energy into creating art. The place I was living did not offer the best quality of life. I was without a quality relationship. I was temporarily without a car in LA (probably the most damning thing of all). I was completely disillusioned with most everything in general. I had cut off most communications with family and friends from my past. My life at the time consisted of a cycle that went: eat, sleep, work, go to the clubs, and have sex with strangers as often as I could manage it.

At the time, getting around was a major issue. Not owning a car in LA was just not done. Getting to and from work was a logistical nightmare. Going to work in the morning took about an hour and thirty minutes on four different buses, the first one being five city blocks from my apartment.

Getting home was even worse; there were fewer buses heading in my direction that left from near my work. If I were to miss the one bus that departed ten minutes after I was supposed to get off work, I would have to wait forty-five minutes for another one, and that one took me about eight miles out of the way, which meant riding two additional buses to arrive five blocks from my home. Sorry, but there is no other way to describe the situation than "full of crap"!

One particular evening, after I had managed to navigate my way home in a reasonable fashion, I was walking the five blocks between where the bus dumped me off and my apartment. I was crossing an intersection about midway home when a BMW sedan slammed on its brakes in time to stop in the middle of the intersection. The driver's side door flung open and a woman emerged. She looked straight at me and loudly called my name. I was a bit startled as I didn't recognize her at first. Leaving her car in the intersection, she walked toward me announcing who she was. Damn! What were the odds? It was Evette, the wife of a couple in northern CA who had been patrons of my artwork a few years prior. She seemed very excited to see me, and I was very happy to see her. We immediately rescued her vehicle from its precarious resting place and decided it might be best to find a place to share an adult beverage together. Evette and I found a place nearby and began unloading each of our stories in turn. After a bit of conversation, we both admitted we had shared an attraction to each other and that we were no longer engaged in our prior relationships.

Naturally, we began to see each other. In a short time, I started my new job in Beverly Hills and was able to get my car out of the shop. It seemed things might be heading in a positive direction, although everything was still a bit out of balance. She was financially sound, residing in an older home located in a beautiful part of Pasadena; I was a financial wreck residing in the bowels of LA. At first, this was not an issue. Obviously, we spent more time out or at her place. One morning over breakfast, Evette expressed that she was seeing another gentleman an older wealthy man, some sort of foreign diplomat. My immediate response was, "What the hell are you doing with me?" She said that in a short time, she had developed very strong feelings for me, as I had for her.

I guess not much had changed in regards to my issues with work-life balance. I had separated from the woman I loved so I could paint without distraction. Now it seemed as though I was giving up one distraction for a bucketload of other distractions. I was just having a wonderful affair with a beautiful, successful, and intelligent woman. I was also keeping in touch with my Kathy, who was expressing that she had grown and was open to the prospect of trying again. Another crossroads. I decided to force the issue and confront my current lover with a choice: him or me. This caused a good deal of turmoil. One might guess the outcome? Yes, she chose the rich dude. I was hurt and dismayed, but I had to transcend my miserable existence. Once again, I threw myself into my work. All through this short period of self-exploration, although I was still flexing my creative muscles, I had not tended much to the creation of art. I had every intention, after separating from Kathy and being freed of the distractions of being involved in and nurturing a relationship, of attacking my artwork with a vengeance.

Wrong! I simply shed one distraction and created several new ones. I should have learned by then: If I wasn't going about creating art, I was simply traveling down the wrong road.

I was getting settled working at a premier department store in Beverly Hills and learning it had a high entertainment value. Celebrities, well-known personalities, and foreign dignitaries roaming the aisles were commonplace. One morning, the store remained closed for two hours after our normal opening hours so that an Arabian princess and her entourage might do a little shopping. It took less than an hour for her highness to snatch up just a bit over a million dollars US in goods. There were also some pretty colorful folks who worked at the store, it being located in Beverly Hills, especially in the visual presentation department. The team was made up of the visual manager and five other folks including myself. The manager was an older English woman, very masculine. She was somewhat reserved, but you did not want to get on her bad side. For some reason she seemed to adore me. Next in line was a proper middle-aged gay man from London. With impeccable taste, he would never dream of doing anything out of sorts, his appearance always perfect. Then there was the head of the fashion department, a middle-aged Parisian gay man with a heavy French accent. Very stout, buff, and overly butch, he enjoyed poking fun at me for being straight. Next, a young lady, the mannequin dresser, was quite interesting: six feet tall, thin as a rail, very well endowed, no hips, and a voice like Betty Boop's. Finally, there was a young gay man, very earnest, very outgoing, heavily into theatrics, and very playful. Putting us all together for coffee in the morning was a daily adventure. The young man I described last became a good friend, but shortly after our friendship began, he expressed that he was having sexual feelings toward me and that if we could not act on those feelings, it would be difficult to continue our friendship. Unfortunately, the friendship ended.

Even though I was in communication with my ex-partner, Kathy and I were entertaining the idea of getting back together, I was not fully convinced it was the right thing to do. I was one of two heterosexual men in the entire store, which made me quite popular with some of the female employees. I was like a kid in a candy store or maybe better said, I was like candy to a bunch of kids in a candy store. It started with the cosmetics department after multiple intimate contacts, then I moved on to jewelry, then to furs and security. It was becoming a wee bit crazy. One older woman offered to pay me in order to secure my services at a specific time. I was elated and demeaned at the same time. Being in demand was great, but it seemed like it was for the wrong reason. I began to grasp the concept that if I wished to be recognized for my creative accomplishments, I needed to seriously consider keeping my stuff in my pants. As much fun as this was, I was still far away from my artwork. This being said, I began to consider my future as an artist a bit more seriously.

One of my first conclusions was that the industry I was currently working in was not only a distraction from fine art but also a breeding ground for other distractions. After turning down the opportunity to work in corporate, I perceived my choice to work at a store to be the lesser evil. Turned out to be not so true. Finally, I was coming face to face with an actual reality the retail industry as a whole was a morally bankrupt industry that held no nourishment for the human spirit, selling a facade based on a facade derived from the foundation built on the facade of a concept. OK, have fun deciphering that. I knew, with my feet planted so solidly in the retail industry, it was going to take both time and energy to escape.

Also, with all my messing about in my personal life, after close to thirty years of drawing breath, I was beginning to recognize a trend in my behavior. Maybe I was a bit slow to catch on? My work in the fine arts was much better served when I was in a stable relationship. Possibly it took me so long to recognize this due to the simple fact that I had spent so much time either single or in unstable relationships. Regarding this particular subject, it seemed opportunity was knocking at my door. As I said, Kathy had relocated back to Los Angeles, and we had kept the lines of communication open. I had never been happier than in the time I had spent with her, and it seemed like only small semantics were keeping us from being together. I called her and expressed my thoughts, and then I listened to hers. It all seemed to make sense to both of us. We would make a new go of it.

It took a few weeks, but then we were together again. I removed myself from the caustic environment of downtown Los Angeles and moved in with Kathy, who was renting a condo with a roommate in an upscale neighborhood in Culver City near her workplace. She had the master bedroom, which she gladly donated half of to accommodate a workspace for myself. This was not the best situation, dealing with a roommate and living and working in the same confined space, but we were both determined to make things work. I immediately began to paint, reverting back to larger representational watercolors. In the years while I was screwing around with prop design and visual presentation in southern California, I had let go of my connections with the galleries I had previously worked with in northern California, and I had not spent much energy on establishing my work in LA.

I began a campaign to find local representation. Not much had changed in the industry since my earlier attempts. It was still a near impossible task to gain an audience with a gallery let alone gain representation by one. After days of visiting galleries and hours on the phone attempting to make contacts, I finally got a break when I presented samples of my work to a commercial gallery located in the Pacific Coast Design Center (the Blue Whale). Acceptance! And shortly after that, a few sales. Things began to look promising. One evening as I returned home from work, I received a call from the manager of the gallery, who informed me that a representative of a large fine arts publisher had come in and expressed an interest in making contact with me. Cool! A day later, I was invited to a meeting at the regional offices of Ira Roberts Publishing. I was a bit confused, but what the hell.

The day came and I arrived at the offices unaware that I was about to meet with the head of the company. We chatted for a while as he looked over my fine arts resume and my portfolio of work. After that, he got right to the point. If I would be willing to explore a few minor adjustments in regards to the content of my work, he would be willing to sign me up and publish it. As a print publisher, there was no consideration for offering original works, it was work to be created for limited edition issue only. Damn! I could not believe my ears. One of the largest art print publishers in the US was asking to represent me.

Once I had recovered from the initial shock, my cursed idealism kicked into gear. I expressed to him it was my understanding that artists who committed to producing commercial limited-edition prints were not taken seriously in the realm of "high art," adding that I was unsure at that point if I was willing to accept that role. He actually agreed with my assumption to a point, but continued his argument. Wouldn't it be better to make a good living at producing what might be considered "lesser art" that was nonetheless enjoyed and consumed by thousands than to suffer through the process of creating original work time and time again only to find myself never being truly recognized as a "fine artist"? Referring to history, he added, "the odds are not in your favor." I listened intently, but could not shake my convictions. We talked back and forth, discussing terms and possibilities. In the end, I humbly conveyed how honored I was to receive such consideration, but that I must decline as I wished to continue on my path to become recognized as a "true artist" who strives to create original work. I often remember this experience with a bit of regret. Life might have been quite different.

Again, change was the only constant I could depend on. I still needed to address my other work you know, the place where I was being paid for spending forty or so hours a week. Like I said, it was going to take some doing to break out of retail. After putting the word out again in regards to my being available, I received a fair number of responses, but only from competitor retail companies. Finally, I followed up on a lead I had received for the position of art director for an internationally published computer magazine. I set up an interview, it went well, and in two weeks I was free from the "evils of retail."

Although I had a good amount of experience working with the graphics industry, I was unfamiliar with publishing. I purchased a couple of cheap suits to serve as my standard uniform, and I was on my way. The publication was the first international magazine for personal computing if you can remember it, this was the time when computers were basically data processors used in large business applications. DOS was the accepted operating system, with Macintosh's OS having just been introduced. Information storage was limited to eight-inch floppy disks, and one megabyte of RAM was cutting-edge. The idea of a computer being used for personal applications was in its infancy.

As art director, I was responsible for the overall look of the publication: the cover, images to accompany feature articles, internal photography/ illustrations. Computer graphics did not exist at this time, so this production was accomplished via traditional means paste-ups, hand-drawn graphics (today called "illustration"), photography, Velox, and whatever one might conceive of in the color separation process. Even knowing as little about the computer industry as I did, I was still able to recognize the rapid growth and the burgeoning importance of the advancement of "personal computing." Immersing myself in the representation of this idea, I must say I did OK at the time, helping to create a new image for the magazine and creating several covers and feature articles that received prestigious Addy awards (advertising awards of Los Angeles). As we all know, personal computing did indeed evolve into the mega-industry we know and love (and often hate) today social media, computer graphics, digital commerce, etc.

I tried my best to fit in to the scene where I found myself. Again, I was left wanting. The folks I was working for were broadly uninspired and lacking in scope and vision, simply wishing to cash in on an emerging industry. Maintaining this position required a good deal of energy. Even though the office was only twenty miles away from where I lived, it was over an hour commute thanks to the LA sprawl. This, added to the reality of working eight to ten-hour days, five days a week, meant a good fifty to sixty hours a week were devoted to the day job that was supposed to be supporting my art. The math was not adding up.

But at least things were going well in my relationship. We were both just working so much and receiving little fulfillment in return. At least, between the two of us, we were bringing in OK money. However, that was beginning to present a new challenge: with our combined incomes and few deductions, we were getting crucified via our taxes. Incredible as it may seem for the time, we made enough money to get slammed on taxes but not quite enough to qualify for a home loan. This balance has always been of interest to me the price of home ownership has long been positioned just barely out of reach of the nation's median income level. Kind of points to the idea that not much has changed in last hundred years?

Considering the financial issues Kathy and I were facing, together we concluded that it was time to think outside the box. I remember my parents talking about my mother's youth and how on a few occasions her family resided on houseboats. It was a stab in the dark, but something to work with. With our limited knowledge and resources, we both began to research the idea. Once we embraced the concept, it seemed to manifest itself as the only direction. Very soon, we were on the path to buying a boat. The process was not an easy one, evolving to a new existence that neither of us were familiar with, but we focused on the particular goal of living aboard a boat.

The next few months were insane, attempting to prepare ourselves for this lifestyle we knew nothing about while trying to maintain a good level of productivity at our respective jobs. The banking industry, then as now, was nothing less than hostile. Endeavoring to convince a conventional lender that a boat was going to serve as our primary residence was met with ridicule. The further we went into the process, the harder it got. Finally, through sheer tenacity, we achieved a foothold. With everything we had in savings, plus my father putting up his house as collateral; Kathy and I agreeing to make ungodly monthly payments at 29 percent interest, the loan was processed and we were seemingly on our way.

One evening as we were finishing up dinner, sitting on the floor of our rented condo, surrounded by boxes as we had sold all of our furniture, the phone rang. It was the bank, calmly informing us that our loan had fallen through. It's sad, today, to remember the angst. We had not only risked everything we had, but also what my parents had. We scrambled to action, and between ourselves and both of our families, rose to the challenge. My parents cosigned the loan. Holy shit! This had better turn out to be good. After recovering from the shock, Kathy and I set ourselves to task to orchestrate the delivery of our new home and make the final move from land to water. To this day, I still cannot believe that this all actually happened. Neither of us had any experience with boats or boating or living on a boat or being on the ocean. If someone were to tell younger me that this was in the cards, I would tell them "you're nuts!"

In our naivete, we purchased a 25' Fishercraft a powerboat designed with a V-hull equipped with the superstructure of a houseboat. Not the most formidable ocean vessel, but it offered a maximal living area. We acquired a slip at a marina located in the backwaters of the LA harbor. Nothing about this transformation was easy. We only had one car at the time, and both of our jobs required commuting. Getting to my job was the most problematic, so I took the car and my partner indulged in an hour-plus bus ride. In order to afford the boat, we had ordered it pretty much empty. Basically, all it had was a head (bathroom) and a steering station. No galley (kitchen), no berth (bedroom), no saloon (living/dining room). It was just a small open space waiting to be made into a home. But I was familiar with construction, and it was a small space. How much trouble could it be?

After moving on board, it was time to begin fashioning the interior of our new home. The first day of construction, I was transporting my tools down the dock to the boat when I encountered one of my neighbors.

He stopped me and pointed at a good size level I was carrying, asking "What are you going to do with that?"

I responded sharply, "I'm building cabinets, why?"

He replied, "You know, you're working on a boat. It is in constant motion." In that moment, I realized how little I knew about my new environment. I discarded my trusty level and began seeking new information. Needless to say, I wasn't getting much artwork done in this era. Because of the restricted space, it would be difficult for me to work onboard something else that would need to transform in our new lifestyle.

Thankfully, we began to acclimate constructing the interior of the boat, meeting new folks, learning about boating on the ocean, taking our first day-long ocean excursions, etc. In fact, it seemed our choice to move to the water suited us. For a short time, we were financially strapped, but that fell into a workable realm before long. We were sucking up new information like sponges. First was acquiring the respected "water bibles": *Chapman's Piloting* and the *Power Squadron's Guide to Seamanship*. It was considered irreverent not to have a copy of at least one, preferably both aboard your vessel. We were gaining a whole new lexicon fathoms, nautical miles, dead reckoning, Loran, RDF, GPS, location determined by hours and minutes, knots, displacement, NOAA, weather fax, blue water, CQR, anchor rode, antifouling paint, zincs, electrolysis, gel-coat, linear-polyurethane, dock box, bilge pump, thru-holes, furling, cleat, toe-rail, bow, stern, etc. We were confronted with not only new mechanics and technologies, but also a new language.

Our new neighborhood was a different world with its own subculture. We were a very diverse group of people placed in close proximity with one common bond. This became most apparent to me one Friday night after work while I was unwinding, enjoying an adult beverage with a neighbor outside in the cockpit of his boat. Before I knew it, there were seven of us there, yakking it up about our experiences of the preceding week. At one point, I looked around and took stock of the attendees: a maintenance diver, an attorney, a surgeon, an insurance salesman, a sign maker, an elevator sales rep, and me. I could not imagine on what planet any of these folks might share a casual end-of-the-week drink together, but there we were, laughing and chatting without any preconceived sociocultural boundaries. It was an amazing moment, all those superficial standards transcended by the simple commonality of boating. Holy crap, was I in heaven? And this cultural experience didn't stop there. I was inundated with it on a daily basis.

A Seemingly Catastrophic Day on the Water

Shortly after moving on board, my parents paid us a visit. My father, being an old Navy man, was keenly excited about the idea of my living aboard a boat my mother did not share his enthusiasm. The plan was for them to stay with us for just a short time. Both Kathy and I were working full-time, so there were a few days my parents were left alone on our new boat. I believe the second day my parents were left unsupervised at the marina, my father decided to prove his usefulness by washing down the outside of the boat. Any other time, his gesture would have been received with a hardy, "Hey, you old salt, thanks for swabbing the decks, hope you had a good time of it," but the reality of his actions hit me in the face like a loaded sucker punch when I arrived home from work that evening. As I said, we had just moved aboard, and moving from land to sea meant we had to condense our belongings we had tons of stuff stashed in every corner of the boat. With my father's innocent and well-meaning action, he had supplied a wee bit of excess water to the front deck of the boat, underneath which lay a compartment filled with important belongings that were now flooded. There were a few things ruined that were replaceable, one of the things not replaceable was a box housing the photos and negatives documenting the last ten years of my artwork. As I lifted the box from the hold, filled with water, totally destroyed, I could not help but express my anguish: "Holy crap." In a short amount of time, with good intent, all that work had been wiped from the planet. I was devastated and could not express the impact this had on me without destroying someone whom

I loved and respected. Ten years gone because someone wished to do something nice. No good deed goes unpunished!

Next-Door Neighbor

The boat next to ours was occupied by a wily maintenance diver who seemed to live his life as a newborn, waking up every morning to a brand-new universe a nice enough fellow, just rough around the edges. Early one Saturday morning (3:00 am) my partner and I were rudely awakened by a pounding on the outside of our boat. I stumbled to the hatch with wild anticipation. Where I found our next-door neighbor "slightly" inebriated and looking a bit sheepish. He muttered "do you have any beer onboard?" I responded "WHAT!" Surprisingly he repeated his initial request. Adding that he had earlier picked up two prostitutes from the "Hollywood on the Pike" (a bar at the lower end of downtown Long Beach) and was viciously wishing to entertain them. Accompanied by a few vulgar words, I expressed my intent desire for him to disappear immediately. Which he was very accommodating. He was a big man with quite an intimidating presence. No matter. A few hours later (7:00am) a reasonable time to wake, I found myself standing next to his boat, holding onto a bit of residual anger at being roused from a perfectly good sleep for such an unacceptable reason. I began to relentlessly pound on the side of his watercraft, yelling his name over and over again. After a time, he emerged in a state of horror.

I exclaimed, "You hear me! There are only two reasons you bang on my goddamn boat in the wee hours of the night. One, my boat's on fire and I'm going to die. Two, my boat's sinking and I'm going to die. Anything else can wait. Got it?"

It took a few minutes for him to collect himself, but he uttered the desired response: "It will never happen again." Surprisingly, this sparked a pretty good relationship between the two of us.

As I said, this new community was rich with diversity that drew me in like a magnet to iron. Embracing this experience was great for life in general, and since my partner shared my enthusiasm, it had a wondrous effect on strengthening our relationship. All seemed to be right with the world except for my artwork. With this massive transformation, I wasn't feeling so compelled to be creative. For the first time in my life, something other than art was my raison d'être. I did not totally stop, but I did revert to representational imagery of my surroundings watercolors of tugboats, the docks, the surrounding industrial area, etc. This did not fall into place with my grand vision of ascending to the "important art" world. It soon became apparent to me that I needed a studio. What a concept! This habit of mine to act with such finality has presented a duality in my life it can be a great tool when it comes to making art, but it can be a bit hazardous to the direction of everyday life.

Weird as it was, a good friend of mine from high school, you know Steve, had a boat in the same marina the same man I had reconnected with and had been working with in display. Even more bizarre, he too had decided to leave the retail visual presentation field, to open his own sign company. Fortuitously, he had an extra room in his business that I sublet with grand intentions. The plan was to use this space mainly to paint and also to handle any freelance graphic projects I could drum up. Interestingly enough, freelance graphic jobs began to materialize in abundance. Before I knew it, I was juggling enough of these projects to generate as much and then more income than I was bringing in as the art director for the magazine. Since things had deteriorated at the magazine to the point that I hated even showing up, much less trying to produce anything of substance, it seemed the obvious direction was to go freelance. My newly formed business, named Visual Concepts, was open for business. Of course, with all the graphic work I could handle, I still had one problem: no time or energy to paint. Due to the fact that I hadn't been painting much prior to this change, it didn't seem to be a big issue, at least for the moment. Little did I know, at this point, painting and creating art had slowly over the years become a defining part of my being. Art, via my ignorance, was defining me as a person. Who knew!

Life was crazy good. Both Kathy and I were happy with our working situations, our relationship was great, we now had a couple of older used cars to get ourselves around with, and boat life was a wonderful adventure. We had been together for a while, and even though we had experienced a bump or two, I was never happier than when she was at my side. Everything was going so well, I thought just one more thing would complete the package: I asked Kathy to be my wife.

I asked, she said yes. We were wed aboard our boat in our marina, my father officiating the ceremony. We had a reception in the marina picnic area with friends, family, and boat folks. A splendid day everyone had a great time, there were no bizarre emotional breakdowns, no family feuds, and all for under $2000. Now that's what I'm talkin' about!

All was right with the world. We were on our way in a life of bliss. The rest of the year was good, along with the first part of the following year. In starting up Visual Concepts (my design business), I recognized that I wasn't the greatest in dealing with finance, so one of the first things I did was to hire an accountant. I found an independent and we agreed on a monthly retainer. I expressed to him early on that my wife and I were playing it pretty close to the line when it came to our finances and that I was new to conducting business in California. I would be relying on his expertise to keep us out of harm's way, adding that I could not afford any substantial surprises when it came to tax time.

I might as well have been talking to a brick. I paid him his monthly retainer and didn't hear a peep from him until the end of February the next year, when he called me and calmly reported that between state and federal taxes, I owed about $15,000. I was unable to constrain myself to a civil response. After sorting out the gruesome details, I found it was true. With him failing to inform me of my progress during the previous year, I had made some money and had paid no quarterly taxes on it. This was an unfortunate development as I could barely come up with $3000 extra in a month, much less $15,000. We pulled together our resources and by April 15th had amazingly produced $5000 for disbursement. Neither California nor the feds were amused. The harassment began. Because our boat was the only thing we had of any worth, it looked like we were going to lose it. In order to avoid losing all we had worked for, I declared bankruptcy. A horrible choice to have to make we lost a lot, but without our home, we would have lost everything. Recovering from this experience took a bit of time and effort.

The lessons I took away from this experience were that one needs to put a good amount of effort into acquiring an accountant, be completely familiar with all of your financial responsibilities, and, if possible, to use a credentialed Tax Attorney Accountant because when things turn to shit, they must represent you in court and when your financials turn to poo, it always ends up in some type of litigation.

Even with all the business/financial weirdness transpiring, I was hopelessly in love with my partner and totally enthralled with my new aquatic life. After being on the water for a while, it was beginning to become apparent to both Kathy and me that mucking around on a "stinkpot" was less desirable than caressing the surface of the ocean powered by the wind. Translated, we were learning that if we wanted to truly embrace the ocean, it would be best accomplished under the power of sail. Now, all we had to do was get rid of the powerboat we had so ignorantly purchased and acquire a sailing vessel.

Although we had completely embraced the challenge, the universe was not quite so ready to accommodate us. This was also apparent in my work with Visual Concepts. After the bankruptcy, I attempted to keep the company going, but after several failed ventures, it seemed to be a dead horse "whip it no more." A person, Rchard, I had connected with during my time in the visual presentation industry made contact with me to possibly assist him with advancing his company. After helping him with his immediate project, he proposed that I might join his company as the head designer, marketing director, and supervisor of his manufacturing facility. I took a look at his company and found it showed great promise. My wife and I discussed the idea and decided, considering our circumstances, it might be a move in the right direction. I negotiated terms to start a base of $30,000 a year with a stipulation that I would receive 3 percent of gross on all profitable contracts. The 3 percent was very important, and one of the reasons he considered bringing me on board. He was at present bringing in over a million a year, but his profit was low. This was almost totally due to his poor manufacturing practices. It was up to me to assess and reorganize these efforts. I attacked this challenge with the veracity of a wild carnivore faced with a pile of raw meat. With my designs and my reorganization, I not only raised the company's income but was able to raise profit levels over 40 percent a good thing for everyone concerned.

During this time, the company Kathy was working with announced they were relocating to Sacramento in (northern California) and they were offering a very handsome package for her to tag along. Hell! Just as things were beginning to fare well, another issue to deal with. At the same time, the owner of the company I was working for expressed that he wished to bring me on as a partner. What a dilemma! We had just had a great year, I was being offered a partnership in a company I had helped develop, and my wife was being offered what seemed to be solid employment with a good income from a progressive company. The only stipulation was that we would have to relocate. Little did we know at the time that one of these offers would prove to be less than honest.

We decided to stay put. As they say in the casino, we "put it all on red." Since Kathy was now without a job, as I negotiated my new partnership with the company, I included a request to bring her on as the front office administrator responsible for bookkeeping, accounting, payroll, phones, etc. We agreed to $25,000 each and a split of 5 percent gross billed. Translated, based on the previous year, between my wife and I, we could easily see $120,000. Fabulous! Kathy and I started gearing up for a stellar year.

In the first three months, both of us noticed that the work was not rolling in as before. I questioned Richard, the owner of the company, about the lack of projects coming in. He assured me it was just a temporary lull. Another month of the same passed. I became suspicious something was not right. I contacted our largest client only to find out the owner of the company was turning down jobs left and right. This made no sense to me. Once again, I confronted Richard, my business partner with my newly acquired information. Having no reasonable excuse to fabricate, he shared the truth: He was going to retire and he needed the company for a tax shelter, which meant he was planning all along to operate the company at a loss for a couple of years before shutting it down. I could not believe what I was hearing, or that this person could be as maniacal as to screw with someone's livelihood for a tax break. With the proverbial poo hitting the fan, Kathy and I left immediately. Kathy took a temp position and I returned to freelance graphic design. We took a hit financially, but somehow managed to stay afloat.

Of course, during this time, once again, I wasn't doing much painting. Just a few small watercolors representing our aquatic environment. I was starting to feel the lack of not creating serious artwork, but I couldn't afford the time it would take to jump back in. We were just getting by with the income we were generating.

We were gaining more experience with life on the water day by day. Trips to Catalina Island, fishing the Horseshoe Kelp, coastal cruising, excursions to the Channel Islands. We befriended a young couple who lived aboard a sailboat in our marina. The male half was a realtor who was transitioning to working with wildcatters' oil exploration. This became important to me as he began to rely on me for all of his graphic and presentation needs for his new endeavors in the oil industry. I started by creating presentation boards for investment groups, which lead to small graphic projects for wildcatters' oil companies, which evolved into doing corporate imagery for the same companies. This progression lead to work from subsidiary companies as varied as a waterpark in Kentucky that was looking for a complete visual makeover. A wild journey. I remember working on all the elements required for this waterpark, Branding, marketing, advertising, corporate imagery, promotion, etc. This was still the era of infancy for digital imagery. Business was conducted by mailing physical projects or by talking on the phone. I had mailed my presentation to the powers that be and received a call upon their receipt. The viewing committee was the board of directors, a group of seven wealthy "good old boys." When I answered the phone, I spoke with a young lady with a heavy southern drawl. She informed me I was to be on a conference call with all the board members. When I was connected, I could hear laughter and chanting "Billy-Bob, Billy-Bob, Billy-Bob." After a moment of everyone speaking at once, finally, I could make out one person's voice.

"Son, are you a southern boy?"

I thought for a moment before answering, "My mom was born and raised in Mississippi, but I was not." There was more conversation among the boys on the other end. Again, I heard one voice speak out above the others.

"What you sent us is good, but we all just love Billy-Bob Catfish." I was taken aback for a moment Billy-Bob Catfish was a very small part of the full package. As I said, this was a full makeover for the entire corporate structure of the waterpark. Total park graphics, signage, advertising, corporate identity, everything. "Billy-Bob Catfish" was a children's menu design I created for one of their four restaurants. The menu was die-cut in the shape of the character with the children's menu on one side and Billy-Bob printed on the other side, fashioned so it could be worn as a mask. Little did I know, after hundreds of hours laboring over creating seemingly brilliant work, that a ridiculous brain fart I used for filler would be the element that closed a near $150,000 project.

The project still ended up kind of sideways. They purchased my concepts outright, negotiating the price to $50,000 with them handling oversight of production and installation. It turned out to be an OK price for what I did. I checked in later to see how everything turned out oh, shit. They changed everything to a sort of polished Walmart quality, not using even a third of the direction I offered. At least I got paid.

Between my work and life on the water, adventure and new experiences were a daily occurrence. My artwork was all over the place I was still doing some representational work while also exploring expressionism and impressionism. It had been a while since I'd devoted serious time and energy to my art. I was still selling some work out of galleries in Sacramento and San Francisco. The studio I had been using for my design business was not very costly to maintain, so I was able to keep it even though Kathy and I were pretty strapped for money. After our last business fiasco, my wife blew through a couple of odd jobs and ended up doing medical transcriptions. I changed things around in the studio with the intent to get back to painting full-time, though in the beginning, I still wasn't doing much of it. Marketing/promoting was the first step, so I prepared promo packages slides of my artwork, artist's resume and statement.

Note: Ever since I can recall, when submitting artwork for consideration (to galleries, exhibitions, juried shows, award shows, whatever), the expected standard was "slides." No photos, no photocopies, no printed images of any type other than "slides." I did not understand this unreasonable demand then, nor will I ever. I do appreciate how in very limited circumstances in larger organizations where decisions are reached by committee, it can be advantageous to have the work available on slides so it can be projected in front of many folks at one time. That makes sense. But as a blanket industry standard, it's bullshit. The number of times I've witnessed decision-makers make a decision based on what they could see by holding a slide up to the light or viewing a sheet of slides on a light table is ridiculous. Today, with the advent of the internet and digital imagery, I believe this insane demand is no longer the standard.

I sent packages out all over the US, with little response. The arena of promoting one's work has always seemed to be more dependent on whether it's "Taco Tuesday" or if "red is the color of the week" or if "Mr. Jones has gas" than on the quality of the work being considered. But maybe I'm a bit cynical in regards to this particular subject.

At this time, I was also working out some issues that I believed were negatively affecting my person. Over the years, I had worked closely with a lot of gay folks, and I had developed a bit of prejudice against flamboyant gay men and gay women who acted like they were more of a man than I. I was also biased against folks of whom it was impossible to tell the whether they had honestly fallen on bad times or if they were attempting to pull your chain for a wee bit of cash. These biases of mine didn't sit right with my sensibilities I wished to change my perceptions. To do so, I went out every morning, walking the streets of the city with the intent to acknowledge everyone I came in contact with in a positive manner. At first, this was a taxing and bizarre experiment. In time, it became a bit more comfortable.

One morning, while I was cruising the city streets with my coffee, practicing my new therapy, I came to an intersection. While I was waiting for the light to change, I saw, directly across from me on the other side of the street, also waiting to cross in the opposite direction, a "bag lady," her shopping cart overflowing with all of her worldly belongings. Not the most attractive sight one could imagine. The light changed, and as I watched her come toward me, I could see she was challenged with some type of crippling disability. Cerebral palsy or muscular dystrophy something that made mobility challenging.

As we neared each other in the middle of the crosswalk. I offered with all the good intent I could muster, a hearty "GOOD MORNING." I wasn't surprised when she did not respond, so I just continued on across the street. As I reached the other side of the intersection, I heard a faint sound coming from the opposite side of the street.

I could barely make it out "Good morning," she offered. I turned to see the woman with her open hand raised high in my direction. I waved back in acknowledgement, then we both turned and continued on our way. I made it a few yards up the street before I was overcome by tears. How had such a brief encounter affected me so deeply?

I cut my walk short and hurried back to the studio, where I immediately laid out the beginnings for a body of work I would call "Human Response." It was a new and interesting approach to paining for me. First off, at that point I had not done a lot of representational figurative work. Also, even though I had been exploring impressionism and expressionism, my norm was to lay out and sketch work first before pushing paint around. With this project, I was truly pushing my comfort zone.

The technique: I started with full sheets of heavy ply Museum Mount (a ridged piece of paper about 32" × 40"). I then masked out a rectangular area in the center of the paper (about 10" × 16"). Next, I applied a combination of gauche, watercolor, and vinyl screening ink inside the masked area to create a perfect rectangle filled with random colors, values, and textures. The next and most important step: I stared into the painted area with only the thought of "human response" to see whatever I might see. Once an image presented itself to me, I then used water to remove paint to various degrees in order to make the image appear. Even by my standards, this was a weird approach.

In the next few months, I produced around 120 pieces. Varied images featuring diverse figures: male, female, children, adults, faces, lone figures, and groups. This being a bit of a psychic approach to painting, I was sometimes surprised at the content revealed in the imagery sublime, disturbing, tender, confrontational, but always emotionally moving and thought-provoking.

Upon completing the project, I took samples to the galleries I was working with in Sacramento and San Francisco. The gallery owners agreed with me that work was strong, of quality, and important, but all the galleries rejected them, saying that it was just too much for their clientele. Fortunately, the gallery in San Francisco had a connection with a gallery in Frankfurt, Germany, that took about fifteen pieces on consignment. I did not have direct contact with the German gallery as the deal was brokered through the gallery in SF. After a few months, I received payment for the sale of thirteen of the works with a request to send more in the next month. Unfortunately, the owner of the gallery in San Francisco suddenly passed away before I had the chance, and the gallery was taken over by folks I was not familiar with. I was informed the gallery would be changing its venue and they would no longer be handling any of my work. If that wasn't bad enough, when I asked about Germany, they said they knew nothing about it and were unwilling to research the matter. This being prior to the internet, research without any contact information was pretty much impossible. Sucked to be me! I not only lost the opportunity to make more sales, I also lost two pieces of art in the deal. I then invested a good deal of time and money to create promo packages for the work, sending them to galleries around the US and Europe.

Not one acceptance. I moved on to creating other work. The remainder of the pieces were either sold by myself individually, given as gifts, or damaged over time. An ill-fitting end to something I believed would prove truly important.

Life on the water was still as wonderful and full of adventure as ever. But as I mentioned before, both of our professional lives seemed to be stagnating. My wife had been reduced to composing doctor's notes and medical records; I was still wandering about in the fine art industry, which was still a bit confusing to me even after so many years. Here I was a pretty decent creative, working in the industry for over a decade and residing in one of the largest metropolitan arenas in the world, but for some reason, it just wasn't happening for me.

A change was in order, both Kathy and I agreed. After much deliberation, we concluded relocation was our course and set our sights on Sacramento for two main reasons. One, this is where the company my wife had previously worked for had moved, and two, in previous years the greater Sacramento area had been considered a prominent area on the west coast of the US for contemporary fine art. As with most things, once we convinced ourselves that the thing was real, we jumped in running. My wife was offered a position with her former employer and I found seemingly good prospects in the fine arts industry. We then set about selling our boat and making arrangements to relocate. The idea of leaving the ocean was tough to swallow, but we both agreed it would be a temporary arrangement, and we had firmly come to grips with the idea that our next boat would be a sailing vessel. Surprisingly enough, we were able to sell our boat in a short time and at not too much of a loss

Northern California

I had secured a small one-bedroom duplex in Fair Oaks, CA, on the outskirts of Sacramento. After boat life, we had no furniture to speak of, so I rented the basics until we could get settled. Acquiring and setting up a studio would have to wait as our move had seriously tapped our financial reserves. Like most folks, we required two incomes to survive. My wife was making OK money, but not enough to make ends meet. I set about signing up with temp agencies while researching and making contact with the local art scene. Before we left Los Angeles, I had purchased a new motorcycle, so my wife had the car and I had my bike. Immediately, I began to pick up temp assignments for a wide range of tasks: removing ice from the arena after the Ice Capades, building fences, light construction work, new store setup, catering, and more. I also found three galleries that were interested in exhibiting my work.

All of this was happening in a relatively short time. We then needed to scramble to secure studio space for myself. We decided upon a two-bedroom house with a large garage in Rancho Cordova, just across the river from where we were living before. Returning the rental furniture, we then purchased only what we needed a bed, a sofa, and two stools so we could eat at the kitchen bar. I set up shop in the garage and began to turn out work in between temp jobs. Although we had not established a solid foundation, things seemed to be progressing OK. But soon a series of events would change everything.

I was working on a temp assignment setting up a new retail store about thirty miles from home. The project was going well so well that I had advanced to supervising the five-man crew. A little extra money. We were in the last stages of work just prior to the store opening. I was searching for a piece of particle board in a vertical rack. As I moved the panels around, one of them that had been cut in an odd shape fell out of the rack and right onto my foot with extreme prejudice. Not being able to see the damage though my boot, I could feel that it was not good. I called the person in charge of the project and they informed me they were tied up and could not come to the site, advising me that if the injury was "not too bad," I could continue to work. Wow, such compassion. I had one of the folks I was working with help me remove my boot, which I was horrified to find had filled with blood. I, with a great deal of pain, put my boot back on, assigned the team duties for the remainder of the day, and then in a daze straddled my motorcycle to ride the thirty miles home.

Finished with Disco and into the 90s

I'll outline the era. I seemed to be moving in a forward direction steered more by outside influence than internal intent. Relocating to a completely different environment is usually taxing on the system, and I was discovering that the flourishing art industry of ten years ago was not quite the same upon my arrival. Even though the industry had diminished, I was able to secure gallery representation at the Artworks Gallery, the Djurovich, the Himovitz/Jenson, the Himovitz/Salomon, the Accurate, the Barbara McDonald, and the Tower Corporate Gallery. Although I was keeping up with my abstract work, I was moving more into the realm of Abstract Expressionism, as well as dabbling in "pure" Expressionism. With our combined incomes, our existence seemed to be stabilizing.

Right around this time, my daughter began experiencing difficulties in her environment, living with my ex-wife. After discussing the issue with Kathy, we offered her the opportunity to come live with us. Surprisingly enough, this idea was not so contested by my ex, but was outright refused by my daughter. Shortly thereafter, I heard my daughter left her home in a hurry, for reasons no one including herself would communicate to me. Later, I would find out both my ex and my daughter were not being completely transparent about what was actually transpiring. What happened after this has very much affected my relationship with my daughter to this day.

Meanwhile, back to my big toe. To my amazement, after a thirty-mile ride on a motorcycle in intense pain, I actually reached the driveway of my house, where I literally dropped my bike on its side and headed for the front door only to collapse on the walkway. After a few minutes, I regained consciousness and crawled inside to the phone. I called my wife and she rushed home to wheel me away to the nearest hospital, where I was patched up and returned home. After this experience, the company I was assigned to agreed to pay for my medical expenses and the temp company I was working with agreed to assign me to work I could "hobble" to. I had been brought up with the ideal that you don't readily sue or openly challenge the folks that you work for an ideal that I have learned, over time and with experience, is not always the most prudent course of action. Working for someone always involves a certain level of trust. When that trust is broken, by either party screw'em. Most all actions demand response.

Crippled for a time, I moved forward regardless. I was sent out on a temporary catering assignment to work with a large technological firm in the area. I began with prepping fruit, vegetables, and lunch meats for meetings and presentations. Of course, I wanted to do well and exceed expectations for whatever was asked of me. I did a little research and found there to be a fair amount of creativity involved in food preparation, especially this type of offering. It came natural to me, using my skills in visual presentation to augment the experience of consuming food. Within a week, I was being requested by various departments in the company. This was all very gratifying and good except for the fact I was making nine dollars an hour as a temp, working almost full time. This was eating into my time to paint without providing adequate financial return. What to do?

After a short time, the company offered me a full-time position. As with all the temp agencies I'd worked with, the assigned company paid around double what the assignee would receive. This company offered me $10.50 per hour with benefits they had been paying over $18.00 per hour to use my services as a temp. I found this offering to be unacceptable. I made a reasonable counter offer of $15.00 per hour, which was immediately rejected. Thus, went my swift goodbye to the culinary experience for large tech companies.

I continued to produce artwork. My wife and I were doing OK, but not yet achieving the monitory rewards we had expected. My foot had pretty much healed and I was painting a fair amount, producing for three galleries, but I still needed to take on temp assignments to augment our income. I was sent on a temp assignment to assist a high-end furnishings store to assist with installing furniture for a special trade event called "Street of Dreams." This entailed a group of high-end homes being constructed and completed with all the trimmings custom landscaping, custom floor coverings, window treatments, lighting, furnishings, and accessories in order to showcase regional architects, contractors, designers, and yes: furniture stores. I was hired just to move furniture, but once I began working, I found myself right back in the world of visual presentation. It was just too hard to listen to buyers, designers, and salespeople anguish over issues that with my experience were no brainers. And while I was presenting an elevated work ethic, completing my assigned tasks with due diligence, I was compelled to surgically and politically offer simple and effective solutions to what was perceived by the folks in charge as major problems. I was becoming a valuable asset. This single project project, working with the furnishing's company, proved to be life changing for me. The folks in charge took immediate notice and offered me a startup position working in their warehouse. Via the temp assignment, I was making $7 an hour, and the company offered me $10 with benefits and unlimited opportunities for advancement. I thought to myself that this quite possibly would be something I could work with. I accepted the offer, already being very familiar with the primaries of the company as well as their general operations.

I began working in the warehouse and showroom accepting, stocking, and placing furnishings, as well as prepping furniture and doing customer deliveries. The company offered residential and commercial furnishings, and CAD layout and installation for modular furnishings. I worked as a stock person/installer for only a few months. Again, by offering input at what I deemed appropriate times, I began to be recognized more for my skills in visual presentation, design, graphic design, marketing, and fine art. After being with the company for only a short time, a new position was created for me: assistant to the residential VP/buyer, Racheal, responsible for assisting in the visual presentation of the showroom, to assist the buyer with acquisitions of artwork and accessories and to counsel the VP in regards to marketing, promoting, and advertising for the residential sector of the company. After taking on this position, things began to change rapidly.

Again, in a very short amount of time, I was traveling about on buying excursions, wining and dining clients, and being wined and dined by clients and vendors. At this point, I was holding down a full-time job (plus) while attempting to paint at the same time. Working 60–70 hours a week, sometimes seven days a week, left me little time to nurture my relationship with my wife. Even though Kathy was also moving up the corporate food chain, she was not on the "bullet train" I was. I perceived what I was doing as not only a viable contribution to our financial status but also a means to the end for my becoming a successful artist. My train of thought had failed me. Although both my wife and I were moving forward financially, we were becoming distant from each other.

How to Blow an Engine

Once you exceed the output capacity of an engine, there will be ramifications in the performance of that engine. How much and in what way the capacity is breached will determine the amount of damage you wind up with. A little analog to what was transpiring. I was so caught up in what was happening to me, once again I didn't see what was happening with my wife and our relationship. As I became more absorbed in my work, I took for granted that my wife would come along with me, not realizing that she was being left in the dust. At one point, she grew so frustrated with our situation that she gave me an ultimatum: "Change this, or we will fail." I, being so caught up in the flash and recognition, refused to accept what she was trying to tell me. To this day I don't know whether my response was for the good or the bad, but I chose to continue on with what I was doing. This ultimately led to our separating, again, which would have a great effect on my life.

"Everybody experiences far more than he/she understands. Yet it is experience, rather than understanding, that influences behavior." –Marshall McLuhan

This event was both tragic and exhilarating. While I understood why Kathy was unwilling to put up with the crap, I was dumping on her, I appeared to be moving in a good direction for my ambitions. Writing this now and reading it back, I perceive myself as being not much more than a self-absorbed ass at that time in my life be that as it may, I continued my course. Kathy and I separated for the second time and I began an indulgent life of debauchery once again, which seemed an appropriate course of action. Even though I was still living life as a pauper, I was experiencing the affluent life, vicariously via my employer. During this time, I became romantically involved with Racheal, the VP, I was working with. It was a grand experience. So many sensations. So much seemed to be correct and leading me to the place I had imagined I wanted to be. Dinner parties, events, meeting new folks who might offer advancement with my artwork. Still traveling at the speed of light and experiencing all sorts of new adventures. But despite all this wondrous input I was bathing in at the moment, I could not rid myself of the feeling that there was something missing. None of it could mask the loss I felt from being separated from the one I loved. This feeling grew to the point that I could no longer ignore it. I was still in close contact with Kathy even though we were living apart. Every time we saw each other, we would both come to tears. You'd think someone I might get a clue?

One afternoon in the not-so-distant future, we both broke down and admitted to each other how ridiculous we were being. After a few hours of tears and rebuking ourselves for our poor judgment, we concluded that it would be best to continue our journey together and truly accept that death would be the only thing that would come between us. That idea would end up coming back on the both of us like bad lasagna.

We ditched all the nonsense, consolidated, and ended up together in a duplex in Fair Oaks. An interesting time we were both making OK money and we were both very dedicated to healing our relationship. We put energy and effort into expanding on my wife's life experience to make sure we were both traveling through life at the same speed. We spent a good deal of time exploring what could offer her challenge and fulfilment in life beyond our simply being together. Interestingly enough, it kept circling around she liked travel, being outside, learning new stuff, and history. We put those ideas altogether and came up with Anthropology and Archeology.

Our labors were fruitful. She immediately enrolled in evening classes to study both disciplines. With both of us working full time and now involved in after-work activities every day, we barely saw each other during the week. Despite this, things were really good. I also had an interest in her studies, so when we got together, we would have in-depth discussions about art, history, and the origins and development of human culture. This was very nurturing to the artwork I was doing at the time. She joined an archeology group at her college and took an internship with a local archeologist. On the weekends, she started going on digs, searching for artifacts left by ancient folks, the explorations were set in the foothills and mid-elevations of the central Sierra Nevada mountain range of northern California. I was very happy to join her on these excursions when I could manage the time. I recall one particular time when I was able to join Kathy and her archeology crew. They were excavating a small area in the woods of the Sierra Nevada Range at about 7000' elevation. They had located the remnants of possibly a small village. From the forest floor they were extracting shrouds of pottery, bone and arrowheads. This was quite the find, as after carbon-dating some of the items, it was estimated the items to be over 400 years old. To actually touch a thing that is thought to have that much history is awe inspiring. To think how those folks existed relative to how we exist today or how we might exist in the future. "Wow." This made me pause and think about humanity as a whole. I had no idea then the important effect this would have on myself and my art in the future.

As I said, we were doing OK financially, and as if we didn't already have enough adventure in our lives, we entertained the idea of moving back onto the water. We could have a sailboat an idea that had been with us since our last houseboat. That being said, we were currently located in Sacramento, California, one hundred miles inland from the Pacific Ocean, even though there were waterways nearby, the idea of having a sailing craft for use on the Sacramento River was a bit of a novelty. It's one thing to sail about and navigate on the ocean it is another story to sail on a river. After adding things up, doing a bit of research, and shopping around, we finally managed to put a package together. We settled on a brand-new Hunter 35.5 sloop, which we picked up in the San Francisco bay and sailed up the river to Sherwood Marina, located just below Sacramento. While living on the boat, I required a separate studio space to work in. I found an historic building in Old Town Sacramento where I leased out about a 1000-square-foot space in the basement.

This period of my life is a good memory. I was with a woman I loved and cared for deeply who felt the same about me, I was living aboard my first sailboat, I was working as a creative in a position I had created, and I was painting and designing in a great workspace. I was the proverbial dog hanging his head out the window of a speeding car with his tongue flapping in the wind.

As I mentioned before, it was a real adventure learning to navigate and maneuver a midsize sailing vessel within the confines of a river. While living aboard in southern California, I had taught myself the basics of sailing on small 10"–14" sailing skiffs. I also had been afforded the opportunity to crew and skipper larger sailboats belonging to my marina friends. I must say, it's a very different experience sailing your very own home, rather than simply being the helmsman on someone else's boat. Exhilarating and powerful. To this day, I have a difficult time finding the appropriate words to express what it is and how it feels to sail one's own vessel.

"There's nothing better than messing about on boats." –Ernest Hemingway

The river and the 1400 miles of navigable delta was so very different from the ocean. I knew how to read charts, tides, and weather, how to use GPS and "dead reckon." But back in the sloughs where 5"–10" can mean the difference between sailing and running aground, moving around in a boat with a keel was a bit "white-knuckle" at times. You might be sailing along through a slough and all at once come to an abrupt halt because you'd run aground on a sandbar that wasn't there a week ago. Or travel twenty miles out into the delta via numerous small sloughs to visit a restaurant/bar suspended on stilts above the reeds only accessible by watercraft to indulge in fresh crawdads and catfish, to then later return to the main waterway after spending the night anchored up in a dead-end slough only to find that your escape has been blocked by a tree a beaver logged during the night. Life on a sailboat up river!

Back on land, I was making full use of my new studio space. It was large enough to dedicate one section to painting and another to graphics and design. Regarding graphics, it was during this time that I began to make the transition from traditional "paste-up" production to what was termed at the time "desktop publishing," meaning I had limited ability to produce my own imagery and copies in-house. I know that may not sound like a big deal, but that little technological advancement would end up changing the graphics industry forever.

Sacramento was not the Mecca of emerging contemporary art that I had known in the 70s. The art market had become settled, at best There were still enough galleries around, but the buzz was gone. I was working mainly with abstract and abstract expressionism, popping out a few representational works from time to time. I was being represented by three galleries in town. This was not a problem as they were not in competition with one another. Two of the traditional galleries were far enough apart and just different enough not to have overlapping clientele. The third was a commercial gallery with a more national reach. I began to develop a small following, and sales were OK.

My schedule was pretty demanding at the time. Working 40–50 hours a week as the creative director for the furnishing store and spending anywhere from 15–20 hours a week at the studio left me little time and energy for much else. I was able to hire an assistant at the furnishing store, which freed me up a little bit, but my position was evolving from being in creative and conceptual work to pure management, budgetary control, and executive meetings. Even though the money was good, I was changing into something I really wasn't comfortable with. Once again, I found myself disillusioned with my involvement in retail.

Around the same time, my wife felt like she had gone as far as she could go with her employer and was in search of a greater challenge. It's funny how sometimes in life when you imagine or visualize things, opportunities arise. My eldest brother had come into some money via investments and real estate, and he approached me with the idea of creating a business together. I was a bit wary, as I recalled warnings from Business 101: "Avoid going into business with friends or family!" But my wife and I were ripe for change, so we ignored the warnings and hopped on board. After much discussion, we decided on a "display house": a business that designs and produces display props, seasonal trim, and store fixturing. This was decided mainly due to the fact we both had experience in the industry. Now was the time for me to put my expertise in marketing to task. We had a limited budget for startup, so I kept my research limited to the western states of the US. After days of mulling over statistical data, we agreed on a site: San Diego, California. Next, we developed a business plan. Next was a working name for the new company: Red Door Studios. The next step was acquiring all the licensing and permits required for conducting business in the area. We then acquired a warehouse in a light industrial complex and moved all our belongs there. All that was left was to move our boat from Sacramento to San Diego, a bit over 500 miles by land and close to 800 by sea. Because in this particular instance money was more important than time, we decided to sail our boat down rather than have it trucked, saving us close to $9,000.

Sailing from Sacramento to San Diego

Our trip was set to begin in early spring off the Pacific coast can easily be classified as an "E-ticket" ride. Big swells, large wave action, high winds, and fast storm movements were characteristic of the season, and all were in evidence on our journey. I enlisted a close friend of mine, John, to help crew. We set out from Sacramento, giving ourselves around fourteen days for an otherwise week-long trip. There were other considerations too. The first was a plan to hook up with family in San Francisco for farewells. This particular objective presented a big challenge right at the start of our journey. We had sailed the hundred or so miles to anchor at the embarcadero harbor in San Francisco, where we had arranged to go ashore for dinner the night prior to our departure south.

We all met at a well-known Italian restaurant in the city. A wonderful time was had by all, but unfortunately, all three of us adventurers were struck with some alien form of food poisoning during the night. John recalls to me, whenever we talk about this journey, how he woke up on board our boat to me moaning, "Please God, kill me" as I pooped and puked my guts out. After a horrendous and mostly sleepless night, we set off at first light, out of the bay to open sea. As I mentioned, the Pacific coast can be a bit tricky in the spring. Upon leaving the Golden Gate, we were immediately confronted with fifteen-foot swells and a six-knot head on current. It made for an uncomfortable ride at best it was a horrid physical experience in our condition. We made our way south, staying 20–50 miles from the coast. The surf and the wind were attacking us from our starboard quarter, very uncomfortable. We were hoping to make it to Monterey Bay by morning. As night fell and the sea had not calmed, I found myself in one of the most intense situations of my life. To this day, when I have attempted to express what transpired, only a few mariners have been able to grasp the intensity of the circumstance.

We had slowly been making our way south all day after leaving the Golden Gate. We were experiencing a following sea with steep swells accompanied by wind chop atop each due to the average wind speed blowing at 35 knots. If one was sailing a heavy displacement 60" blue-water boat in these conditions, it would not be such an issue. But we were on a light displacement 35.5" performance boat a whole different story. I had the mainsail down to the third reef and nothing but a little patch of cloth showing for the jib (to help steer the boat). I also had to motor to help climb the backs of the swells. From the trough of each swell, we would slowly creep up the back of the next at about a 25–30-degree angle. Upon hitting the crest of each wave, the bow of the boat would come completely out of the water and point toward the sky, then drop like a rock a good 20–30 feet, placing us at the face of the wave. Then the boat would surf down the face of the wave, right into the next trough. Because we would pick up speed during that surfing phase, we would bury the bow of the boat underwater to almost midship, and as the bow rose again, hundreds of gallons of sea would rush aft to flood the cockpit. This pattern repeated about once every six to eight swells, and we did this for about thirteen hours before we decided to tuck in to Santa Cruz to anchor for the night. It was now dark, and that harbor was about an hour away.

Right about this time, the wind and the swells began to pick up a bit. The boat had already been "battened down," meaning made water-tight. The crew was below deck grabbing a bite to eat, and I was at the helm. There was no moon, so all I could see was the illumination from the cabin lights through the deck hatches, the instrument lights, and the navigation lights. At this point I was steering only by compass and GPS as there was no line of sight available. I moved off course a bit and got hit abroad by waves, so I corrected. In doing so, I pointed the boat directly south. As the boat crested the next wave, it felt a little different, like the downward angle of the boat was greater. Visibility being limited, I wasn't quite sure what to expect. When I hit the trough of the swell, I could feel the resistance to the forward movement of the boat. In the next moment, watching the yellow illumination of the cabin lights turn green through the enormous amount of water washing over the boat, I realized that my actions had temporarily turned our boat into a submarine. As the water moved aft rushing over me hip deep in the cockpit, a great feeling of humility welled up inside of me how small and insignificant I was to face the power of the sea.

We made it into Santa Cruz without damage, the three of us simply exhausted. The next morning, we had planned to make it to Moro Bay, but cut things short and tucked into Monterey as there was a weather front moving through and the winds were pushing 45 knots. Laying over the night there, hoping for the winds to die down, we left the next morning at 4:00 a.m. knowing we had a long trek in front of us. The winds had only lessened to 35 knots, so it was pretty bumpy getting out of the harbor. As the day progressed, the winds evened out at around 20–25 knots and the swells widened and lessened to around ten feet. The day was not quite so hair-raising as the last few had been. After having to navigate extra-long tacks, the journey we had estimated would take twelve hours ended up taking closer to eighteen. Normally, this would not be an issue, but we were going into Moro Bay. The entrance to the harbor is historic for its large breaking waves, as illustrated in a famous maritime photo of George C. Scott's 50" Chris-Craft, with nose to the sky, breaking through a large wave while attempting to exit the harbor. Armed with this type of information, I wanted to do everything in my power not to roll into the harbor in the dark of night. Yeah, well nothing I could do. We were coming in at night. We were still a few hours off when I hopped on the radio to raise the Coast Guard/Harbor Master no response. Little did we know that everyone in Moro Bay apparently goes home at 5:00 pm, Including the goddamn Coast

Guard. So, not only were we coming in under the cover of night, we also didn't have a clue what to expect. Needless to say, I was a bit anxious.

Fortunately, the waves at the entrance of the channel were about the same size as the swells we had been dealing with pretty much the whole trip. No sweat! Well, maybe a little. We found a dock to berth at, and early next morning, off we sailed. The plan was to push all the way to Point Hueneme in Oxnard, CA. Our only challenge on this leg of the journey was that to get to Point Hueneme, we would have to round Point Conception another challenging area off the coast of California. If you look at a map of California, you might notice that the northern coastline of the state runs pretty much north to south. About halfway down, the coastline has a sharp change of direction, with the southern coast line running northwest to southeast. Point Conception is where this change occurs. This point is also where the Pacific coastal waters change the northern ocean waters tend to be colder and rougher, while south of this point the waters tend to be warmer and more, well, Pacific. So, it's safe to assume that where these two different waters meet, a type of "storm front" condition occurs in ocean, making it a challenge for mariners to navigate safely.

There are two trains of thought in regards to navigating these waters: (1) Head out to sea and avoid the naughty place altogether, or (2) attempt to choose a time to pass when conditions are the least screwy. If you have chosen the latter option and you find you chose poorly, you can always run for the shelter of Cojo Cove which is precisely what happened with us. We had already dealt with some fairly antagonizing conditions, but this was brutal we tucked tail appropriately between our legs and ran for the shelter of Cojo. Interestingly, upon entering the sanctuary of the cove, there was not one boat to be found. After being at anchor for a few hours, the number of boats in the cove had grown to eight. Later on, we watched the weather and found a moment to escape, continuing on to Oxnard. We laid over at the Channel Islands marina at Point Hueneme for the night in a seemly well-deserved respite.

Heading out the next morning with much calmer seas and a lot less wind was a welcome pleasure, and it was easy sailing ahead all the way to our layover in the LA harbor before the final leg to San Diego. The next day was a long one but offered no major challenges. As we closed in on our final destination, we noticed an abundant amount of boat traffic just outside of San Diego Harbor. Little did we know it was the final competition of the America's Cup. We were coming into the harbor right after the end of the races. So, we were welcomed to San Diego by all the finalist 12-meter boats along with a flotilla of hundreds of spectator boats pretty festive. At last, after too many days of adventure, we had arrived at a new chapter in our life. We had a day to rest up before attacking the preparations to open Red Door Studios.

San Diego was more incredible than I could dream, more horrifying and devastating than I could possibly image. A bit of a dichotomy? After sailing over 800 nautical miles down the coast of California from San Francisco to San Diego, I had taken the first steps to becoming a mariner. As time progressed, I became much more experienced in boat-handling, sailing, navigation, and just about all things involved in messing about on boats.

Red Door Studios

Upon visiting the facility where we would house Red Door, we made a disturbing discovery. During our voyage south, there had been heavy rains in the area, and the warehouse where we had stored everything had flooded. A few of our personal items were damaged, but worse, quite a bit of my artwork had water damage. Once again, water turned out not to be my friend when it came to artwork. We got right to it my wife hustled up some temp work while I set about buying tools, equipment, and materials. After getting the shop in working order, the first order of business was to design and construct one of each of the Red Door product offerings. This would serve a few purposes. Once a prop was made, I could then figure how best to replicate it efficiently. Also, I could estimate quantities for material use as well as which materials to use. With this information, I could develop pricing. Once I had a line of goods completed, it was time to photograph everything for our promotional/marketing elements. Finally, after completing the full line, I then had a bunch of cool stuff to display in the showroom.

This whole process took a little over two months, after which it was time to get down to the business of sales. Everything was moving forward pretty much as planned, with one small hitch. In all the preliminary research I conducted before choosing the San Diego area, nothing indicated that General Dynamics would pull the plug and close down operations in the city. Had I known that a major organ in the economic body of the region was about to fail, I wouldn't even have considered it much less staked our entire lives on it. General Dynamics' closing its doors during a time of otherwise moderate economic stability sent the area into a three-year financial tailspin. Under normal circumstances, this challenge might had been survivable, but Red Door with its limited funding had only a two-year shelf life.

The next few years proved frustrating and hard. Every call I made gave us a similar response: "We love what you have to offer, but we can't afford any expenditures right now; like everyone else, we're tightening our belts." Even with all of this heavy resistance, I was able to secure and maintain a few accounts, but in the end, it was just not enough to keep the business afloat. During this time, I managed to paint and secure a couple of local gallery contacts. All of this craziness continued for about a year until it became brutally apparent that the only way Red Door would survive was to secure SBA (small business administration) financing. The smallest amount available to us was a quarter million. My brother and I considered this amount in the context of the current depressed economy and concluded it might not be a good bet. We then began the process of dissolving the company.

My wife and I considered that our credit was in good health and that in the near future with the business closing, we might be unable to make any changes. So, we decided to upgrade to a larger boat. I know this may sound a bit insane, but it turned out to be one of the better decisions we made back then. We were able to readily sell our current Hunter 35.5" for a reasonable price and buy a 43" Westsail sloop. Fifty feet overall, she was a tried and true heavy displacement, blue water, world cruiser an impressive hunk of fiberglass that opened up new doors to adventure on the water.

A note for all you folks who hate "moving," which I believe represents most every sentient being on the planet. After buying the Westsail, we had to move all our belongings from one boat to the other. We simply pulled the two boats next to each other in adjacent slips and handed everything over from cockpit to cockpit. The whole process took the two of us about two and a half hours. It was the fastest and by far the easiest move I have ever been involved with.

We also moved to a new marina on Harbor Island. After Red Door closed, I no longer had a studio to work on my art. This presented a challenge as our marina was just off of downtown, which was a high-rent district. One Saturday afternoon, Kathy and I stopped into a well-known restaurant not far from home, only to find out that it was owned by a gentleman I had become acquainted with in northern CA. As we were talking, the subject came up that I was looking for studio space. He immediately took us out to a small cottage located to the side of the restaurant. It was old and not in the best condition, but he offered it to me for $125 per month. Equal square footage in the area would easily go for $500–800. An obvious "hell yes" was given in response, and with a handshake, I had a studio to work in no more than two miles from my home.

But everything was still in flux. Both my wife and I were without steady employment, and San Diego wasn't getting any cheaper. These were challenging times that required drastic measures. I mentioned that I had been working on boats, and an opportunity arose for me to work underwater. I immediately went out and got myself certified to scuba dive an ordeal in itself. Nonetheless, I achieved a certificate quickly and went to work underwater: cleaning the bottom of boats, doing underwater repairs and underwater retrieval (people who hang around boats drop stuff in the water all the time). Signing on with an already established company, I worked out of my boat (home). This was brutal, physically demanding work at the going rate of $10 per hour, usually in cash. Living aboard a boat and waking up five days a week to have coffee in the cockpit, then slipping over the side to the finger where you don your wetsuit and gather your tools and tanks of air before heading out to the other boats surrounding you in the harbor. Spending your day scraping barnacles from the bottom of hulls, replacing zincs and props, and retrieving objects dropped overboard might seem difficult to most folks, but I actually gravitated to this way of life. If not for the incessant ear infections (due to how polluted the water was) and the low rate of pay, I would have continued in this occupation longer than I did.

As I mentioned before, at this time I also acted as crew. I became acquainted with a young man in the marina who captained a 45' Egg Harbor for fishing excursions. Soon after we got to know each other, he offered me the position of "first mate" on the vessel, although this position was a non-salaried agreement. I was simply paid a percentage of the take on any cruise I assisted with. I also applied my skills in marketing/promoting at an extra charge to the owner of the boat. I was working underwater during the week and playing first mate on a fishing boat on the weekends. And of course, I was painting and doing freelance graphic work with any spare time/energy I might have. A wild ride.

One of the many memories I retain from this experience was during the America's Cup. The boat I was working on had been retained as a "photo boat" for the races. We had six international photographers aboard, from France, Japan, England, Canada, Germany, and the US. We were also hosting a race official who was supposed to "officiate/regulate our positioning near and about the race course." As first mate, besides seeing to the needs of our guests, I was also the navigator. The night prior, I had plotted a course, reviewed it with the race official, and set up a schedule to place us near the starting line just before the start of the race. Due to a huge amount of traffic and above average winds, we were forced to redirect, which I was plotting on the fly. To help those of you who have never navigated around the America's Cup, the race boundaries are not physically visible they are only waypoints on a chart. For so many unforeseeable reasons, we ended up near the starting line about 20 minutes later than expected and about 30 yards from where we'd intended thanks to wind, traffic, and the idiot official who demanded we alter our course after he had already OK'd it. Unfortunately or perhaps fortunately, whichever way you might wish to look at it we ended up right on the starting line, right at the start of the race!

It is difficult for me to express in words the rage and intensity that followed. All at once, everything changed to confusion and insanity. There were 12-meter boats traveling within feet of us, and the main contender the New Zealand boat was fast heading directly at our midship as the skipper and crew of the New Zealand boat screamed obscenities and called for our immediate gruesome death. The moment passed; thankfully, there were no collisions and no casualties. Being so caught up in making sure of this, I didn't take notice that we had unintentionally placed all of our guests in nirvana: all of the photographers on board were snapping shots in overdrive, capturing images that if not for us being in the wrong place at the wrong time would not have been impossible.

Within seconds, over the VHF, a demanding voice rang out, "You are required to leave the area immediately. Upon returning to port, report immediately to the race committee staging area." So, the skipper and I hung our heads in shame and turned the boat around to head back. As I came down from the fly bridge to deliver the sad news to the photographers, I noticed they were all laughing and hugging each other with great joy. When I reached the lower deck, the French photographer grabbed me, kissing me wildly on each cheek, followed by each photographer hugging me in turn. One even declared us gods.

I was agog. I was trying to tell them that we were kicked off the course and would more than likely be disqualified from working the rest of the series. Finally, the photographer from the US grabbed me by the shoulders and looked me square in the eyes, expressing with grand elation "In those few crazy minutes, we all got prize-winning shots; prize-winning, man!" So, why be sad? I broke out the champagne and we had a very happy trip back to port.

When we arrived at the docks, one by one as the photographers disembarked, they kept handing me what seemed to be lots of cash as tips. I stuffed it all away and accompanied the skipper to visit the race committee. Judgment was swift and harsh: we were disqualified from the rest of the races. This was a big deal as we were looking to gross over $15,000 for the whole event, which after fuel, food, and drink would more than likely translate to about $9,000 net.

When I offered to the committee that the onboard race official had OK'd our course plan, the response was "There is no appeal, you're out." We sadly returned to the boat to review our take for the day. Surprisingly, we found that with our one day of fees and the generous tips, we had grossed over $8,000 and netted about $6,800. Not bad for such a horrendous day. The skipper and I headed out to visit a local watering hole to drown our sorrows and possibly pick up new clients.

There weren't many more excursions on the chartered boat, nor much more time spent working underwater. As always, the creative was calling me, as well as an internal awareness that there just might be something with a wee bit more substance waiting out there for me.

My wife, meanwhile, was looking for better employment. She was offered an administrative position at the regional headquarters of Hertz auto rentals. She went through the process and before we knew it, she was involved with Hertz. Right around the same time, myself also wishing to progress my employment status, I answered an ad in the local newspaper calling for professionals in the marketing and graphic design industry to offer instruction at a local private post-secondary college. I know, what the hell was I thinking given my past failed attempts in academia, the fact that I did not have a degree, and the ever-pressing issue that all I really wanted was to create art? What drew me in was that in the past, outside of an academic environment, I had been pretty successful at offering information to others in a constructive way, by way of conducting classes, working with interns, and tutoring a couple of protégés. Also, the offering was a part-time gig, which would afford me time to continue with my artwork. Maybe a bit of a stretch, but after talking it over with my wife, it seemed to make some kind of sense. I answered the ad and was surprised when I was contacted to set up an interview.

Back to School

I hosed off, threw on a suit, gathered my seemingly impressive resume, and headed out to the school for the interview, completely unaware that my life was about to change in a big way. Upon my arrival, I noticed a single parking lot (totally full) and one single-story building. Not exactly what I had imagined. Upon entering what I presumed to be the main entrance I was greeted by a receptionist, I expressed I was there to interview for a teaching position. the next thing I knew I was sitting in the dean's office, being interviewed by one of the administration's elite. I have to admit I wasn't very optimistic, considering how the interview was going. The young man conducting the session was quick and sharp with both questions and responses, almost to the point of being antagonistic or accusatory. It felt more like an inquisition than an interview. I left feeling like there was no chance in hell I would be considered. A few days later, I received a call from the school inquiring if I might be willing to return to the campus to meet with the president of the college.

A bit bewildered, I agreed. Once again, I found myself being interviewed in a similar manner, only this time without the animosity. This was something I could work with, so I joined right in with the play. Even thought we were very different personalities, the president and I seemed to connect on some level. After a long interview, I was given a tour of the campus, after which I returned to the president's office and was offered a part-time position teaching third-year student "ad campaign development." The one hour and forty-five-minute class was offered twice a week, which added up to 2.9 hours per week, or a bit over $400 per month. I agreed to take on the position, which I saw as a perfect way to supplement my art and graphic work. The position was offered to me with the stipulation that I would actively work on obtaining a BA degree. Both my wife and I were completely amazed. Here I was, a person who barely made it out of high school, being given the opportunity to teach at the undergraduate level. Damn! I was very much in line with the doctrine of the school, which took a "real world, hands on" approach. The president and owner of the school came from the ad industry and simply wished to educate and train students to become active in that industry. Pretty simple, right?

Not really. Preparing students for the industry in everything from production to creative to administration and financial budgeting was, at least, a huge undertaking. This being a private post-secondary college, it was not only important that the curricula were qualitative I would also be judged on my ability to place graduates into the industry.

As I've said before, with most all things, both my wife and myself, when afforded an opportunity, jump in with both feet. True to form, I embraced this project with great passion and seriousness. Once I began teaching my first class, I realized that in this particular environment, the only similarities to the academia I had experienced in the past were that class started and ended at a specific time, roll call was taken, and there was a loosely followed syllabus. Everything else was different the ages of the students ranged from 20–38 years (most students being in their mid-twenties), tuition was not cheap so most students actually wanted to be there, and they expected something from each and every class. It was more like having a room full of apprentices whom I would interact with on both a group and an individual basis. After teaching for a while, I thought I had died and gone to heaven. I was getting paid to share my knowledge and experience with people who desired it. What a concept.

I had learned from being in the industry that a level of professionalism was required for people to take you seriously, and I brought this lesson to the classroom. I also made myself approachable and available to every student. I tried to set a standard at the beginning of the course that the only stupid questions are the ones that aren't asked, and would describe in detail how to achieve a 4.0 in the class as well as how to achieve a 0. I treated students with respect, and I required it in return.

At the end of every quarter, each student of the college was asked to fill out an evaluation for each of their classes and instructors, after which the instructors would meet with the president of the school to review the results. At the end of the first quarter, I was filled with anticipation as I waited to be informed of the outcome. I'd had no indication whether I would be continuing on at the school, or how my students might evaluate me. I received my critiques as well as a scheduled appointment to discuss them with the president of the school. Reading them, I feared for my seemingly short life as an educator. "Very hard class," "too much expected," "teacher demands too much from us," "teacher needs to lighten up," "The worst class I've ever had here" along with comments like "I learned more in this class than any other I've taken here," "keep this instructor," "instructor offers real world information," "really hard class but good."

Regardless, I saw more negative responses than positive. I was devastated, convinced my short term as an educator was going up in flames. When my appointment with the president came, I was completely surprised to find that this was exactly what he was hoping for. He then shared some thoughts with me that he had not expressed when he brought me on board. Apparently, he had noticed in the last year that the evaluation process had become a bit like a popularity contest that the quality of student work was diminishing and possibly some of the faculty had become complacent. He added that he had hoped to shake things up a bit by introducing someone like myself into the mix. I believe it was sort of a compliment. I was given two classes for the next quarter. Not only had I made the cut, I was getting results.

I mentioned before that this was not a conventional college. For example, one of my classes was third-year Ad Campaign Development. The college had aligned itself with various nonprofit organizations. At the beginning of the quarter, a representative from one of the organizations would come to the school and present to the class the advertising, marketing, promotional, and/or graphic needs the organization had for a specific project or program. Next, with my guidance, each student would have about ten weeks to go through the process of developing their solution for the client's request via the creation of first thumbnails, then semi-comps, and finally finished comps ready to present to the client. The final week was spent preparing each student to pitch their concept. On the last day of class, each student would present their seemingly grand campaign to a group of representatives from the organization. I found this means of education to be nothing less than brilliant. It was a great way to transfer knowledge while being highly fulfilling for me as the instructor, and in most cases, everybody won the nonprofit organizations received fresh new ideas pro bono, the students were guided through hands-on industry experience, and I got tons of gratification and fulfillment. What's not to like!

Still the Damn Tremors

During this time, I was still painting and doing occasional graphic work. I was also still cursed with the damn tremors in fact, the disability seemed to be progressing. They were a bit more pronounced, and not just in my right arm and hand, but were now present in my upper trunk as well as my left hand. A real goddamn nuisance. I had tried all the drugs available with very little effect. What was worse, all the medications prescribed for this condition came with nasty side effects, most of them especially hard on the liver and heart. In my research, I found that in the old days, alcohol, especially wine, was prescribed to lessen tremors, with the only big side effects being drunkenness (along with the very real probability of addiction). Armed with the information from my doctors that my cursed disability was not going to miraculously disappear and, in all likelihood, would become more problematic, I began the process of seriously experimenting with different painting techniques in the hope I might develop a technique I could sustain as long as possible despite the advancement of my condition. The basic technique I settled on was a combination of methods I had used in the past: working with water paints on canvas, laying down a foundation of brightly colored brush strokes and shapes, then applying multicolored, nonpermanent water paint, then using water to remove the top layers of paint so that the foundation layer would show through. I would vary the amounts of paint I removed to create images, shapes, and symbols; once the painting was complete, I would apply varnish to make the work permanent.

Over the next year, life on all levels seemed to progress at an unbelievable rate. Kathy moved up the corporate ladder to Regional VP of Operations for Hertz, and at the school, I went from one class to full time.

I was really in my element at the college. I had developed a good rapport with the student body as well as the faculty, and I was making headway in the community, dealing on behalf of the school with their nonprofit partners. I was asked to sit on the board of the San Diego chapter of the Ad Club as well as the boards of two of the nonprofits. It was all so crazy! A few years prior, my wife and I were barely scraping by, with me working underwater and my wife basically an administrative assistant. Now we were pulling down six figures with the prestigious titles to match, along with my recognition in the San Diego community.

It was a lot to digest, but what came next was even more bizarre: the president of the college asked me if I would take over as acting dean of the school. This was big. Even though I exhibited all the qualifications, I could not in title be called the "dean" because I had not yet completed my degree. So, in title, I would be deemed the "Career Development Administrator." In this position, I would be responsible for hiring, firing, and managing a faculty of twenty-five instructors as well as conducting all graduate exit interviews, the career development program, overseeing the library and its staff, directing the student council, counseling and disciplining the student body, and overseeing research and development of current and new curricula. Holy crap, where the hell did this come from? Surprisingly, it wasn't a huge jump in salary, but after a bit of discussion with Kathy, I accepted the offer. I had always possessed an overdeveloped imagination, but as a younger man, even in my wildest of thoughts I never imagined being married to an exceptional and beautiful VP of a major corporation while acting as the dean of a private college, sitting on the board of directors for three organizations, and living on a 50" sailboat in one of the most desirable cities in the US. Just damn! In a Hollywood movie, this would be the perfect place for a happy and successful conclusion to my story. But wait there's more.

Life was better in this time than I had ever experienced prior. Both my wife and I rolled in it, like a dog happily rolls in dead stuff. We embraced our newfound existence with great exuberance. The demands on my time and energy were unbelievable. Up and above fifty hours at the school, easily another 10–15 hours in community involvement, the same at the studio, painting. I was averaging a whopping 60–75 hours a week working, with whatever minutes of time that was left spent on life.

Unlike many other folks we knew who also lived on boats, my wife and I saw it important to experience everything the lifestyle had to offer, which very much included going out and about on the ocean. Both Kathy and I agreed early on that since we lived on a mobile vessel, if we could not ready the boat for travel in less than fifteen minutes, we were living in the wrong place. We were both adept at handling the boat, and I had become comfortable with single-handing the vessel. A quality inexpensive weekend for us consisted of meeting at the boat on Friday evening after work, sharing an adult beverage, readying the boat, leaving the slip, motoring out to the mouth of the San Diego harbor, finding a good point of sail according to the wind and sea, setting the autopilot so we might enjoy preparing and eating dinner, and enjoying an after-dinner adult beverage while we sailed into the night. When we were done with sailing, we would make sure we were clear of the shipping lanes, set the boat alee, and drift in the ocean while we slept, waking the next morning anywhere from 35-50 miles off shore. Those next mornings were such a gift. Usually waking before sunrise, whoever was up first would get the coffee going. The sensation of walking up into the cockpit, fresh coffee in hand, to survey your surroundings of nothing less than 360 degrees of incredible ocean with no land in sight was much more powerful than any of the hallucinogenic chemicals I had experienced in my youth. We would then take in the morning, after which we would make the leisurely sail back home. It was a small way to afford ourselves a wee bit of real quality time amid the insanity we had created on land. We used the boat as much as we possibly could: short trips to Mission Bay just to hang out for the weekend, sailing down to the Coronado Islands to dive and fish, sailing to Catalina Island for diving, fishing, hiking, and a wee bit of island night life. On days when Kathy had to work and I could squeeze in a few hours of leisure, I'd take the boat out alone, try to anchor on top of some fish, and do my best to bring a few tasty brutes onboard, then head back to the slip where I would gut and filet my catch, preparing a little fresh feast for when my honey returned home from work.

Taking on Water

One Christmas, my wife and I decided to shed the family obligations and just do something for each other. We planned to sail from San Diego to Cat Harbor (the bay on the west side of Catalina Island). Approximately 100 miles of sailing. Under good sailing conditions, this would be about an 18–22-hour trip. We left San Diego first thing in the morning, two days before Christmas. The day was overcast with totally calm winds and sea. So, we were looking at no sailing, just motoring for the first part of the journey. Once we were about thirty miles off the coast, it became very eerie. It was still very grey out from the overcast, and the sea was "swimming pool" calm completely flat, not a ripple, no wind anywhere. It was very surreal looking out from the deck of *Terrapin*, it was impossible to distinguish the horizon. It was as if we were suspended in a universe of grey. As if this wasn't weird enough, suddenly we saw breaks in the surface of the water. Around the boat was a crowd of porpoises. Before we knew it, we could see thousands breaking the water in every direction. I truly cannot express the impact of this experience, which lasted for a few hours.

We motored on into the night. Sometime after dinner, the wind started to pick up not much, just a steady breeze, but still: off with the engine and up go the sails. By just before daybreak, the wind and the ocean were up. We had been sailing for a few hours laid over at about 30 degrees. Both my wife and I had been up in the cockpit for last few hours. Thinking about breakfast, my wife went below to prepare our mobile morning feast. Upon entering the cabin, she screamed: She found about three inches of sea washing around above the floorboards in the saloon. For anyone who knows nothing about boats the water is supposed to stay *outside* the boat. We were both highly alarmed. I went below to survey things. Knowing that the boat had a 38-ton displacement, I became very afraid. Although we did not know at the moment why, we had to assume the boat was sinking. And remember, this was our home I immediately instructed my wife to gather all documents, photos, and anything else too important to lose to the sea. I did a quick assessment and found that if things were to carry on as they were, we were going to be at the point of total loss in a very short time. While standing below in the cabin in now about five inches of seawater, I placed "the call" on the VHF radio, being very sure of my wording. The word "MAYDAY," in my understanding, is reserved for imminent disaster and death. The words "vessel in distress" are reserved for a boat that was imminently heading in that direction.

With a meek tone on the Coast Guard radio band of the VHF radio, I offered my call numbers, next repeating "vessel in distress" three times. An immediate response came from the Coast Guard, acknowledging the transition. Shakily, I described our current situation. I was dismayed at the response I received. The Coast Guard expressed that it would be anywhere from an hour and a half to two hours before they might arrive at our location. This being said, a common practice of mariners out at sea is monitor the Coast Guard channel. I knew other folks were listening to this call. All three of my automatic bilge pumps were working at full capacity. Both my wife and I were using available hand pumps and even buckets to get the water where it was supposed to be. With all of our so-called "important stuff" piled in an inflatable tethered next to our sinking vessel, the situation was not looking like it would end well. Right about then, a boat that was in the area and had heard our distress call showed up alongside prepared for a possible extraction. I thought we were making headway in our efforts and asked if instead of an extraction, they might have any hand pumps on board. They offered what they had, and Kathy and I frantically continued our pursuit. In a short time, with the other boat standing by, we were able to get the immediate issue resolved. I found that the flange connecting the water exhaust had broken. For all you folks that do not grasp what this means: This six-inch hole in the hull, located just above the water line, would allow seawater to flow into the boat at a rate of hundreds of gallons per minute. Not a good thing. Once the immediate threat was removed, I was able to repair the broken flange with emergency epoxy, which I hoped would last for the remainder of our journey. After a few hours of pure torture adrift at sea, not knowing whether we were going to lose almost all of our belongings, we were on our tenuous way to Cat Harbor to "enjoy" the relaxing holiday we had imagined. We arrived at port, anchored, and spent the rest of the day pretty much like zombies and yes, downing a few adult beverages to adjust our frazzled nerves, retiring very early.

The next day, Christmas morning, was much different. We woke just before sunrise, put the coffee on, and threw some eggs and veggies together just in time for Christmas breakfast in the cockpit with a beautiful sunrise. It was a glorious crisp morning, just a slight breeze; we were anchored in about fifty feet of crystal-clear water so clear I could see even the small fish swimming on the bottom of the bay. Kathy, still a bit tweaked from the day before, went back to bed. I had spied some nice-sized fish hanging on the bottom near the boat. Woo-woo! It was time for one of my favorite things fishing! I slipped into my wetsuit, slapped a full tank on my back, and grabbed my trusty "Hawaiian Sling" (a thin eight-foot pole with a rubber loop attached to one end and three sharp prongs at the other, used for spearing fish). Into the water I went. It was surreal visibility was a good eighty feet. It seemed like I could see forever. I descended to the bottom and before I knew it, I was tracking a good size sheepshead let loose my sling and "pop" tagged him. I returned to the surface near the boat to find Kathy up and about in the cockpit. I handed my prize fish off to her and headed back down to the bottom. Within about ten minutes, I had tagged another two: a good-sized kelp bass and a sizable sculpin (poisonous spines on its back and gills, but tasty fluffy white meat inside). That was it. With those three fish, we had enough for lunch and dinner for the next two days. I got back on board, hosed off, and donned some shorts and my favorite Tommy Bahama shirt my customary Christmas attire while on or near the ocean. As I was cleaning the fish while enjoying a pretty high-octane eggnog, I was watching an older gentleman sail in to anchor about 100 yards off our stern. Sailing in to anchor is a tricky process. Most folks drop the sails and use the motor to anchor. If you're using your sails to anchor, it usually means you either don't have a motor or it's broken. He appeared to be single-handing the boat, with his first mate being a small brown dachshund. He did just fine dropped his sails and then he and his mate retired to the cockpit to enjoy a smoke.

I talked it over with Kathy, and we both agreed it being Christmas and all that we would prepare a "goodie basket" and row it over to him. So, we went all out: we filled a wicker clothesbasket with fruits and vegetables, nuts, homemade bread, cookies, crackers, cheese, ham, one of the fish I caught, a bottle of wine, and since I saw he smoked, I threw in a few packs of cigarettes. We even had a leftover ham bone that we wrapped a ribbon around for the first mate. Made it all nice and tidy, lowered it into the inflatable, and motored it over to our new neighbor. As I neared the boat, I could see it was pretty well worn.

I announced my arrival: "Ahoy, Merry Christmas." First, I was greeted by "Skipper," the dachshund. Then I met the captain of the boat, Martin. He was a thin older man with a face well carved with experience. I offered the gift basket to him and he seemed very grateful to the point of tearing up. I came aboard and we sat in the cockpit sharing a cup of wine and a smoke while he told me a bit of his story. Martin was a retired Merchant Marine. His boat and his dog were everything he owned. His boat was a 28" Robert's sloop no engine, no galley, no head, no radio, no navigational equipment. Not much more than a bare hull with a bunk and a water tank. He explained he had just come up from Mexico on his way to make contact with some folks in Ventura. For the last four days, he and his mate had been getting by on hardtack and water, and the smoke he had when he arrived was his last one. Not having a tender and not having a motor made it a challenge to fill his water tank. This guy was a real adventurer at seventy years old.

We talked a little more, then I dove into the logistics of how we might assist him in his journey. I returned to *Terrapin* and shared with Kathy what I had learned. She was on board with the plan to offer assistance. We spent the next day gathering supplies and helping him get his water tank filled. We ended up leaving at the same time. He sailed north stocked with a pirate's necessities water, a jug of rum, coffee, tobacco, and of course some other foodstuffs; ourselves heading south back to San Diego with a good holiday feeling. Our boat didn't sink, we had a great time, and became a part of someone's odyssey.

Meanwhile, back on land, life was hectic. My wife was addressing her duties as a VP and I was teaching, administrating, and painting. I had been moving slowly from an abstract-expressionism approach to a more representational, intuitive means of addressing my artwork, which I found to offer more fulfillment. I was entering a new chapter of work, somewhat combining techniques and sensibilities I had addressed in the past with new ideas that I had gained along the way. Together, we were doing well financially, which allowed us the opportunity to travel. To get more bang for our buck, we decided it best to stay in the western hemisphere. Our travels had been pretty limited thus far Hawaii, just across the border in Canada, and the same in Mexico. Both of us had an affinity for Latin culture, so we looked south. We narrowed it down to the Amazon or Costa Rica, settling on Costa Rica because it was about half the cost and we could spend more time there. We both had about six weeks of vacation time coming to us.

We flew into San Jose and rented a car before driving to Manuel Antonio, located on the west coast of the country. Spent about ten days in a beautiful small hotel (only four large suites) that looked out over the jungle canopy to the Pacific. The wildlife was abundant one afternoon, I heard a lot of loud barking sounds right outside our room. I went out on the balcony to be greeted by a large troop of howler monkeys messing about in the trees, some almost close enough to shake hands with. We drove back to San Jose and snagged a ride on a small four-seat plane south to Golfito, a small pueblo situated on the edge of a large bay near the Osa Peninsula. We dropped out of the sky to land on a short dirt path they were calling a runway to find no ticket office, no baggage claim nothing but the thin dirt path. We could see our hotel a short distance away nestled in the jungle at the edge of town. We were dropped off at the so-called airport, with the plane circling around to take off as soon as we disembarked. We were very excited because Golfito was not a tourist destination and we had already done the tourist thing. We wanted to experience the "real" Costa Rica. As we neared the entrance to our hotel, we couldn't help but notice a few men dressed in military uniforms sporting automatic weapons. As we drew nearer, two of the men came toward us saying *"Alto-alto."* All at once it became very uncomfortable.

One of the men, his weapon raised, said *"No entrar, hotel es cerato."* Holy crap! There we were in the middle of nowhere, in a foreign country, with very little command of the language, and no place to stay. We didn't know if there was another hotel, and the plane was not returning for us for almost a month. The soldiers were of no help. We also had a fair amount of luggage to drag around. We were able to ascertain from one of the soldiers which direction we should head to get to town. Did I forget to mention it was the "green season" of summer? This meant it rained most every afternoon with the high daytime temp being 80–90 degrees at 90–100 percent humidity. Just brutal for a couple of west coast gringos. Luckily, about half a mile down the road, we were able to flag down one of the three taxis in town. We agonized while communicating our situation in a mixture of Spanish and English somehow, were able to make our point. The driver took us to the only other place in the area: a small resort about five miles south of town. It was a little run-down, kind of charming at the same time, and it had all the requirements a bar, restaurant, and individual *casitas* overlooking the bay. It was actually better than where we were planning to stay.

We stayed for the week, exploring the area. We had made contact with an older *Tico* (the term for a native Costa Rican), a boat skipper who ferried us around on various excursions. A big plus was that the gentleman spoke a little English. He hit us with a wild idea: he would gather all the necessary provisions to ferry us to a small uninhabited jungle island, located on the bay below the Osa Peninsula, that he knew had fresh water and a good amount of wildlife. Hell yes! We were picked up before first light at the hotel by his son, who then delivered us to the beach where his father's panga was waiting. It was loaded with two large ice chests, a few boxes of dry goods, hammocks, tarps for the rain, sleeping bags, fishing and snorkeling equipment, a Hawaiian Sling (a long light metal rod, with an elastic rubber band attached to one end and three eight inch sharpened prongs sticking out of the other end), rum, beer, drinking water, a solar shower, and walkie-talkies. Wow! This guy was crazy good at this. We agreed to stay for four days. We took a short boat ride out on the bay, arriving on a small beach located on a jungle oasis about a half a mile across. After offloading all the supplies and giving us a few instructions on what to do (and not to do), the panga motored off into the distance. What an exhilarating feeling, to intentionally maroon yourself on a tropical island. We had a stellar time. Ran around naked or half naked most of the time, caught fish to eat, collected various crustaceans to tickle our taste buds, munched on fresh fruit, made weird umbrella drinks with Costa Rican rum, ate Costa Rican beef (Costa Rican beef bears little resemblance to the meat product we call beef in the US), it is simply better meat, and only saw a few fishing boats pass by to remind us of civilization. We were joined by a fair number of coatimundis, iguanas, turtles, crabs, macaws, kestrels, and more. All in all, it remains one of the most wonderful recreational experiences of my life. When we were picked up, we both were giddy as schoolkids. After that, we spent a few more days lounging at the hotel, then it was back to San Jose and on to San Diego.

As I said before, I was toying with new painting techniques. I began painting on canvas more and more, instead of paper or board. Experimenting with texture and underpainting, equipped with my new experiences, I began to paint more people, influenced by Kathy's interest in anthropology, archeology, and in an attempt to express my take on the "human experience." A whole new realm was opening up in my work. In the past, I had focused on illustrating the environments people might be in. Now, I wished to explore the people themselves. At the same time, I was becoming disillusioned with what was being called "contemporary art." In my opinion, as far back as the 1930s the definitions of visual art were being systematically challenged. Not necessarily a bad thing it just opened the door to anyone who wished to express themselves to do so. It did not matter much whether the artist might be skilled in a discipline, if they possessed a specific skillset or talent, or if they were simply someone who wished to express themselves. This ideal directly translated to the idea that "anything is art." An emotionally disturbed individual moving pigment around on a panel, a pachyderm randomly placing paint on a canvas, a person staying in bed for an extended period of time, a person piling rat excrement in the corner of an exclusive NY gallery all of it was "art." According to what I had learned, art required some form of application or at least some discipline. To be called an artist, or in my case more specifically a painter, one needed to have skills or expertise in moving pigment about with the intent to express an aesthetic or conceptual premise, and/or the skill or expertise to transform an aesthetic idea or concept to a three-dimensional work (sculptor).

NOTE: This all makes me wonder if, in the not-too-distant future, our culture will even require painters and sculptors.

I had come in contact with a gallery owner in San Diego who ended up exhibiting my work for a few years. One afternoon Susie and I were having a friendly chat, the subject of Mexico came up, more specifically Yelapa, and she insisted I should go there. This was very intriguing to me, as in my past on two separate occasions, two completely unrelated folks had expressed to me the very same thing. One was a young man who lived in my marina in Sacramento, California who had told me he was raised in Yelapa. The second was Thomas, whom I met via the furniture store I worked at, a painter who had shared with me that he had a house in Yelapa where he spent his winters.

OK, enough, I should go to Yelapa! I returned home and shared the conversation with Kathy, and after doing a little snooping around on the internet, we both agreed our next trip would be to Yelapa.

Yelapa was a small fishing village set on a small bay connecting to the Bay of Banderas on the west coast of Jalisco, Mexico, about twenty nautical miles south of Puerta Vallarta. I say nautical miles because even though Yelapa was fixed on the mainland, there were no developed roads attaching it to the rest of the world. It was only accessible by boat or a very long journey through the jungle by *burro*. Yelapa was also *Hecho* land roughly translated as "protected Indian land." It seems that prior to the meager development of the small village, the area had been inhabited by three different groups of indigenous peoples, adding to its interesting history.

Night of the Iguana (1964) was a film directed by John Huston and starring Richard Burton, Eva Gardner, and Deborah Kerr, based on the 1961 play of the same name by Tennessee Williams. The film was shot on location in Mismaloya, located just a few miles up the coast from Yelapa. Even though the film was being shot in a remote location, the folks involved needed a place to refuel and get away from it all. Yelapa was that place. The mega-stars and crew would descend on the sleepy village to escape the invading pressures of the media. This action I believe set the pace for the future of Yelapa as "the place to get away from it all." After the film was released, more gringos descended upon the little village in attempt to experience the same thing. Not long after, in the late 60s and early 70s, with the advancement in popularity of both rock and pop culture, well-known artists began to make pilgrimages to Yelapa.

On our first visit to Yelapa, I had no idea it would soon become an integral part of my existence. Kathy and I stepped off the panga onto the pier at the north end of the village, and I felt a bizarre feeling of "home" rush over me. In that first week of our stay, we made instantaneous connections with both locals and expatriate gringos in the area. It was an almost spiritual experience. Both Kathy and I returned from our visit wondering "what the hell happened?" We returned to Yelapa four or five times in the next few years, building on the connections and relationships we had found there. I even painted and sketched while I was there, something I never did while vacationing.

Meanwhile, we were growing in all directions. My wife was gaining respect and recognition in her field, and I was growing in my involvement in academia as well as with my artwork I was bursting out at the seams. I had settled in with a somewhat new technique that had evolved from the practices I mentioned previously. I looked at it as a "semi-permanent path to permanence."

The market for boats was good at the time, and we found *Terrapin* to be turning into a bit of a money pit. We were able to sell her in a short time at a small profit pretty much unheard of in the boating industry. We found her replacement a few hundred miles up the coast: a 42' Cheoy Lee Golden Wave. We were in love; she was such a beautiful thing such a beauty that "Bugle Boy" (fashion retail brand) was planning on shooting a commercial in the area where we picked up the boat and we were approached by a representative of the project who offered us $1500 per day to shoot on our new boat. We were very flattered, but declined as we were on a tight schedule to return home.

I could never have imagined this time of existence for myself. I was being challenged, growing, connecting with not only my community but with the world around me on more levels than I can describe without boring you. I was experiencing the self-awareness of "being there."

With all of this wild life experience transpiring about us, we started to consider the prospect of putting down roots possibly selling the boat and buying a landbound house. Wow, this was in and of itself a wild change. After sixteen years of living aboard, we agreed it was time. We put the boat up for sale just a few short years after we bought it and began looking around at possible properties. So much happened in this short transition period. We moved ashore, right into an artist's loft in the epicenter of the "Gaslamp" district of San Diego. We began a time of great self-expansion while experiencing a new side of culture we had not truly indulged before as a couple: the urban scene. Again, like two hungry kids in a candy store, we wanted to taste everything. It was a little weird not being on the water, but we were so adapting to our environment. One of the most prominent changes was that I no longer required an offsite studio, and so once again, my work was brought into the home. Possibly due to the excessive amount of new input, my artistic endeavors flourished. It all seemed to be somehow connected. I was surprised to find that at such a time when I was so overly taxed in terms of my output of energy as well as the amount of new experiences I was being offered, my work would develop as it did. I began to produce an abundance of work that had primitive content, addressing what appeared to me to represent some of the fundamentals of the human experience.

What a brilliant time to be alive and working. I intuitively laid out a particular work that would be titled "Alone in the Jungle," a large piece depicting a subject I had not directly addressed in the past: me. A sort of self-portrait, surrounded by cryptic markings petroglyphs, symbols, and primal images. After its completion, I stood back and looked at it only to conclude, "It's not bad, but what the hell is your point?" A short time later, this question would be poignantly answered.

Our hunt for a house in our price range was taking a bit of time which really didn't bother us too much, as we were enjoying our current lifestyle. The main reasons we were considering the purchase of a home were (1) to become property owners and (2) because we were getting hammered on taxes. Finally, we found something, put an offer in that was accepted, and put the house into escrow. We had already planned a short trip back to Yelapa, so we thought what the hell and took off.

A few days into our stay in Yelapa, while we were attending a party up in the pueblo, things began to change. At one point during the evening, Kathy disappeared to the bathroom a few times. The last time, when she returned to the table, she was white as a ghost. She was on her period, but expressed she was losing a lot of blood! It was quite a frightening mile walk back to the hotel; she became so weak I ended up carrying her for the last leg of it. During the night, she continued bleeding. There was no clinic or medical service in Yelapa at that time, so we arranged for a panga to take us to Puerta Vallarta at first light, then caught a cab to the hospital. After seeing a doctor, we were told that without running a lot of tests, the only thing they would consider was an emergency hysterectomy. Not something we wished to entertain in a foreign country on the fly. They set her up so that she might make the trip to San Diego and helped arrange to get us on the next flight out. By the time we got back home, Kathy's issues had subsided a bit. She went to see her gynecologist the next day and was scheduled for a hysterectomy around the same time escrow was supposed to be closing on the house. Kathy attempted to return to work, only making it for a few hours. Something was just not right, she had very little energy. So, she took some sick leave she had accrued, having never missed a day of work in her time with Hertz.

1998, Tragic Times

The day came for Kathy to go in for her surgery. We got her to the hospital around 9:00; she was prepped and into surgery by 11:00. It was supposed to be no more than a couple hours, so I waited there at the hospital. Two hours went by, then three and then four. By that time, I was freaking out, asking anyone who would listen to me "What the hell is going on?" Her doctor sent out word from surgery just before 4:00 p.m.

"There were some problems during Kathy's surgery," the doctor said, adding that she was "sure Kathy would make it out of surgery OK." Finally, more than seven hours after it all began, I was informed that I would soon be able to visit her in recovery, but the doctor wanted to speak with me beforehand. I was a wreck! Waiting around the hospital for seven hours with little or no information, and now the doctor wanted to talk with me before I could see my wife. On my way to meet with Kathy's physician, the thought that something was seriously wrong kept repeating over and over again in my mind. There were a couple of chairs and a table set at the end of a corridor. I was told to have a seat and the doctor would be out shortly. So, I sat and waited some more. A door across the way opened and out came the doctor. I had met her before, and besides the fact of her being a doctor, she had struck me as being an OK person. I immediately noticed her eyes were red and swollen.

When she began her conversation with "I'm not quite sure how to say this to you," my eyes began to well up. She proceeded to tell me the procedure went quite well but then came the goddamn hook. She went on to say that during the procedure, they found present a large amount of a rare form of cancer, leiomyosarcoma, that had already spread to several other organs. She added with an encouraging note that they felt they had removed upwards of 90 percent of the cancerous tissue. Not wishing to seem totally and completely destroyed by this information, I asked, OK, so what's the prognosis?

The doctor added "it doesn't look good," and that she had found in her limited experience with this particular form of cancer, "it was definitely terminal," with rapid advancement. The longest a person with this form of cancer had lived was about five months, but there was no record of anyone ever surviving this. We briefly discussed possible treatments and the "what the hell to do from this point." It's impossible to express in words everything that surrounded me at this moment. The doctor explained that she had not shared this with Kathy yet, as she wanted to wait till, she was out of recovery. Going in to see my wife became a challenge I knew she had a terminal illness, but she did not know, and I couldn't tell her at the moment. I guess it didn't matter to her that much she was still pretty out of it from being sedated for so long.

A little later I met her in her room for a quick goodnight; she was ready for sleep. I went out to the car to drive home and it all hit me I broke into uncontrollable sobbing. I just didn't get it. Kathy was always healthy and on the go; hell, she was only forty. By this time, it was already tomorrow. I found a local bar and closed it down, then headed home. I turned on the tube and pretty much drank till I could not keep my eyes open. Lying down on the sofa, I actually slept for a couple of hours. I got up, made some coffee, and made a list of who I needed to call. This may not sound so hard, but I just could not fight the tears. I pulled myself together so I could go back to the hospital and meet with Kathy and the doctor. Parking at the hospital was challenging at best there simply weren't enough spots, which would bring about a bad moment in the near future. I got up to see Kathy, who was doing much better than when I had left her the night before. Surprisingly, the doctor showed up right after me and then proceeded to lay everything out for Kathy, who seemed to be taking the news with a stiff upper lip. There was bit of Q&A, then the doc hugged us both and wished us the best. Right after the doctor left, we looked at one another while we were holding each other tight and broke into tears.

Kathy muttered through her tears, "I don't want to die. We've both worked so hard and everything is so good!" We cried, talked, and held each other for the rest of the day till the nurses kicked me out. This marked the beginning of a very surreal time for myself as well as the beginning of the end for my beautiful wife.

From the time I first began writing this book, I have found it to be difficult to capture a period from my past in words. I actually have to revisit that period of time in my conscious mind to remember, relive, and rehash the events. This is one period in time that pushes the boundaries of being "too hard."

After a few days of trying to get our affairs in order to prepare for what was to come. I tried to return to work at the school what a stupid idea! All of the faculty and many of the student body had met or known Kathy. From the moment I hit the front door, it was nothing but tears and hugs. I barely made it through my first class. I spoke with the president of the school and he graciously suggested I take an extended paid leave of absence. "OK!"

Kathy was in the hospital for about a week. I had made arrangements for a hospital bed and daily nurse visitation at our apartment. I also received instructions on giving shots, changing IVs, and changing waste bags. I charged into the role of "caregiver." I was also behaving as I believe every other person would while dealing with a loved one's cancer. I spent hours researching possible treatments. Kathy had a few chemo and radiation treatments while she was still in the hospital, but by the time she returned to our home, she was "over it." The treatments were invasive and almost completely incapacitated her. As I shared with her remote possibilities of obscure treatments in South America, she demanded that I stop the lunacy "I know I'm dying, please let me have a little bit of life." I tried to take on her request, running interference between her relatives and friends who were completely convinced they had stumbled upon the latest trendy cure as well as the droves of medical shits who basically wanted to prod and probe her in regards to further medical trials. I was simply trying to take care of the shit storm taking place all around us and eking out moments to love and be with her as she met her end a tall order. I took on the task with nothing less than total commitment to her happiness loaded our patio with growing flowers, carriage rides morning and night though the park, recounting stories of our existence, greeting her needs with smiles and loving candlelit dinners on the beach. If she had a thought, I would do everything in my power to make it come to pass. Working with the president of the school, we arranged for Kathy to visit Marine World in San Diego and get in the water to interact with the dolphins there. No matter what was done, Kathy's condition was progressing and she ended up back in the hospital. A tragic time for everyone involved.

Kathy had deteriorated into critical condition. It was coming to a point where she was doing mass quantities of morphine to handle the pain. She could no longer walk and could barely rise out of bed. She had only been back in the hospital for a few days when we began to discuss moving her to hospice. It was right about this time I had the bad moment I spoke of earlier. As I said, parking was impossible at the hospital. I did not mention the hospital was Catholic.

I had left the hospital earlier in the day, but was called to return because Kathy had taken a turn for the worse. I jammed back to the hospital, circling the area frantically without success trying to find a place to park. I must add, I was wound a wee bit tight with all that was transpiring. I finally said "screw it" and parked in front of the main entrance. I had already spent a great deal of time getting there as well as looking for a place to park, and I kind of assumed it might be important for me to be there in a timely manner. With all that was going on, mentally and emotionally, I was right at the edge.

As I walked through the front door, I was immediately met by two nuns who proceeded to block my forward movement, both of them expressing almost in unison, "Sir, you can't park there."

My response was "This is an emergency; I will move the car as soon as I can." My response fell on deaf ears.

They continued to block my path, both of them pushing their hands against my chest in an attempt to stop me, repeating "you cannot leave your vehicle there." A vision passed before my eyes where I finally reached Kathy in her hospital room only to find she had already died, before I could get there, totally overcome with grief, returning to the lobby to, with great joy, brutally slay the same two nuns who were currently providing me with a huge amount of crap. While one of the worthless pieces of skin continued to physically block my movement, the other was calling for security. Security arrived immediately and grabbed me by the arm.

I held my arms to the sky, screaming at the top of my lungs while sobbing, "ARE YOU PEOPLE FUCKING INSANE? MY WIFE IS UPSTAIRS DYING AND YOU WANT TO SCREW WITH ME ABOUT PARKING! DAMN YOU ALL TO HELL YOU WORTHLESS PIECES OF SHIT!" The security guard grabbed me by both arms, temporarily restraining me. I said to him, "Let me go you piece of shit. If my wife dies and I'm not there because of this bullshit, I'll hunt you down and end your fucking life. Now let me go!" At this point, everything was way out of hand.

Fortunately for everyone involved, there was a young man waiting in the lobby witnessing these events unfold. He ran to my side and offered, "Give me your keys, I'll move your car and find you later." I instantly gave the young man my keys, broke loose the grip of the mindless security guard, and with great disdain for the preceding events, headed to my wife's side. Lucky for me and others, she had not passed, but she was in dire straits.

The nurses and doctor asked what took me so long. I replied "Ask your board of directors and the assholes in the lobby." This whole experience reeked of a misunderstanding of what is truly important. That day, we worked through the process of moving Kathy to hospice. Later, I met with and apologized to the nuns and security for my vulgarity, but added that they might want to take a second look at their priorities. The young man who had helped defuse the insanity earlier found me and returned my keys, letting me know where he parked the car. I embraced him and thanked him with all my heart.

Also, that afternoon, our realtor and the folks from escrow kept frantically calling. Finally, I took a minute to answer. I was informed that everything was in order and that we needed to sign the papers that day or the house was going to fall out of escrow. I did my best to explain what was going on, adding that I really didn't give a rat's ass about the house, escrow, or anything else that did not have to with Kathy's life or what was left of it at that very moment. Thanks to a few folks and some fancy footwork, we lost the house but did not lose all the funds we had dedicated to the process.

We moved Kathy to the hospice facility. My wife, my love, my friend was slipping away. I had involved myself so much in her life, it was impossible for me to consider her death. The counselors at the hospice facility made sure I understood the concept. Basically, Kathy was going to die there. There was not going to be any healing, treating, or making better. Interestingly enough, a few days earlier I had been contacted by a representative of the "Hemlock Society." I understood what they were presenting to me, but could not in clear conscience take an active hand in my wife's passing. There have been times, thinking back to that moment, when I wonder if that direction might have been a kinder path for Kathy. Incredibly, in her last days, a few of her "Catholic" relatives had found out that we were going to have her body cremated. Can you believe they actually contacted me to express that we were committing a sinful act in the eyes of the church and that if we wished for Kathy to be admitted into heaven, we could not possibly go forward with our plans? As you might imagine, my response was harsh and sharp as a knife. To this day I am amazed at the audacity and lack of consideration those worthless pukes had for Kathy. It was a representation of the brutal and horrific acts demonstrated throughout history by folks who say they are acting in the name of "God" or "the church"!

Kathy was only in hospice for a few days. The staff at the facility were incredible. Basically, it was all about the patient being in the worst possible end situation with hospice attempting to make that horrible time a wee bit more tolerable.

She passed in the evening, and even completely saturated with pain meds, she fought for her last breaths. Again, it is impossible to express in written words what it is like to witness your love being taken from you in such a horrible way. I held her, not wishing to let go. The nurses had to physically pry me from her. With the help of her parents, we addressed the immediate required functions. Then I tearfully embraced Kathy's parents and drove home. As an act of kindness, they offered to stay at the facility because it was going to take a few hours for hospice to ready her body and inform the morgue. I was not aware when I said goodbye to those two fine people with whom I had at that time spent half my life that I would only see them once again. Surprisingly, I was able to navigate my way home. When I arrived, I entered our apartment, a place that at that moment felt foreign to me. I was a stranger in a strange land. Everything I had known was gone. I had no idea at that moment whether I wanted to continue on. The apartment was cluttered with medical supplies, including enough morphine to sedate a small city into the next century. I could not stop weeping. I tried to muscle down a few drinks in the hopes I would just pass out. I made the required calls, then turned on some music and began to paint. Through the tears, I painted a woman's torso with lacerations and scars. I worked and drank until the sun came up. Then I finally passed out for a couple of hours. When I awoke for a few seconds, it all seemed like a bad dream. Then reality kicked in and I began to weep again. The next week was a blur. Surprising to me, there was so much business, paperwork, documentation to do. After surviving the first night, I dumped all the morphine down the toilet. Not the brightest idea, but it was better than dumping it into me, which I had considered in a couple of weaker moments.

There was an outpouring of kindness and well-wishing from a great many people. I was humbled by it; at the same time, it felt like pouring acid into an open wound. And yes, I painted over the hideous image I had made the night of my lover's death. I shut myself off from most everyone, just trying to do what needed to be done. One day, I was getting rid of all the flowers on the balcony that I had placed there for Kathy's sake when my next-door neighbor came out to ask me what I was doing. As with every other action at this time, in tears, I tried to explain. He expressed that he had lost his wife and that he understood. Thinking that I might gain some insight in this horrid situation, I invited the man over for a drink. A very bad move!

Later on, he showed up and I tearfully shared my experience with him. He seemed to be listening with understanding and compassion. Then I inquired about his experience. He got about a sentence out before he began sobbing uncontrollably. I tried my best to console him, with little success. After about an hour of him sobbing and muttering a few words in between, I finally made out that his wife had died suddenly around eight years ago and that he had never recovered. He was pretty much an empty shell, totally reclusive, moving from job to job just to survive. He added that this was the first time he had actually visited with someone in quite a few years. Holy crap! It was devastating for me. I couldn't help but wonder, was I looking at a mirror of myself in eight years? If so, I should probably just off myself right now because I could not imagine just surviving in such a pathetic manner. I thanked the man for visiting, then hurried him out, hoping never to lay eyes on him again.

After about a week, I contacted the school to say I was going to come back to work. The president of the college urged me not to and reminded me that my job was secure "take whatever time you need," he said. Not listening to his advice, I returned. I was met with a wave of tears, hugs, and kindness. I barely made it through my first class before I had to go. I returned home to seriously contemplate what the hell I was going to do. It was right about that time when all the calls and notices started coming in from the different medical and insurance agencies.

Even though Kathy and I were covered by supposedly one of the best medical insurance plans money could buy, over the last couple of months, the total medical expenses added up to near $800,000, and after all the smoke cleared, I was responsible for nearly $250,000. Another dose of reality. I quickly retained an attorney who specialized in medical insurance. After a ridiculous amount of headache and nonsense, it was all settled that I would have to put out less than $25,000. Fortunately, Kathy and I had a bit of life insurance and I was able to make the nightmare go away without becoming a casualty of it myself. In all of this experience, I was becoming more and more disenchanted with the medical and insurance industries also with financial agencies, state and federal governing agencies, and any religious convictions that might be left. All the things that I had been taught were in place to benefit a "good life" were failing.

Prior to Kathy's passing, I prayed to the Christian god I was brought up with. "Please, here is a good soul, I will do anything in your service if you might not take her from here." No response. As a last resort, I asked "the devil" too. It was interesting that in this time of great need, there was nothing offered to me from the religious conscript I was familiar with. I was even willing to embrace the doctrines of Allah and the Muslim faith, Krishna, Buddha it didn't matter to me what dogma, doctrine, religion, or spiritual belief. There was no response from anywhere in the religious universe. This challenged everything I had been taught about god. After going through this experience, I could not in good faith recognize any forms of organized religious dogma. I was convinced they are all conceived by man to serve man. Whatever spirituality exists in the universe, I believe it is far beyond the confines of a church or any ancient text. Being confronted and dealing with Kathy's death was highly influential in solidifying the belief structure I maintain to this day.

It seemed that most all the debris had fallen to the ground from the recent blast, and it was finally time for me to address myself and how I found myself emotionally devastated, mentally impaired, and spiritually challenged, I wasn't quite sure at that time whether I was a casualty or not. I could not function in my job as an educator, I could not paint, and I was very poor at functioning in any social or professional environment.

After adding it all up, it occurred to me that I was unable to exist in the world I had previously designed for myself. This was confusing for me, as I had always considered myself to be somewhat adaptable to most any situations. With that being said, I was completely ignorant of what was required of me in this particular time. I was standing at the edge of a precipice, and if I wished to continue on, major changes accompanied by a leap of faith were in order. I pondered different scenarios. I could take a leave of absence from the school until such time as I might return to my previous to my life, at which time I would be able to function as I had before. Sell everything, buy a boat, and sail away. Stay where I was and try to heal myself as quickly as possible. Find a place in the woods and get off the grid. Move to a simpler environment where I could just paint. Sign on to a commercial fishing boat. Move out of state or country. Immerse myself in some cause so that I might have an effect. Or simply end it all and stop the nonsense.

I've realized in the process of inputting all these words to regale you with a story about a person who creates art, and after rereading what I've put down, that in yapping about my life as an artist, I have only made references here and there on these many pages to my actual artwork.

One might think that a biography about a painter might contain a great deal of information about the physical process of producing art, detailed descriptions of how one goes about developing new techniques, and information about how to address and work with new materials. I stated at the very beginning of this tale that this art has affected my life and my life has affected my art. Yes, there is much more to say about this life that has affected my art. I am pretty convinced that if I had filled these pages with detailed notes on process, technique, style, materials, and my dealings with the business side of the art industry, I would have lost everyone in the first part of the story. I believe it might be more interesting to read about an artist's experiences as they develop their skill set than to simply offer a chronological tale of actuating their discipline, no?

I ended up scheduling a bit of time to possibly think a bit more about all the possibilities mentioned above. So, I booked a trip to Yelapa, Mexico. It was the logical place for me to regroup and sort things out. I put stuff in order at home, packed my clothes and some painting supplies, and then hopped on a plane to Puerta Vallarta.

Little did I know that this quick "find myself" trip would become another life-changing event. After disembarking the plane, catching a cab into town, and arriving at Playa Los Muertos in the south of Puerta Vallarta, I was greeted by familiar faces who shared in my sorrow at Kathy's passing. Then it was onto the water taxi for the 40-minute trip to Yelapa. I knew the skipper as well as several people on board and again was warmly greeted, again everyone sharing in my sadness. Once I arrived at Lagunita (the main hotel in Yelapa), where Kathy and I were familiar with the owners as well as most of the staff, there were tears and embraces all around. In that short amount of time, I felt more at ease than I had in the three months prior. After a lot of talking, tears, and tequila, I got myself set up in one of the thirty-two casitas located right on the bay, out near the pier. I fell asleep that night to the sounds of the ocean and the singing cicadas, chachalacas, and coatimundis.

I awoke the next morning and headed across the beach for the mile-long trek to the pueblo. I wanted to let the other folks my wife and I had made contact with there in the past know what had happened. Surprisingly, on my journey I was met with a constant stream of tears and hugs. I guess news travels faster than one can walk in a small village. The day was filled with remembering Kathy. Once again, I was astonished to find how "right" it all felt. At the time, I couldn't have known more than twenty words of Spanish, but communication was abundant, amazing. I was able to make it through the next few days with a bit less angst. I then set up my paints and boards to work. I began to move about, taking photos, sketching, and doing a few watercolors. Of course, that was in between the times I was sobbing uncontrollably and being so depressed I felt like I was lower than a snake's belly in a wagon rut. There was nothing I could do to curb the flow of tears, but it seemed at the time that alcohol would numb the pain. I was spending a good deal of time by myself either exploring or working. Folks would track me down periodically to check on how I was holding up.

During my visit, I ran into Thomas, the artist who had first told me about Yelapa years before in Sacramento. He invited me to his place over on the other side of the river a sweet little one-room (plus bath) a cement structure with a palapa roof, nestled into the side of the hill overlooking the lagoon. As I mentioned before, Yelapa was somewhat primitive only accessible by boat or burro, no roads, no cars, no electricity, and you had to have a military-grade satellite phone to get any sort of signal. There were two landlines in the area, one at the hotel, Lagunita, and a pay phone in the pueblo. Beyond that, the closest civilization was about ten miles up the coast. During our conversation, I expressed that even though it might appear I was doing poorly, I was feeling and functioning much better in Yelapa than I was back home in San Diego.

Then he tossed out an idea for me to consider. He suggested that I stay in his house for the summer. You see, Yelapa is a seasonal destination for gringos. During the winter months, when it's temperate and dry, Yelapa is flooded with tourists (the High-Season). During the summer months, when it's hot, humid, and rainy, the gringo population dropped down to about five or six. My friend said that he usually contracted a local to care take his place for those 4–5 months when he was back in the States, but he was willing to contract it to me with the condition that I would have to agree to stay for at least four months. The more I thought about it, the more it seemed to make sense. I sure as hell wasn't going to be ready to return to my old life anytime soon, and here was an opportunity to have a wee bit of responsibility with limited social demands, and I would get a little pay while I took the time to heal. It began to sound like the right thing to do.

Even with the language barrier, I was getting to know more locals every day, whose company I came to prefer over most of the gringo population. I shared the idea of staying in Yelapa with a few of the people I had become close with there they all a offered a positive response.

I had about a week left before I was to return to San Diego, and things for me in Yelapa had been evolving at a rapid rate. I had decided not only to return to Yelapa for the four months, but perhaps for an even more extended period of time. Overlooking the fact that I was a complete train wreck of an individual at that period in time, I had still managed to impress folks with my ethical behavior and the fact that I treated others with respect. An administrator with the hotel had taken notice of this and asked to meet with me. Another "holy crap" moment.

Before then, I had simply been a guest at the hotel. I was vaguely familiar with the history of Yelapa and its relationship with the Lagunita. I would soon find out much more. I met on the beach with the man whom I guess one might call the operations manager of the hotel. He was a quiet gentleman a bit my senior who had been raised in Yelapa. It was obvious to me that he took great pride in the responsibility of his station at the hotel and in the community. His command of the English language was enough that we were able to communicate and establish common ground. As he laid out a tale of the distant past and recent history of both the hotel and the community, it reeked of the "Wild West" laced with dysfunction, adventure and corruption. I was captivated by his yarn. When he expressed that the hotel was in dire straits, I was concerned, knowing that the hotel was by far the largest employer in Yelapa. The conversation went on for a couple of hours. He concluded by sharing his perception of me over our few years of contact he believed my presence in Yelapa along with my endorsement of the hotel could possibly have an effect on the future of Yelapa itself. That was a lot to take in at the moment.

He expressed that the two gringo partners who had been running the hotel were experiencing issues mismanaging the hotel, bar, and restaurant and with the hotel doing poorly, the *comunidad* might take the opportunity to seize control as it had done in the past. The hotel employed about twenty-eight locals, which meant family incomes supporting over 180 people at that time, almost one third of the total local population. I knew most of the employees of the hotel and I considered some to be close friends. I knew enough about the political and social structure in Yelapa to imagine what might happen there with the Lagunita: it wouldn't be pretty. I spoke with one of the partners and one member of the hotel's management. They assured me that, yes there were some issues, but that all was OK. By the time I would return to Yelapa, I would hear a wee bit different tune.

I returned to San Diego. I felt empty inside, out of sorts, like I was in a foreign place. Within days of my return, I stopped wrestling with my decisions. I now had a mission. I immediately began to put things in order. First thing, I organized and scheduled a memorial service for Kathy. I also set up with some good folks I knew in the boating community to assist me in releasing Kathy's ashes to the ocean. I am really unsure how I was able to manage so much in such a short period of time, taking into consideration what a mess I was. Next, I began researching the prospects of permanently relocating to Yelapa. I contacted the Mexican embassy in San Diego with a great deal of effort much time on the phone, filling out and obtaining piles of documents, residency papers, preparing my financials so it was possible to make the transition. Also, during this time, I was communicating my intentions to friends and family. I wasn't completely surprised (but maybe just a little) at the amount of negative responses I was receiving from those I held close to me, my family most of all. I knew I was a mess at the time, but I believed that since nothing else was making sense, it might be best to rely on my own instincts.

Within several weeks of intensive activity, I was ready to go. I was embarking on one of the most incredible adventures I had ever encountered in my existence. My plans were to make it through the summer, to paint, and to become acclimated to the area and culture. I brought with me enough paint, illustration board, and watercolor board to last me a bit over a month, hopefully giving me enough time to locate a possible source for more supplies in Puerto Vallarta. My do-it-yourself solar kit included one large solar panel, one electrical output regulator, one inverter, and two six-volt golf cart batteries that I picked up in Boca on my way to Yelapa enough power to run my laptop, a small printer-scanner, and a small stereo. The rest of my luggage was mainly shorts, T-shirts, and all my Tommy Bahama shirts. I figured I could pick up everything else as I needed it. I don't believe I mentioned that when Kathy and I first met, we both smoked cigarettes, but seven years prior I had quit while Kathy continued to smoke. The night Kathy passed, there was a pack of her smokes left at home. It seemed like it was time for me to start again many of the people I knew in Yelapa smoked and besides, it was a cheap habit in Jalisco one carton of Camels was the equivalent of $10.00 US.

Once I arrived in Mexico, I began to settle in as much as one could in my state. It was unbelievably hot, with 80–100 percent humidity every day. Oh, and yes, it rained most every afternoon and evening. Because I found myself walking in sand or in the river a lot, my canvas shoes and sandals were toast within a week. I started going barefoot except for when I would travel to Puerto Vallarta. Even though many of the locals did this, several cautioned me against the practice because "you might step on a scorpion." I know, sounds kind of weird, but this advice was not without merit. In the years I had been visiting Yelapa, I had seen my fair share of the little stingers. There were big-ass black ones that look real menacing, and when they sting you it hurts like a, well, you know. Then there's the *alacrans*, little flat-tailed suckers, two inches up to maybe five inches long. When these bad boys sting you, it's like rolling the dice. From what I found in doing a little research, they can deliver a multitude of toxins in a single sting, and basically, the amount of toxin as well the mix of the cocktail is determined by how much the little critter is threatened. The sting could feel like a real bad bee sting or it could mean days of "Doc, take the leg cause I'm dying!" Pain, pins and needles, numbness, etc.

The reason I mention this is because I had been in Yelapa for less than two weeks when I was at a friend's house one evening for a drink. As I was sitting there, I felt something on my pant leg; without looking, I brushed it off with my hand. I felt the sting immediately and upon lifting my hand to see what the problem was, I found a three-inch *alacran* hanging from my middle finger, just pumping his little heart out. I flung the little bastard off. My friend saw what happened and informed me that he was going to run to the hotel because they had an EpiPen in their first aid kit. He expressed that if I was going to go into anaphylactic shock, it would more than likely happen within the first thirty minutes. He had me lie down the pain was intense and making its way up my arm; the tip of my finger was completely numb; I was feeling pins and needles under my eyes and around my lips and shoulder. I remembered what my friend had said just before he left about "within thirty minutes." I started doing the math It was a fifteen-minute walk from his house to the hotel, and fifteen minutes back. Then I thought, to myself "I hope he was serious about *running* to the hotel." He returned in about twenty minutes with the EpiPen and accompanied by a couple of local folks.

I had a bit of mucous building up in my throat, so I was spitting a lot, plus my throat was becoming a bit tight and my sight was blurring. I was getting a little freaked out and was wondering why he was in such a rush to get the shot if he wasn't going to give it to me. He explained that although administering the shot would keep me from entering full-on anaphylactic shock, mixing it with the other toxins already present in my body could possibly worsen or create other issues. So, these guys sat, drank tequila, and watched me for about an hour and a half. I stopped spitting and my breathing went back to normal, although the pain and numbness had worsened. Around that time, they poured me glass of tequila and toasted *"todos está bien"* "it's all good." I was not convinced due to the fact that I still felt like warmed-over dog poo. It was explained to me that I was possibly going to feel like crap for the next couple of days, but the good news was that I was not going to die! Over the next five years of my residence in Yelapa, I would be stung four more times. Once on the morning when I was to be wed in hindsight, I probably should have paid more attention to that particular omen. But I don't want to get ahead of myself.

Back to getting settled in Yelapa. I still found myself in tears dozens of times every day. I was doing some painting and still keeping pretty much to myself. I remember one rainy afternoon; I was finishing off a watercolor in my casita when I heard someone at the front door. Opening it, I found a young man whom I had come to know over the years in Yelapa. We had fished together and had developed a mutual respect. Standing there in the rain, I could see he had a six-pack of Corona and a bottle of tequila. I invited him in, at which time he attempted to explain why he was there. Not an easy task, as he spoke no English and I was still limited to just a few basic words in *español*. After a bit of banter back and forth accompanied by a great many hand gestures, I finally put together what he was doing there. Simply explained I was his friend, I was hurting and sad, and he felt that it was his duty as a friend to come and share time with me. Damn this is why I was falling in love with the culture. We sat and watched the rain, drank, talked very little. He spent all afternoon with me and into the evening, when he politely excused himself and headed home for dinner with his family. I can still feel the impact of his gesture as if it happened today. The definition of a good friend.

Next, the people from the hotel approached me once again. The Lagunita was failing. If something did not happen real soon, the hotel would go down. At the same time, the young man I mentioned approached me to become his partner in his fishing charter business. It was a lot for a broken man to digest. I wished so much to go into business with the young man, but it was all for personal reasons. If I were to become involved with the hotel and had any degree of success, I could create a positive effect for the whole village. I chose the hotel. I began negotiations with the administrators and the one partner only the one partner because the other one was in the hospital with a broken hip that he got by falling down some stairs, drunk. I should have taken it as a clue! But instead, I agreed to invest a good deal of money and to take on the responsibility of marketing and promotions. In return, I would receive food, accommodations, drink, smokes, and the equivalent of around $450 per month for as long as I was involved. Such a deal? My friend as well as a few other folks in the community weren't as excited as myself about my decision. Nevertheless, it happened. I was now the proud one-third owner of a hotel, restaurant, and bar located on the beach in a third-world country. This was a wild concept, beyond crazy. In my past experience, I was told by folks I knew in the food and bar industry to "never buy a restaurant or a bar." Damn! And I had just bought into a failing one. I was flying by the seat of my pants.

After agreeing to go forward with the hotel, I soon found I was completely unprepared for it. Not only was I jumping into new and unfamiliar financial, legal, political, and social environments in a foreign country, but there were other unforeseen consequences:

- I was immediately perceived differently by the employees of the hotel, for better and worse.

- I was immediately perceived differently by the gringo population of Yelapa also had some good and some bad.

- I was immediately perceived differently by the locals.

- I was accepted as a business owner rather than a tourist in Puerto Vallarta.

- I was personally feeling like I might have jumped out of a plane without a parachute.

- I was about to become politically involved in my community.

- I immediately became a target of the "coyotes" of Yelapa (explanation to come).

This all had a big effect on my acclimatizing to my new environment. Here I was a new resident to the community, in all respects an emotional train wreck, an artist, a business owner, and a marketer. In looking back at the reality of the time, it seemed like not much had changed from my previous existence, I was just actuating things in a simpler form and in another country.

At the time, I was still being given consideration by most everyone with regard to my recent loss. Even though my pain and tears weren't going away, I found that the people around me were becoming a bit less sympathetic to my situation. Funny how emotional support is often short-lived.

So, here we are, back at learning to be involved in running a hotel in a remote area in a third-world country. I'm still brand-new, I have one partner Jim, in Puerto Vallarta in the hospital with a broken hip he got after being too drunk to stand up, and now my other partner Sam, gets shipped off to Puerto Vallarta for rehab. Who the hell in their right mind would sign up for this kind of stuff? Holy crap! I'm new to the country, I'm new to the area, brand-new to the business, I'm totally lacking in language skills, I'm an emotional wreck, and I by no means signed up for what was about to happen. It only took a couple of days without the other partners for things to go south. What was about to transpire would challenge me in ways I could not have imagined. One afternoon, the head bartender (who also happened to be the *comissario* (law enforcement officer), for Yelapa at the time sort of like a sheriff) announced to me that the *comunidad* was going to seize the hotel that evening. I happened to be having a tequila with him at the hotel's empty bar at that very moment. I was a bit bewildered and asked him to please explain.

"What do you mean?" He went on to explain that the *comunidad* had been observing the dysfunction of the hotel for a while and they were not pleased that I had become a partner, adding that since both the recognized partners were incapacitated, this would be an appropriate time to take control of the hotel.

I then asked, "what does that mean?"

He then casually expressed, "I am offering you warning so that you might evacuate the hotel guests to Puerto Vallarta and alert any employees that they must leave the property."

I thought to myself, "What the hell!" My response to him was "OK. Let me get this straight. You, my head bartender, are informing me that I need to evacuate the hotel guests as well as hotel employees, so that a bunch of community yahoos can take over the hotel?"

He answered "Yes."

I queried, "What if I refuse?"

He responded, "It will be bad for everyone."

I thought for a minute and then offered, "Thank you for your warning. I will evacuate the hotel guests and employees. As for myself, I'm not leaving."

He added, "We'll have to beat you."

I responded with, "I just lost the love of my life and dumped every penny I have into this crappy hotel. If you wish to take it from me, you'll have to take my life."

He paused for a moment and then said, "We'll be back at 7:00."

As the bartender was leaving after he offered his ultimatum, I reminded him of my background and told him that when he left, I would be preparing a statement to release over the internet and for the media in Puerto Vallarta at the first sign of trouble, after which they'd be lucky to find a tourist within forty miles of Yelapa in the next five years. After collecting myself, I arranged for the hotel guests to be taken to Puerto Vallarta, and then informed all the employees about the situation. I was planning to stay the course by myself in the hotel office.

I was surprised to find that the night watchman for the hotel, Mateo, requested to stay with me. The hotel was empty except for the two of us. Seven o'clock passed, eight o'clock passed, then nine and ten. The night watchman suggested I go home; nothing was going to happen. I slept in the hotel office that night. Morning came without incident and the employees showed up for work one by one.

I was waiting at the bar when the head bartender showed up for his shift. He greeted me with a meek "Buen dia." I responded in kind.

Then there was a long, uncomfortable silence that I broke with a loud "What the hell?" He began to explain, saying that the folks who were planning to seize the hotel decided not to, adding they were willing to give me a chance.

I responded with "Really?" as I was thinking to myself *What the hell have, I stepped in?*

He asked if I was going to fire him. I offered, "No, you're a good bartender and besides you were just the messenger 'don't kill the messenger.'" We brought the hotel guests back from Puerto Vallarta and things continued on like nothing had happened. I was hopeful that this type of drama would be an isolated incident no such luck.

The one dysfunctional but working partner Sam, returned from rehab, and soon after the other "non-functioning" partner Jim, returned to Yelapa from his hospital stay in Puerto Vallarta. From what I could gather in conversation with other folks and the man himself (when he was somewhat coherent), he was born in the 60s with a bit of a colorful past who at one point was a budding entomologist. Unfortunately, what I got to experience of this man was less than good. He was a worthless drunk, in poor health, leeching off an agreement he had set up years in the past. After a short period of involvement, I found Jim to be an empty shell of a person, proving himself to be simply a liability to my person and to the hotel. My other partner Sam, a seemingly clumsy but lovable individual, was much more complex. I don't think too many folks respected him, but they did find him likable and so they tolerated him. In the beginning, I was astonished at how he had seemingly held the hotel together in what one might be considered a working model. Later, I would find him to be much less than I originally perceived.

I went about attempting to organize what might be called a marketing and promotional direction for the hotel. At every turn, I ran into opposition. Not enough perceived return for money spent (which was a crock, because the hotel had never been marketed before). Too flashy for "low-key Yelapa." It was a primitive area with little or no tech support, and on and on. I was fighting an uphill battle, although in time I did manage to get through a new corporate image, some signage, and some web presence.

I dove into everything room pricing, food service, bar service, resources, maintenance. I made it a point that I was willing to do anything I might ask an employee to do. This was a new concept for the staff, and it got me a lot of instant respect. As well as doing graphic, marketing, and administrative work at the hotel, I dove into a lot of physical work as well, which seemed to help with my emotional state. I was drinking quite a bit and not eating a lot; it was summer very hot. I would occasionally indulge in a little "Bolivian marching powder." I didn't notice so much at first, but as time progressed, it became pretty apparent that I was losing weight. When I first arrived in Yelapa, I weighed in at around 205 lbs.; after three months had passed, I weighed in at 142. I was a stick with a 28 waist. I became a bit concerned and started to eat a bit more until I leveled out at around 150 lbs.

Every day was an adventure, filled with new experiences, painting, dealing with the hotel, trying to fit in to a new culture, learning a new language, exploring the jungle, fishing, and simply trying to feel human again. I had been in Yelapa for about three months, and I had not been intimate with a woman in about six months. I know, so what. After spending the previous twenty or so years sharing intimacy with Kathy on a regular basis (two to times a week), going cold turkey for four months was not good for me. At first, I didn't have a clue as to how to rectify the situation. I was in no way able to spark up a relationship with a woman, as I was still quite the mess. I would accompany my partner on supply runs to Puerto Vallarta about once every two weeks, where we would usually stay in town for at least one night. On one of these trips, we were having a drink after dinner when I worked up the courage to ask him if he had any information regarding professional women. Whoa! It was as if I had pushed the plunger on a load of dynamite. He being single, not the most attractive man in the world, and having resided in the area for years exploded with information. Then he took it as his duty to show me the ropes. Prostitution was legal in Puerto Vallarta; in fact, it was a booming business. Go figure? He explained the ins and outs (pun intended) of approaching the industry: where to go, the going prices, who to talk to, what not to do, etc. That night, he took me to a couple of clubs and introduced me to the management. I could tell immediately this was going to add a whole new dynamic to my already adventurous experience. I did not involve myself with any interaction that evening, but I remained in town for an extra day on my own, returning to one of the clubs in the afternoon.

I was nervous and unsettled about going forward with this, but it seemed the only option. So, there I was. It being early, there were only a few customers in the club. The manager recognized me from the night before and invited me in, instantly providing me with a drink on the house, then calling all his professionals to the table.

"*Uno para ti,*" he asked. There were about ten women, most very attractive. I hesitated for a moment, when one strikingly beautiful woman stepped forward and put her arms around me, saying "*es mio.*" Worked for me.

I arranged for her to accompany me back to the hotel. Once we were in the room, we shared some tequila as I did my best in my limited *español* to ask about her and express my situation. She spoke and understood zero English, but she was very patient as well as kind and sweet. I had been informed that it was professionally correct for the client to ask if kissing was OK, so I did, and she responded with a kiss.

I then asked if it would be OK with her if she just held me for a while. She smiled, removing my clothes and then laying me on the bed before she snuggled up next to me. It took about a minute for the tears to come. I had a good cry and she shed some tears with me, after which we engaged in what I would call some pretty wonderful sex. After that, we talked and laughed at each other's language skills (or lack thereof).

It came time for her to leave. As she was going, she offered *"Por favor, me gusta mucho, otro tiempo in la futura"* "I responded, Yes, I would like that too." She smiled, I walked her to the street, she hopped in a taxi, waved adios, and it was all over. About three hours of good, sad, great, tender, and wild. Including her fee, tip, and taxi fares, it came to around the equivalent of $150.00 US. All things considered, one of the better investments I have made. This would mark the beginning of many trips to Puerto Vallarta over the next four years to engage in similar negotiations.

As per my artwork along with everything else, I was still committing serious time and energy to painting. Throughout this period of exploration, I had managed to produce quite a few representational watercolors, all ranging in the size of 2' × 3', all depicting my geographic area. It seemed the best I might offer at the moment was a representation. I was in no shape to delve into conceptual work that would have been too much for me. I was just beginning to deal with my emotions and already had a great deal on my plate. I had managed to sell a few of the works I created to tourists in Yelapa and to a couple of folks in Puerto Vallarta.

As I mentioned earlier, during my time in Yelapa, a few celebrities would occasionally show up to revisit the "primitive Mecca." I recall one happy memory of running into one such celebrity. It was a beautiful morning with the high season (a term used by both locals and seasonal visitors to describe the winter months, when the gringos would return to Yelapa) just kicking into gear. I was doing my routine inspection of the beach in front of the hotel; there was only one person out there, a woman who looked to be around my age sitting quietly under one of the hotel's beach palapas. I figured she might be a guest of the hotel, so I stopped by to wish her a pleasant morning and to see if she needed anything. She responded by saying, no, it's a beautiful day, I have a great margarita and I have my book. Excellent, I replied; "*buen dia.*"

As I was about to leave, I turned back and said, "Excuse me, you look somewhat familiar to me." The woman smiled and told me her name. I in return exclaimed, "Oh my god, I read your book and I'm fan of yours!" She smiled again and asked if I would like to join her. I said yes, excusing myself to dash back to the bar, returning with two top-shelf margaritas, one for her and one for me. We sat, sharing stories, laughing, and drinking for several hours. I then excused myself, exclaiming what a pleasure and privilege it was to have shared this time with her. She politely expressed the same in return. Later on in the day, I returned to the beach and found her at the same table with two young men preparing to retire, possibly to a place less populated. A very fond memory indeed!

Meanwhile, things were heating up with the coyotes. For those who don't know, coyotes in Yelapa were people who worked the tourists in order to get them to go to a certain business or use a certain service. In the US we might call them "barkers," but coyotes were possibly just a little bit more aggressive. For the most part in Yelapa, the folks that were coyotes weren't good for much else. There existed a geographic issue in Yelapa that set the stage for static with other local businesses, especially on the beach. The only pier to disembark from the water taxis to Yelapa was located at the far end of the hotel. This meant that most people who came to Yelapa, especially tourists, had to disembark at the pier and walk through the hotel property, past the hotel bar and restaurant, before they might hit other businesses on the beach. Kind of a monopoly on traffic. Inevitably, the coyotes would strategically place themselves on hotel property in order to convince tourists to use businesses or services other than those offered by the hotel. Since the hotel was beginning to show signs of life, the coyote presence was growing like an out-of-control virus.

It was evolving into a real problem. I could sit on the beach at the hotel restaurant and watch individual coyotes escort groups of tourists off of the hotel grounds and down the beach. It wasn't that I wished the hotel to have a monopoly on tourists visiting Yelapa, but since the coyote issue had escalated, I was seeing the hotel lose more of its "share" of clientele. Now there were over twice the number of coyotes, with a good percentage representing the lower life forms of Yelapa. After quizzing tourists on a few occasions. I was told that some of the coyotes were not only misrepresenting the other businesses and services but also telling tourists stories about, for example, people getting sick or dying after eating at the hotel restaurant, people being kidnapped and held for ransom while staying at the hotel, how the owners of the hotel were connected to the local cartel, that there had been a recent outbreak of crabs and lice at the hotel, and more.

Enough already! After about a month of this nonsense, my partner and I went to the *comunidad* equipped with documentation of what was going on to ask for help. Of course, this was ridiculous because some of the representatives of the *comunidad* were the same folks who had earlier wished to seize the hotel. You might imagine our surprise to find that most of the members of the *comunidad* were in favor of working with the hotel in order to solve the problem. After a few meetings and a lot of talk, the general consensus was that anyone who wished to act as a coyote needed to register with the *comunidad*. Next, coyotes representing other businesses/ services were not allowed to operate on hotel property. This looked pretty good on paper, but would later develop into something else altogether.

Now we had to find and mark the hotel's actual property line on the beach, which was in itself a real challenge. After that was done, it was left to the hotel to police the property line on the beach as well as the pier. In the beginning, this job fell to me. Sucks to be me! I would make sure I was out on the pier to supervise each day when the water taxis arrived, then I would follow the tourist through the hotel to the property line on the beach, where I would be confronted with up to fifteen coyotes yelling out their offers and sending insults in my direction. This practice continued daily for a while; I soon realized that this might not end well.

While all this turbulence was going on, my housing agreement was soon going to come to an end and it was becoming important for me to arrange a new place to live. In my short time in Yelapa, I had looked into alternate properties but had not found anything suited to my needs. By this point, however, my investments had grown enough that I felt the confidence to seek out a property to build on, so I secured a plot of land not too far from the hotel. This was an amazing act of faith. I was living in a foreign country, not totally immersed in the culture, I was limited in language, I had limited funding, and I had limited scope as to my future. So, I put everything on red, and hope it turned up.

All went well with negotiations for the property; next came designing and building a habitable structure. I mentioned before that Yelapa was considered "*hecho*" land: this meant that no one but indigenous people could own property. So, to get around this, the few family property owners would lease plots of land with terms between six and fifteen years and annual payments that were quite low for undeveloped property. All leases on undeveloped property included the condition that the lessee of the property would add improvements within the first quarter of the lease and that subsequent lease renewals would carry considerably higher annual payments. I was able to negotiate a little over two hectares of prime real estate not too far from the hotel for the equivalent of less than $1000 US a year for eight years.

Of course, I had wildly wonderful concepts in mind for my new home: tree house, subterranean, multi-level hacienda with waterfalls and ponds throughout. All of these were possible, except for the fact that I had to accomplish this task with limited funding. Without eating up my investment funds too much, I had about $10,000 to work with. In Yelapa at that time, a person could construct an OK-sized palapa for around $6,000. Palapa roofs, made of palm fronds, were very beautiful, but came with some drawbacks. They needed to be refurbished or replaced every six years or so. They would sustain damage in high winds, and they were a favorite place for scorpions to hang out. Considering all of the above, I came up with a simple two-story cement block structure on a poured cement slab. I did this with the intent of adding on to the structure over time. Downstairs was a living area, studio, kitchen, and bath. Upstairs had my bedroom with an open deck space. Not what I truly wanted, but it met all my design and construction criteria, it was easy to care for and maintain, and it was nearly indestructible.

I contacted a man who lived in the pueblo who had a reputation for doing good cement and block work. We went over the plans I had drawn up, after which he agreed via handshake that he and his son would help me to construct the house. If all went well, it could be completed in less than ninety days. OK under normal conditions in the States, this small project would be complete in under two weeks. Considering the conditions in Yelapa at the time, I expected this project to take more like six to twelve months.

Clearing the land was done by ax, machete, and shovel. All building materials had to be brought in by panga, offloaded onto the beach, and then transported to the property via mule or person. All tasks were accomplished by hand because there was no electricity. The cement blocks were not premade: we made them ourselves with a couple of "two blocks per set" wooden molds on an empty slab of cement down near the beach, and once they had cured, we transported them via mule or person to the site. The people I had contracted to work with me on the project were only contracted to do cement work all woodwork, metalwork, plumbing, and electrical had to be accomplished by myself or someone else. The gentleman I had contracted to assist me, when he had the money, liked to get drunk in the afternoon. Plying him with a daily beer or two was a part of our original agreement, but attempting to control the amount of beer he might have access to on any given day was a battle for me. If he had no beer, he was an asshole, impossible to work with. With some beer, he was tolerable and quite efficient. Too much beer, he was an asshole, impossible to work with. And, it being the summer, the weather was not always cooperative with our schedules.

I forgot to include "water" in all the foregoing rambles. Access to water was a big deal in Yelapa. Due mainly to the limited availability of electricity, all the wells in the area were of the "open" type. You know: a large hole in the ground with the sides lined with rock or block, where you can stand at the top, look down, and see water. Because digging one of these suckers was quite the project, not all properties had wells, which in turn made it necessary for folks to enter into "water agreements." Yelapa being still somewhat primitive, a lot of these water agreements were handshake deals. Especially up in the pueblo where folks were a bit more concentrated, there was a maze of above-ground PVC pipe running everywhere. The pipes would get old and break, mules or donkeys would step on them, and coconuts would fall and break them. Yes, it would be better if the pipes were buried, except for the fact that the agreements were constantly being changed or renegotiated.

The other ongoing problem was people disconnecting and reconnecting water lines without permission this was a constant annoyance. I had made an agreement with my partner form the hotel, who lived next door for water access; he was hardly ever at his place and had a preexisting pump on a well just down from his property. However, he in turn had a water agreement with someone else: a couple of women from the east coast of the US who had recently taken over the lease on the property where the well was located. Even though they would frequent the hotel bar and restaurant while they were in Yelapa, they were openly hostile toward the hotel. Moreover, they seemed to not like me for reasons I would never be made aware of. On their next visit, they learned via the grapevine that I was tapped into my partner's water. All hell broke loose, with the two witches confronting me and demanding that I stop immediately. Thankfully, my partner intervened and was able to get them to back off for the present. Just prior to the two witches returning home from their stay in Yelapa, they stormed into the hotel office with a new water agreement for my partner, basically stating that he was the only one who could access the well.

There was a lot happening in the office at that very moment, so simply to get these two annoyances out of his face, he signed the agreement, understanding that they would not return until next season. However, I immediately began researching alternatives. My plate was pretty full at the moment attempting to maintain the hotel, restaurant, and bar while dealing with the coyote situation, trying to complete the construction of my house, attempting to heal, and oh yes, trying to paint. I looked into digging a well on the lower end of my property, which seemed like a suitable site because of the immediate rise in elevation of the property and the size of a large rock deposit. The lowest bid for digging such a well was about $10,000 more than it cost to build my house. This was not going to happen. There was a small property just across the trail from me that included a well, but finding a contact for the owner required no less than Sherlock Holmes.

Time passed. I still didn't have enough money to dig a well and I could not find the elusive entity who would show up once every few years to the property across from me. So, we just continued on using the witches' well. The funny thing was, it's not like we were endangering their water source. It was simply that they didn't like me, and in turn they did not wish to share their water with me.

High-season was upon us, once again. I had moved out of my artist friend's *casita* and was staying at the hotel for the interim. Meanwhile, the cement and block work were completed on my house in three months. Considering all the complications detailed above, it is still amazing to me that it happened at all, much less within such a reasonable timeframe. It was now time to finish it off so I could move in this included the septic tank. I had designed it with a leach line and field. Most folks just had cesspools: they would throw a bunch of land crabs in prior to shutting the lid and burying them. (This was done due to the fact that land crabs eat anything, including shit.) Even though I designed my tank to last for years, I too dumped a bunch of land crabs in before I closed it up. This action actually brought a bit of joy to me I'll explain later.

Back to the "water witches." The two women returned to Yelapa at the beginning of the season and came straight to confront me about the water situation. I shared truthfully with them what had transpired, adding that there was good possibility that things would be set to their liking during this season. This went over like a lead balloon. They made a scene, called me a lot of bad names, then hurried off to their *casita*. My partner and I were inundated with work at the time, as it was the beginning of the season, so the hotel, restaurant, and bar were all hopping. After putting in over sixteen hours at the hotel, I went back to crash in my partner's back *casita*. When I walked up his path, my flashlight illuminated a water pump along with pipe and fittings sitting on his front porch. I instantly knew what had happened. While my partner and I were working our asses off

149

welcoming folks to Yelapa, the two vindictive bitches had hired someone to affect an immediate stop to our water access. Even considering Yelapa's standards, this was a brutally hostile action. Things became ugly and the landlords got involved. After the gnashing of teeth and a great amount of crap being thrown about, the pump was reinstalled, the water flowed, and soon after, the gentleman who leased the property across from me showed up, at which time I was able to negotiate a workable water agreement. So much unnecessary energy, time, hurt, and money was wasted because a couple of people didn't like me. Damn! I consider it gravely inhumane to deny another person reasonable access to water.

But about the land crabs. Other than being used to line the bottom of one's septic tank, I can find little use or redeeming qualities in these little suckers. All they do is eat anything and everything, multiply in vast numbers, and stink when they die. They range in size up to about eight inches across, sport reddish-orange colorings on top and tan on the bottom, and brandish two claws with black tips. For the most part, they hang out near the shoreline or in the ocean, but once a year they come ashore to mate, covering the ground up to around a half mile inland. They wind up entangled in mass orgies in corners, in showers, on countertops, around trees all of them just screwing away then after a few days, they head back to the ocean, but not without leaving a trail of destruction in their path. I said they eat anything and everything: this includes food, plants, cloth, paper, wood, and yes, they'll even chew on plastic. I lost eight Tommy Bahama shirts to these little horrors.

The first time I experienced this phenomenon, I became so frustrated at listening to the crabs all night and not being able to sleep and having to clear upwards of fifty of them out of every corner in the house and yes, because they ate my Tommy Bahama shirts that for nearly a week, right around sundown, I would arm myself with a seven-iron golf club that I kept in the hotel office. I'd stop by the hotel's bar on the beach to equip myself with a bit of tequila, then I would then grab a five-gallon bucket and fill it with the evil little crabs. Next, I would make my way to an isolated part of the beach where I would go about sipping tequila in between strokes. I would reach into the bucket to collect a single crab, then

I would place him belly-up in the sand at my feet, then I would announce the customary "fore" just prior to whacking the little sucker's entrails out to sea with my best power swing. To this day, I really don't know if it was the tequila or the symbolic whacking of the crabs or both, but I always felt a little calmer after doing this.

I now had a stack of paintings and drawings that resembled a body of work. Via a friend I had made in Puerto Vallarta, I scheduled an appointment with an art gallery located in a nice part of town. I showed them my work, told them my story, and I was in. This was the easiest and quickest arrangement for gallery representation I had ever made in my life. I would end up exhibiting with them for a few years, being in a couple of group shows, and having one solo exhibit. Over the short time I would be involved with the gallery, I would do a bit over $7000 US in sales of my artwork.

At the hotel, I was spending a good deal of time with the maintenance man, Herardo. He was a younger man with a family, very bright, spoke a little English; in time, we became very close. Beyond his station at the hotel, he also had a boat that he chartered out for fishing. He was very generous and fair with me when I contracted his help to finish off my house. I was also becoming very familiar with the hotel's generator, which he tended to daily. It was an old military-style Caterpillar diesel, very temperamental, and put out AC electric at 50 hertz. The fact that the generator's output was 50 hertz and not the standard 60 hertz normally found in most US households would end up being quite costly for me. I ended up frying a fair number of electronic devices telephones, computers, printers, fax machines, scanners etc. Oops! Hard learning curve.

My nonfunctioning partner from the hotel, Jim, was becoming more of an issue. It had reached the point where he was no longer a viable part of the hotel. In fact, he had become a detriment as well as a liability. At this point, his daily routine went like this: He would stumble from his residence to the hotel restaurant for breakfast around 10:00 a.m., just about the time hotel quests were arriving. He would then occupy a table and proceed to annoy anyone in close proximity with his drunken babblings. After an hour or so, he would stumble back to his casita, where he would drink away the afternoon and evening. Often quests would complain about loud music emanating from his residence. He also had, amazingly, managed to collect a live-in girlfriend who was a real piece of work herself. These two characters were occupying two prime adjoining *casitas* overlooking the hotel's swimming pool. This was becoming more and more problematic: Not only was he taking up these prime spots in the hotel but his daily drunken presence and his pathetic attempts to unsuccessfully interact with clientele was at best an embarrassment to the hotel. Attempting to deal with this issue as well as the persistent coyote problem was vexing me. I didn't know which issue was going to blow up in my face first.

My house was completed enough that I could at least sleep there, and it had a functional toilet, shower, bed, fridge, and oven. Its DC lights worked off of solar, and I had a line to the hotel generator for AC power. My oven/range ran on propane, my fridge was AC/DC (not the rock band) electric, and there was a gravity-flow water tank and a solar collector for hot water. I had ironwork for the windows and a spiral staircase fabricated in Puerto Vallarta. Like most of the buildings in Yelapa, there were no "glass" windows, just iron/wood frames and maybe screens for the window opening.

Dealing with the coyote issue on a daily basis was becoming especially hard for me. Mine was the only face they would see when they heard "No, you can't cross this line," "No, you can't be on the pier," "No, you can't talk to those people" no, no, no. Systematically, they were being conditioned to think that I personally was the problem not the hotel, not the community. Every day, they threw around insults and harsh words. This one day, almost all the coyotes seemed to be a bit more aggressive than usual, with one particularly nasty gent becoming physical. I was standing just inside the hotel property line when he stepped across and began to push me back while wheeling insults at me in Spanish. I kept pushing his hands away, expressing to him that I would not fight with him in front of the tourists. All the other coyotes, of course, were egging him on. It just so happened that the hotel's night watchman was nearby and saw what was going on. He ran over, picked the guy up, and threw him back across the property line, onto the sand. Everyone was a little surprised; it seemed to ease the tension a bit. The man got to his feet, dusted himself off, then walked up to the edge of the property line.

He looked at me and said, "He [the night watchman] is not always going to be around to save you. One of these nights you'll be walking home in the dark, then no one will ever see you again."

I responded, "Are telling me you're going to kill me, in front all of these people?"

"No" he answered, "I'm just saying bad things sometimes happen in Yelapa." After that day and for quite a while after, he would taunt me every time we passed each other.

This would change in the not-so-distant future. He and a couple of his lowlife friends were really becoming a nuisance. I did not take their threats completely to heart, but I also did not completely ignore them. I had become pretty comfortable with using a machete clearing brush, removing bark from trees, shaving wood, and cutting the heads off of critters I was about to skin. I began the practice of carrying a machete with me when I was out and about at night. I also had one attached to the inside of my front door and one under the mattress of my bed. Paranoid, you ask? No, just cautious. I opted for a machete mainly because it was the only form of protection other than baseball bats that was used in Yelapa at the time, no one in Yelapa owned firearms.

The coyote problem wasn't going away. My partner, Sam and I went back to the *communidad* to see if anything else could be done. Most of the representatives were very aware of the problem, either through hearsay or direct contact, some being related to coyotes. The general mood was that the coyote's actions gave the tourists a bad impression of Yelapa. Although the *communidad* wanted the coyotes to stop, they felt there was nothing more they could do at their level. We returned to the hotel where we decided that my partner, Sam and two representatives from Yelapa would go to the state office in Puerto Vallarta to voice these concerns.

In hindsight, this was not the best plan. You see, Puerto Vallarta in fact, the whole area was highly dependent on tourism. So, if you walked into an official office and used the words "tourist" and "bad" in the same sentence, everyone would get a little crazy, and that is exactly what happened. After the folks in Yelapa met with state officials, the state officials decided that the state police should intervene. After the meeting, the hotel was informed that a squad of fourteen state troopers would be arriving the next week and that the hotel was responsible for their housing and food; other than that, the police would know what to do.

What a stupid idea! The hotel was already seen as an enemy of the community. Now, it was going to be the base of the *Gustavo*. Everything was already in motion; we could do nothing to stop it. Around four days later, in the late morning, two fully dressed inflatable attack boats made a landing on the beach in front of the hotel. It was like something out of a movie. Black boats with manned, high-mounted, 50-caliber machine guns, loaded with officers decked out in full combat gear, all carrying assault rifles. This attracted a lot of attention from folks on the beach. I went down to the surf to greet them, as I knew they were about to be guests of the hotel. I immediately noticed by the signets on their uniforms that these were not state police they were *federales*.

Damn! I was party to having brought *federales* to Yelapa. After the initial shock died down, we got them all checked in and their stuff stowed in their *casitas*. The hotel restaurant, bar, and office were full of tourists and locals inquiring about what was happening. Prior to the arrival of the feds from the office in Puerto Vallarta, the hotel was sent instructions on what to tell folks when the officers arrived: "The *federales* are here on a routine inspection to check on the safety of rural resort areas." Most of the tourists bought it, but many of the locals knew better. After the initial drama was over, we gathered the hotel staff and had a little meet-and-greet with the troops, during which time the lieutenant in charge of the operation announced that his team was there to correct the coyote problem and that they had been deployed to Yelapa indefinitely or until the problem was deemed "resolved." This information was not at all music to my ears. Yelapa was known to be quite the "free spirit" destination ganja, cocaine, and mushrooms were openly tolerated. With a bunch of feds running around, this would have to change.

During our introductions to the troops, I could not help but notice two female officers, one of whom was a real hottie. Furthermore, the hottie had not stopped smiling at me since they landed. It was noticeable enough that my partner, Sam and some of the staff were already congratulating me on my upcoming engagement.

Immediately, the coyote issue showed improvement. It seemed that everyone in Yelapa was on their best behavior. This wasn't such a bad thing, and it just wasn't Yelapa. I soon worked up the courage to actually talk to the female officer who continued to smile affectionately every time we passed. She spoke actual Spanish, not the Mexican or indigenous dialect that I had become somewhat familiar with which meant communication was going to be a struggle. Our first conversation was uncomfortable at best, we were able to get our names established, she was Lucia and I Renzo. After alleviating all the preconceived notions, we both concluded that we both desired each other and were willing to chance the possible consequences. This was so totally unexpected as well as completely desired it was like some kind of dream: "Barefoot gringo meets Mexico City *federale*." As we talked more, Lucia set up some ground rules. She could not come to my house alone, we could not be seen alone together other than in casual conversation, we could not have dinner or drinks together in public basically no contact in public. Anything we did together had to be done stealthily and within the confines of her *casita, due to the language barrier, establishing the ground rules took over an hour.* So began my clandestine affair with the young and most beautiful Mexican *federale*. At first it was fun and somewhat easy; after a while, it became difficult and uneasy. I don't know if you have ever tried to sneak around in a military encampment without being discovered. Try doing it three to four times a week for over a month. It ain't easy. I would sneak to her casita under the cover of darkness and we would do our best not be at the same place at the same time during the day. Fortunately, we pulled it off and did not get caught. The feds were only in Yelapa for a bit over a month. After enforcing some law and order, causing disturbance, rousting tourists and locals, costing the hotel a fair bit of funds in food, bar, and *casita*, arresting a few lowlifes, and basically being overkill for a lesser issue, it was time for them to leave. One afternoon they loaded their patrol boats with little fanfare and motored off into the sunset. The night before, Lucia, my sweet *federale* and I shed some tears knowing that we both would miss our strange connection. All in all, I guess it worked out afterward, the coyote problem was somewhat manageable. Unfortunately, during this occupation, the feds were overly tolerant of my nonfunctioning drunkard partner. I had actually entertained the thought of planting a suitcase of cocaine under his bed and then leading the *federales* to it, exclaiming, "It's his, he did it!" I just couldn't bring myself to do it. In hindsight, it probably would have been the best plan for all concerned.

In regards to my painting at this time, I was beginning to branch out a bit with my technique. I was experimenting with multiple layers on canvas once again, and building up the courage to explore more conceptual subject matter, although I was still producing quite a few mid-sized representational water colors.

It seems I have been portraying only conflict and upheaval during my residence in Yelapa, but there was so much more. Small experiences that were good and reeked of quality. I noticed, as I was building my house, a mid-sized hawk like bird that would show up from time to time. I tried to identify it via Audubon references and by quizzing the locals, but never was able to. Nevertheless, it would show up on my property once or twice every year. Over the course of the time I was there, it not only returned but, one year, it returned with a mate. They nested and produced offspring, who then returned to the property. A few other folks also saw the elusive bird, but it never was truly identified, and I had to chalk it up to "something that happens in nature."

Because of all the turmoil I was thrown into when I came to Yelapa, it took a while for me to become aware of the existence of baseball there. There were two existing teams: the "Pan Bimbos," referencing a certain brand of white bread and representing the gringo population, and the local team known as the "Riacillas," after the name of Jalisco's local moonshine, *riacilla*. During the season, there was a game every week. I became known as "the pitcher slayer" due to the fact that I wasn't very consistent at hitting out of the park, but I was pretty consistent at hitting really hard line drives straight up the middle just about chest high directed right at the pitcher. I will always remember these games as good times.

I had a good rapport with one of the older maintenance folks at the hotel, Angel. He was a stout seventy-year-old man indigenous to Yelapa whose sons also worked at the hotel. He was the sweetest and kindest of souls. Due to the language barrier, we didn't talk much, but we always seemed to communicate a great deal. Whenever I think of him, I always become warm. One time, I was sitting alone on the beach after a long, hard day of attempting to heal myself while at the same time trying to apply Band-Aids to what one could perceive as a critical patient the hotel. I was feeling so broken at the moment. This gentle man pulled a chair up next to me not too close, just close enough for me to know he was there. I turned to him, in tears, and he simply nodded to me with a reassuring glance. Over the next hour while the sun went down, no words were exchanged he just sat there with me. Just as the sun had set, he got up and moved toward me. He placed his callused hand gently on the back of my neck, softly offering "*Mi amigo.*" A special moment I was granted to spend in the presence of a great man. I guess the reasons I reflect on my time in Yelapa as being so special is that just about every moment, good and bad, was loaded with passion. Just so you know, happy and good stuff happened too. It just seems like the crazy, hard, bad stuff is more exciting!

My house was pretty much complete. Tile work, fixtures, paint, and furniture. I had split the downstairs living area in half, devoting the back half to my studio not a bad place to work, with pretty good light. As I mentioned before, life in less developed areas can offer some unique challenges. Due to the fact there was no electricity offered as a utility in Yelapa, I had set up my house to use both DC and AC applications. I installed both DC and AC light fixtures, and my fridge was both DC and AC. When it came to "tunes," it was most efficient for me to have a DC unit, so I purchased a really powerful car stereo in Puerto Vallarta along with eight box speakers to mount around the house. I had previously been torturing my ears with a little boombox, so when I finally got all the system's parts together back at the house, needless to say, I was very eager to hook it all up so I might finally enjoy some quality sound in the jungle. It was toward the end of the dry season and the weather was already starting to turn. I took an afternoon off just to install my stereo system, which was no less than a three-hour job. As I began the instillation, I noticed the clouds forming outside. I hurried things along, knowing a storm was imminent. The storm moved in rapidly with heavy rain, thunder, and lightning. As I was finishing off the last connections for the stereo, I heard a deafening blast. I looked out the window and I could see illuminated electrical current traveling down the barbed wire fence on the property line near the house. The last thing I saw was a flash at the window, at which time I hit the floor. From my position on the floor, I heard several loud pops and felt an intense tingle rush through my body, leaving all my hairs standing at attention. After the initial shock, I rose to my feet to find small pillars of smoke wafting from different places in my house. Apparently, lightning had struck the fence just above my house, run down the wire, and then jumped to the metal frames in my window. From the window, it had then passed through every receptor in that part of the house. Luckily, I offered more resistance than some other stuff in the house. There were burn marks on the metalwork in the window, and my stereo and wiring were smoking and fried. I had to replace my stereo, four speakers, some light fixtures, my inverter, my fridge, and some other metal odds and ends. I did leave the scorch marks on the metalwork in the one window just as a reminder.

My next interaction with Mother Nature was just as strange, albeit not as costly. Soon after my electrifying experience, I was painting in my studio one quiet afternoon when I could not help but notice seeing more little critters than usual moving about the floor so much so that I actually began to pay attention; the critters were obviously moving in one direction. Beetles, scorpions, bugs of all types were scurrying across my floor in the middle of the day in great numbers toward a singular destination. What the hell? I looked up at one of the back windows of the house and could see a few large black ants coming inside. At first, I didn't pay too much attention. Then there seemed to be a few more ants present around the window. I went out back to survey the area outside of the windows damn! The ground behind my house, for as far as I could see, looked like it was moving. I had read about them, I had seen nature programs about them, and now I was going to experience them up close and personal: army ants. Millions of the little guys, and they were headed in my direction. Fortunately, I had heard locals talk about them before, which included them saying what to do should you encounter them. After establishing that yes, they were going to be occupying my house, I went back inside, gathered some things together, closed up, and headed down to the hotel. As I neared the hotel, I checked the grounds for signs of infiltration all clear. I informed the staff members who I knew lived in my vicinity so that they might flee as I did.

An invasion of army ants has its good and its bad. It's good because the little monsters devour every living thing in their path that cannot run away from them, so you get rid of a lot of unwanted pests for a while. It's bad for the same reason. Tethered, caged, or enclosed animals of any type will be eaten. If you are unable to flee the masses, you will become food for the ants as well. I spent the night at the hotel, returning to my place the next day. As I walked up the path to my house, I could see the entire structure covered with the little things. I returned to the hotel and stayed another night. The following day, I checked the house once again. No activity! I gathered my things and returned to my home. It was a bit eerie standing at my front door. I looked down and could see a couple of piles of small bones a rodent and possibly some type of lizard. It was also absolutely quiet. The jungle is usually a very noisy place, but after the ants' passage, there was simply nothing left to make noise. I bid my new little friends farewell, until next time.

Things at the hotel were beginning to pick up a bit. We were becoming more successful at attracting and servicing specialty groups yoga, meditation retreats, nurses, naturalists etc. This was a good thing not just for the hotel but for all of Yelapa. We would have these groups set up for anywhere from five to fourteen days, which meant that all these folks were also going to the other restaurants in the area, buying souvenirs from local vendors, going on guided excursions basically enjoying all that Yelapa had to offer.

An added benefit for myself was that most of the groups were made up of females from their late twenties to late fifties. During the season, I was never wanting for female companionship although there were a few times when I got a little overindulgent and my partner along with some of the staff would greet me with rolling eyes and call me "gigolo" in an accusatory manner. This is not the only name I was being called at the time. Generally, in the community I was called Lorenzo (the Spanish version of Laurence) by most folks, but some of the kids in Yelapa called me Renzo for short. I liked the name, although it did not catch on with everyone; some folks called me Lorenzo, others referred to me in the shortened form Renzo.

Altogether, things were kind of OK for a while. I was becoming more socially active, I was only crying a few times a day, I was painting on a regular basis, the hotel was doing a bit better, I had a home of my own to live in, intimacy with women was readily available to me on an ongoing basis (paid for or not), I was spending a fair amount of time on or in the ocean fishing, I was learning new stuff about culture, nature, society, and politics on a daily basis, I was becoming familiar with a new language I was like an attentive child in school open to absorbing the new.

I don't know if you might have noticed this in your life, but sometimes when things are going along seemingly just nice, all of a sudden, things turn to poo in a heartbeat. You might have noticed a pattern arising in my story? That concept might have some validity. My nonfunctioning Partner, Jim, who had in all of this time just been a worthless leech, was now reaching critical mass. As I mentioned before, he had somehow attracted a woman the only logic I could find for it was that she might have thought he was near death and there may have been a payout waiting for her. Whatever the case might be, he was now a totally useless drunk and she was the epitome of a waste of skin. Not only were they occupying two prime *casitas* in the hotel, but our guests were always complaining of abusive noise and the constant smell of ganja; daily, they would pathetically make their way to the hotel's restaurant where they would continue to drink themselves silly and annoy the guests with their pathological rhetoric, or they would arbitrarily lash out at anyone who might displease them at the moment. This recurring nightmare was worsening and becoming all too much.

Everything had been tried; it was time to crap or get off the pot. He had elevated himself to being a real threat to the existence of the hotel. My functioning partner and I pleaded with him to move out of the hotel and offered that the company would still pay for his subsistence: "NO!" Would he move to a less popular room in the hotel? "NO!" Would he and his piece of crap girlfriend please not interact with the hotel guests? "NO!"

There were other scenarios offered, with the same response received. This individual still perceived himself as a valuable representative of the business. It had come time for the unthinkable: we began the process to evict him. In Jalisco, Mexico, this is not a pretty process. We followed every procedure to the letter, with him simply pissing off every effort to make things come to any good end. After a long legal process which could only lead to incarceration (if enforced) and many failed attempts to just get the guy to leave, it was time. Myself, my functioning partner, Sam, the hotel staff, and most of the folks in the community agreed this needed to happen. We delivered the official notice in person: It's over, you either need to agree to work with us and move out of the hotel or the police will show up tomorrow and remove you to jail in Puerto Vallarta. Even after the weeks of going back and forth, now that we were standing there in front of this man offering in no uncertain terms what was about to happen, his response to me was, "You don't have the balls to do this."

Little did he know it was already done. The next day, the police came and removed his sorry ass from Yelapa. Immediately we received verbal attacks from a few of the older expats in the community but also praise and congratulations from many others. I was fully aware that my involvement in this coup would bring about consequences in the future. Jim would never return to Yelapa, living out the rest of his short pathetic life in Puerto Vallarta. The general air at the hotel was uplifted, like a great sigh of relief. Business continued to improve, slow but steady.

Tasting the Sweetness of My Surroundings

After making it through the first two years, it was beginning to look like I might have possibly made an appropriate decision in embarking on this life. Traveling back and forth to Puerto Vallarta by boat, I was becoming very familiar with the coast line along the way. Not more than a few miles up the coast from Yelapa, I had spied a small cove with a beach. I asked Herardo, the maintenance man at the hotel if he was familiar with it, and if so, would he be willing to take me there and drop me off for a couple of days? He knew the cove and expressed there was pretty good spear fishing there.

I made arrangements with the hotel to take a couple of days off. Herardo picked me up on the beach at first light. We took a quick trip up to the cove, where there were good-sized waves hitting the beach, so bringing the panga close to shore was a bit wild. With a bit of difficulty, he dropped me and my supplies off on the beach. After this excitement, I found myself standing on a small beach accompanied by an ice chest, some fishing and diving gear, and some damp supplies that were supposed to be dry. As I watched my friend in his boat disappear around the coastline, a feeling of uneasy calm washed over me. In the past, I had watched this cove at different tides to see that the beach never totally disappeared. I set my camp up high on the shore among the rocks. After setting up camp and constructing a palm frond lean-to, I began fishing. Because of the big surf, surface fishing was nonproductive, so I threw on my diving gear and grabbed my "sling spear" to see what I might find under the waves. It was a bit of a challenge getting beyond the surf, but once I did, it was magical. Unveiled to me was a wonderland of beauty and bounty. In less than thirty feet of water, I speared two good fish in a short amount of time. I returned to the beach where I prepped my catch for dinner. In setting up my firepit, I had specifically constructed it so I could have a small outcrop of flat stones that were supported just above the heat of the fire. I was able to get the rocks heated up and placed the fish on the hot surface. I had gathered some fruit and had some other items to accompany my catch. I indulged in an exceptional dining experience while watching the afternoon turn to a brilliant sunset. I lay there in the sand remembering all that had happened and pondering what the future might bring.

The waves continued to crash on the shore as the sun left the sky. I was a little uneasy as I had never visited this place before. All was dark around me, except for the light of the embers of the fire. I looked into the jungle surrounding me and saw many pairs of green-illuminated eyes. Right about that time, the calls began to ring out. I knew from the alien sound that it was coatimundis. I stoked the fire one last time and eventually fell asleep, waking just before the sun rose. In the dim light, I could see a couple of coatimundis mucking about on the beach. I got up and stoked the fire to prepare for breakfast. I had not come unprepared. Fresh pork belly, fresh eggs, handmade tortillas from Yelapa. Again, I added some things I found nearby and mixed up a *cielo rojo* beer, lime, and tomato juice with jalapenos for a glorious breakfast feast for one, set on the beach. I explored the jungle around me, angled and spearfished the rest of the day, and stopped in the afternoon to enjoy some passionfruit and papaya I had found nearby. Once again, I brought my catch ashore to cook it on my fire. At the end of the second night, I had reached nirvana. I was almost convinced that this was the place I was intended to be. How could one possibly contest this existence?

Yes, it was possible. I found that although my idyllic isolation was having a great effect on my own personal enlightenment, I was having little or no effect on persons around me. The social experience is as important for me as communing with myself. I am an artist, and in taking on the role of creating art, what is its worth if no one else sees it? I began to really understand that I was destined to be around other folks that is, if I wished to call myself an artist. In the time I lived in Yelapa, I would return to this magical place about eight times, only twice sharing it with female counterparts.

It was time to start another "high season." Soon Yelapa would be inundated with more white folks than you could shake a stick at. There was always a fair bit of anticipation in the days just prior to the start of the season. This was especially true for me and for this particular season. As I said, a few months earlier I had played a major part in removing one of my partners from Yelapa in fact, having him thrown in jail. I also mentioned that there would be future consequences, one of which I was about to face. Jim, after spending around five days in jail, was now living in an apartment in Puerto Vallarta, paid for by the hotel, along with his skank girlfriend. What I did not mention before is that this partner had a son in his mid-thirties who would usually stay in Yelapa during the high season and head north during the low season to involve himself in some less-than-legal business. I was not looking forward to our meeting this year. I knew the young man; we were by no means best buddies, but in the past we had always acknowledged each other in a friendly way. Did I mention, he was pretty stout, liked to drink a fair bit, and had a short fuse?

I hadn't run into him yet but had heard he was back in town, and, yes, he was already talking smack about me and the hotel. Unlike Sam, my somewhat functioning partner, I enjoyed getting out and about in Yelapa. I frequented other restaurants and bars in town. My partner suggested that I just stick to the hotel and wait for everything to blow over. HELL NO! This was my home. I refused to be bullied into hiding away. It was a Friday night, and my norm was to head to the other end of the beach to a bar that offered live music. That night, I walked into a full house at the bar, and, sure enough, there he was, already pretty high, sitting at a table with several friends. As soon as he saw my face, it began.

"There's the asshole who had my father thrown in a Mexican jail." This accusation was accompanied by a lot of derogatory remarks regarding my character and embellished with a lot of cuss words. The place got pretty quiet; I believe most folks there were figuring on a showdown.

I responded, calling him by name, : " Brad, You've had a bit to drink, this ain't the time nor the place to do this." My response did not find favor with him. He bolted out of his chair and lunged toward me; I in turn assumed a defensive stance. Several folks moved in between us, with a few holding him back.

The owner of the bar and some of his help grabbed ahold of me, with the owner of the bar proclaiming "Renzo is right, this isn't happening here or now."

The owner turned me loose and I said, "Thanks. The owner of the establishment offered to me, maybe it's best if I play somewhere else tonight." I left and made my way home in the dark. When I woke the next morning, I couldn't shake off the negative crap that had happened the night before. Yelapa was my home; it didn't sit right with me that some punk who crashed here a few months out of the year should be dictating my actions. I concluded that this could not continue.

I knew he had more than likely stayed out late, drugging and drinking. I waited till almost noon, then headed over to where I knew he was staying. As I approached his place, I could see him sitting on the front porch having a beer.

As I neared the porch, he came to his feet, abruptly expressing "What do you want?"

I responded, "I want this shit to end, right here and right now!" This was indeed a bold statement coming from a 150-pound artist pushing fifty. I added, "If you want to talk and find out what actually happened with your dad, cool. If you feel you need a piece of me, cool. Let's go right here, right now!" I don't know whether my actions simply took him by surprise or whether he couldn't picture himself beating the crap out of an old man, but whichever it was, we opted to talk. The conversation did not last long; he knew what I was saying about his father was the truth. When we seemed to be done, I offered "Are we done here?" I received a positive response. From that time on, neither of us were exactly friendly toward each other, but there was no more hostility.

I was coming up on the half-century mark an age that in my youth, I never thought I'd actually physically witness. The folks at the hotel organized a grand fifty-year birthday bash for me, with a little more than fifty folks showing up for the festivities. At one point during the night, I looked around at all the folks having a good time and thought to myself, "Here I am, fifty years old I'm in better shape than I have been in over twenty years, I live in a small jungle village in a foreign country, I'm living by myself, and in all my life I've never had fifty people show up for my birthday." It was an incredible evening. Interestingly enough, this was not the only birthday celebration held in my honor. As I mentioned, I was making frequent visits to the men's clubs in Puerto Vallarta. I had a favorite club where most everyone knew me by name. The manager of this club had found out it was my birthday through my partner, then contacted me in Yelapa to ask if I would consider making my way to Puerto Vallarta on a certain day because he was organizing a special night for me.

"Hell yes!" I was not quite sure what to expect party hats and a cake, or maybe something else entirely? I made the boat trip to Puerto Vallarta, checked into the hotel I always stayed at when I was in town, hosed myself off, grabbed some dinner, then I was into a taxi on my way to the club. I believe it was a Sunday night (usually a very slow night of the week for the clubs). When I arrived, I could see only one car in the parking lot. This surprised me, as even on slow nights there would be a few cars and taxis around.

When I neared the front door, I saw a sign posted: "Closed for private event." The door was also locked. I knocked and quickly the manager was there to greet me with big hugs and a bounding "*Cumpleaños, mi amigo!*" Like in most clubs of this type, the room was dimly lit. As I entered, I noticed the place was empty. No bouncers, no bartender, no customers, only four lovely women seated around a table in the middle of the club. As I got closer to the table, I recognized three of the women from earlier encounters. In the middle of the table was a good-sized flan supporting a lit sparkler; off to the side of the table was a full bar set up including a little mountain of Bolivian marching powder. The girls greeted me warmly, sat me down, and sang me a beautiful rendition of "*Feliz Cumpleaños.*" I was completely taken aback by such regal treatment.

After the song and some toasting, one of the girls offered up, "We did not buy you any presents because we are your presents." I was amazed, humbled, and frightened at the same time. I will leave the happenings of the next few hours to your imagination, though I do need to share what happened afterward. The sun was coming up soon, and it was time for everyone to go home. Interestingly, I do not completely recall leaving the club I was feeling a bit higher than normal, feeling a bit strange as well, as if I, had ingested some drug (other than the booze, cocaine, and sex). Since the club was closed up, there were no taxis to be found. I sort of remember wandering around an unfamiliar area of Puerto Vallarta. Although I could walk, I was not in complete control of my faculties, and I was hallucinating a bit. I wondered for a while, then it came to me: If I could make my way to the ocean, I might find my way back to the hotel.

Not the best idea. I did make it down to the beach, but the tide was high and the shoreline was not navigable. I found this out by getting trashed by waves, losing my shoes and shirt. Now I was on a strange shoreline soaking wet, no shoes, no shirt, and wasted out of my mind.

I'd guess by now it was around 7:00 a.m. I found myself on an outcropping of rocks with lots of deep tidepools. I distinctly remember seeing the hotel maintenance man Herardo, crash his boat onto the rocks in front of me. I became frantic and alerted folks nearby, who in turn alerted the authorities. I somehow contacted the hotel back in Yelapa to report what I had witnessed. I was surprised to find out, when I spoke with my partner, Sam, that the maintenance man and his boat were sitting on the beach in front of the hotel in Yelapa. All at once, I found myself standing shirtless, shoeless, and way out of my element in an upscale beachfront community in south Puerto Vallarta, attempting to explain the recent fantastic events to an officer of the law. All this just after I was in contact with my people at the hotel and hearing them explain to me that I was nuts.

As the investigation came to a close, one of the officers involved, who spoke a bit of English, took me aside and quietly offered, "If I ever see you again, you're going to jail." I was still in not the best state I was lost in an unfamiliar area about four miles from the hotel I desperately needed to reach. I did have my wallet, ID, and a few wet pesos. To this day, I have no idea how I actually made it back to the hotel, but when I finally did, I looked like something the cat just threw up. As I walked through the lobby, I could feel the eyes of the staff upon me with great disdain. I had finally reached the status of Ugly American. After recovering, I was amazed I had managed to survive the ordeal in one piece. Later, I contacted the manager of the club to inquire "what the hell." After a bit of digging, he found one girl had slipped me some ecstasy and another gave me some acid. The girls confessed openly, saying they just wanted me to have the most fun. Holy crap, how much fun can one person endure? This event luckily faded into the past in regards to damaging my reputation in the area, but it will be imprinted in my mind forever.

I was continuing to expand on my revised painting techniques, digging deeper into more profound concepts regarding my subject matter. To improve upon my understanding of this new work, I set about creating a series of human faces. I masked out similar sized areas on individual sheets of watercolor boards, then flooded the interior of the masked area with random, bright, translucent, permanent colors. After the applied paint dried, I would then add a thin layer of semipermanent, dark-valued paint over the top of the same surface. Once this application dried, I would use water to remove those areas of paint I wished to have a lesser value while exposing the initial colors I had laid down. Each work was a quick exercise, so I was able to produce a lot in a short amount of time.

As with my "Human Response" series, I was surprised to find that even without sketching first or having the intent to represent anything other than a person's face, I could gather such a variety of expressions, ethnicities, and emotions from each work upon its completion. After completing over fifty of these exercises, it dawned on me that I might have created an effective educational device. I had developed a technique that could be modified for easy application, and the application of paint could be accomplished on a small scale. Under my direction, a person with little or no experience with painting could use this process to develop at least a moderate skill set in applying pigment with the intent of achieving a recognizable image. This was the first time I had entertained the idea of opening up my studio to the public for the purpose of art instruction. This was pretty good timing because I really wanted to complete the plans I had originally set for my house, which included constructing an area downstairs to accommodate a bedroom and patio, leaving the complete second story devoted to studio space. I even had a bit of funds to make it happen. Wow, what a concept intent and funding! What was not to like about this? The hotel was doing OK and did not require my presence 24/7, I was opening new avenues and directions in my artwork, I was beginning to recover from the devastation of Kathy's death, I was becoming settled and accepted in my new community, I had the opportunity to instruct, and I was somewhat financially able to at least entertain all of this. I know, this all sounds like it has the makings of a "good outcome."

Right around this time, a brutal storm hit Yelapa. Water fell from the sky like I had never seen before, to the tune of twenty-five inches in less than twenty-four hours. The storm moved fast (which was good), directly up the canyon where Yelapa and its river were situated (which was very bad). I also learned by in-your-face catastrophic illustration an historical fact about the hotel at this time: It seemed that when the hotel was first constructed, the river emptied out to the bay right next to the hotel, and when it rained a lot, it would sometimes be a nuisance. So the original directors of the hotel went to a great deal of trouble to redirect the river such that it would empty into the bay at the other end of the beach about a quarter-mile away. This pre-Lorenzo historical event became terribly apparent to me when the river crested and chose to follow its original path. This wouldn't have been such a problem except for the fact that after diverting the river, the hotel expanded, building the restaurant's kitchen and storage, public restrooms, and half the bar right atop the newly dry riverbed.

Just up from the restaurant and bar was a creek bed that ran between a few of the *casitas*. It was dry more often than not, and when it was running, it was never more than a trickle. During the storm, that trickle turned to a raging mass of churning water and debris eight to ten feet high and more than twenty feet across. Along with several rock slides on the property, the damage was substantial. We completely lost one large *casita*, five others sustained major damage, six others lost walls or bathrooms, the kitchen and bar were wrecks, and, finally, there were two new 30' wide by 20' deep gorges formed in the hotel's beach, making most of it inaccessible. This was a true disaster. The hotel received a little federal assistance along with a little more from the *communidad*, but most of the repairs and reconstruction would be financed by the hotel.

Beyond the financial burden, this disaster affected me in other ways. I would now be devoting most of my time and energy to the reconstruction of the hotel. First on the list was flushing out the well, as the flood had filled it with debris and it had gone rancid. I worked with the staff to reclaim the well, which meant days of working in waist-deep not-so-clean water at the bottom of a twenty-foot hole in the ground. I was unaware that during this work, I had sustained a cut on my lower back. Just after we had completed work on the well, I became ill. I had no idea what was wrong whatever it was, I was not getting better, and in fact it was kicking my butt. It just so happened my partner, Sam, was friends with an MD from Puerto Vallarta and he and his family were vacationing in Yelapa. I was hunkered down at my home, feeling like death warmed over. The doctor came to my *casa* and, after a quick look, jumped into action. He ordered up an immediate boat to take us to Boca, where he had left his car, after which he whisked me away to a hospital in Puerto Vallarta. I don't remember a whole lot about this particular time. I do remember being cared for and receiving massive doses of antibiotics. I had contracted a staph infection from the dirty water via the cut on my back. I was indisposed for about a week. Just before I returned to Yelapa, the doctor who had come to my rescue visited me and explained what had transpired. He expressed that when he visited me in my home, I was exhibiting signs of a critical staph infection, adding if something had not been done in short order, I would have more than likely expired in the next few days. Damn!

I returned to Yelapa, and after a bit of regrouping, I returned to the tasks at hand. Not only did this event almost take me out of the picture for good, it changed what I was going to be doing in the near future. It was decided that if I was going to be expanding my job duties at the hotel, it might be in order for me to be compensated accordingly. I then went about applying myself to different parts of the hotel redesigning as well as constructing *casitas*, building bridges, building and rebuilding structural areas on the property. This would not only keep me really busy for the next couple of years, it would also afford me with a wee bit of "chump change."

Please, may I add that right around this time of enlightenment, personal growth, and a hell of a lot of hard work, I was just coming to grips with the idea that I was living alone in small village in a foreign country. The idea that I had better get a handle on this because it may be the rest of my life was becoming very real to me. I was going to live my life out with no more meaningful relationships, only chance encounters and paid visitations. Amazingly enough, this was beginning to make sense to me, enough so that I was becoming comfortable and accepting of my existence as well as my future. Finally, I was becoming whole again.

Enter the devil! An energetic young gentleman from San Francisco who visited Yelapa every couple of years and whom I had befriended early on. We had kept in touch via email and he had informed me of his plans to visit Yelapa once again. In his correspondence, he made clear his concerns about my being sad and alone. This person, convinced of his need to fix me, would in the near future help orchestrate events that would change the course of my life.

At the same, time Yelapa was evolving. High tension structures carrying electricity had been erected in the hills nearby, which meant Yelapa was about to be electrified. This came about very quickly, and phone service was fast on its heels. In an amazingly short time a matter of months Yelapa was thrust into a new age. At the time, I was unsure this was a good thing, but it happened anyway, and all of a sudden, I was on the grid again. With as much power available to me as I could pay for, I could now communicate with anyone at any time I wished, and in very short order I even had water available to me as a utility. Damn! Within a matter of months, everything I had worked so hard to familiarize myself with had changed in the direction of what I had left behind in San Diego. It was a bittersweet moment.

But back to the lad from San Francisco. He arrived in Yelapa and, without delay, headed straight for me, hell-bent on bringing about change to my life. He came to my house in the afternoon and shared his concerns with me over some tequila, about his perceptions regarding my not having a woman to share my life with. This in itself was not so strange because we had discussed the subject many times before. The only difference this time was that it seemed like he had found religion for the first time and he had been chosen to resurrect my miserable existence. We bantered back and forth, him expressing how miserable I was, me trying to convince him I was just fine. It all ended with me saying I was fine and him saying he was going to return that evening to make sure he physically escorted me to the "bailey" (dance) that night, in order to expose me to available female prospects. I was uncomfortable with the idea, but figured, "What the hell?" After he left, I got some things taken care of, then hosed off in preparation to party. He showed up just as he said, and we made our way to the pueblo. It was the beginning of the season, so the only dance club in Yelapa was hopping that night. I really did not want to be there. I was thinking I'd have a couple of drinks, talk a little, and make my way home. But it was either the tequila or there was some sort of voodoo in the air, because once we got settled at the dancehall and he began to point out possibilities to me, by some obscure rationale, his bantering started to make some sense. He pointed out one woman whom I had always considered a bit of a flake and really didn't find that attractive. Incredibly, as the night went on and we discussed the issues more, I ended up asking this woman to dance, after which we sat and talked for a bit. I couldn't help but think to myself that this was a person who, in the past, I could not see myself interacting with, much less starting up a relationship with. Something was happening that I did not seem to have much control over. This woman and I sat and talked for the rest of the evening in fact, we ended up closing the place down. I saw her home to the place she was staying, after which I made the almost two-mile walk back to my home. That night, I tossed and turned in my bed, wrestling with my own conflicting thoughts. This should have been a clue to myself to run for my life! Instead, I woke the next morning completely smitten with this woman. Fortunately, this viral attack on my soul would take a wee bit of time to fully kick into gear.

I involved myself with the completion of my house, projects at the hotel, and my artwork. The renovation to my house required a lot of manhours. I hired locals to help me with the project; some worked out, some did not. It was an ongoing challenge. A lot of the work involved ferrocement, which was a process not too many folks in the area were familiar with. Just as in building the original structure, it was a real feat to complete the house as I had originally intended. This was all taking time as I was simultaneously attempting to sort out my emotional issues, but at least the second-floor studio space was complete. I had constructed a roof over the top of the open deck space and installed a built-in workbench around the entire patio. This was done so I could seat up to fifteen students, and soon I would get my first chance to put my labors to good use. The remodeling of the main floor turned out pretty good. I had broken through two sides of the house to make three archways. On the back wall was a doorway to the raised level bedroom, and two large openings on the side of the house opened out to a walled patio. I then built a water pond. The bedroom opened up to the patio and pond with an eight-foot waterfall built into one side that emptied into the pond. Being totally open to the jungle, it was not a bad place to hang out.

My First Opportunity to Offer Art Instruction on Foreign Soil

There was a husband-and-wife team who had been successfully bringing a group of nurses to the hotel on retreat for a few years. Prior to the group's arrival, I had talked with my partner Sam and expressed my intent to offer art instruction at my studio. He thought it was a great idea, and if it went well, the hotel should incorporate it into future group offerings. I met with the couple over drinks when they arrived and pitched my plan. They happily agreed to let me offer the program to the nurses. On the day that groups arrived in Yelapa, my partner and I would give presentations on stuff to do as well as stuff not to do, and would talk about some of the diversions available while in Yelapa. During this presentation, I pitched my art class to twenty nurses. I was a bit surprised to find that twelve were eager to sign up. They already had a pretty full schedule, but I was able to squeeze in three days at two hours per day; $150 per student for six hours of instruction times twelve was $1,800. It wasn't a gold mine, but it represented a great place to start. The first program was a smashing success. All the nurses who attended raved about how much fun they had, how much they learned, and most importantly, how they all thought it was well worth the expense and would do it again. Wow! Touchdown! This definitely exceeded my expectations.

Just before the group was going to leave, the organizers came to me and expressed that they wanted to make the art instruction an integral part of their group offering and asked if it was possible for me to supply them with any promotional material. This was the birth of what would become known as the "Art Asylum," through which over the next two and a half years I would provide instruction in the arts to a few hundred folks.

I continued to battle with myself in regards to why I was so drawn to pursuing this woman whom I didn't particularly like. Nevertheless, I continued to see her. The process of dating her was hit or miss at best. While I perceived her to be a free spirit, I would later find that she was actually a total loon. But I wouldn't come to this reality till it was much too late. Looking back on the process where weird on-and-off dating turned to an actual courtship, there were so many red flags that I can't believe that I hadn't already run for my life. The challenge was that I was falling in love with this crazy woman, and it seemed I was powerless to do anything to stop it. I would eventually come to learn, after five years of involvement, that "love" is ambivalent: it can be good, bad, wonderful, dangerous, fulfilling, destructive, and stupid all at the same time.

OK enough disclaimer, I'm giving away the plot. I was beginning to make the over two-mile walk to where she lived across the bay more and more often. It was becoming apparent that we were an item. Muffy was very taken with the fact that I was an artist; moreover, she liked the idea of me offering art instruction. She wanted in. Muffy had somewhat of a job where she was living. In order to bring us closer, we devised the idea that she could move in with me and work to promote my art instruction. It was done, and soon we began to face the ramifications of our decision. Without immediate income from our business venture, I was now feeding two people instead of one with my food allotment from the hotel, which would grow into an issue in the near future. Also, as a couple we had developed an affinity for Bolivian marching powder as a recreational enchantment. My relationship with this woman was immediately developing into a dilemma. On one front, it was servicing my imagined need to be in a relationship with a woman; on another, it was bringing about financial challenges as well as damaging my standing in the community. Regardless, I continued with this wild adventure. We played house together, making some advancement with the "Art Asylum." Interestingly, my artwork was becoming more emotionally driven.

Via my new relationship, I was making contact with folks in Yelapa who had previously been unavailable to me. I connected with a glass artist from Washington State (a protégé of Chihuly, the world-renowned glass artist) who had been visiting Yelapa for a couple of years. Upon his visits to Yelapa, we began to develop a strong connection. Whenever he was in town, we would get together and share information about the arts. One time in particular I remember, he showed up and sought me out straight away to ask a very poignant question he'd been pondering: "Does the art we create define us as a person?" Holy crap! This was big. I was dumbfounded and requested a bit of time before I might respond. I know this might not seem to be that big of a question, but posed to anyone who has devoted a lifetime to making art, it's the quantum question. I did respond "yes," taking a quote often attributed to Marshall McLuhan: "We shape our tools, then our tools shape us." I think this concept also applies to artists and the art they create. After I left Yelapa, I lost contact with this particular artist.

I was driving myself into a much more demanding existence dealing with a new relationship, living with a woman after learning to live alone, painting, promoting my artwork, teaching art, growing the Art Asylum, working with administration and promotion at the hotel, construction work on the hotel, coyote duty at the hotel. I was not aware of the fact that I had been systematically pushing myself toward a much more complex existence that I had worked so hard to deconstruct. Though it seemed I had limitless energy, I did not. I turned to "artificials" in order to enhance my productivity a dumb idea. Cocaine was readily available and very affordable since it was produced right up the valley from Yelapa. The perceived value to me was that for minimal expenditure, I could change ten hours of production time to twenty hours of production time. Although this sounded pretty good in theory, the opposite would become apparent soon enough. I was also quite surprised to find how ready my new girlfriend was to embrace this idea, she being the "peace, love, and veggies" kind of girl. Time progressed with myself getting a lot accomplished, some good and some not so good.

Hurricane Patricia came along a nasty piece of weather. She passed right in front of Yelapa, causing a fair amount of destruction to the area. At the time, there were only about twenty folks staying at the hotel. Just prior to Patricia's impact, we evacuated everyone from the hotel to my *casa*, mainly because my house was located a bit more inland and constructed completely out of cement. It was not such a bad plan, since a few of the *casitas* these folks had been occupying sustained a fair amount of damage in the storm. Yelapa sustained a bit of damage as well, but overall faired pretty well. There was a lot of cleanup to do at the hotel, along with more construction work for myself.

Financially, my new girlfriend, Muffy and I were getting by. I had my small salary from the hotel, payment for construction work at the hotel, periodic money from art instruction, and funds from the sale of my artwork. Altogether, this didn't amount to a whole lot, but if I was bringing in this type of money in and living alone, I'd have been doing pretty well. Muffy and I did enjoy "having a good time," and considering there were two of us as opposed to just one, I accepted the fact that it would require more funds to get by, although it did seem like money was dissipating at a rapid rate. In hindsight, I should have paid more attention to this particular issue because it would soon become a clear and present danger.

There was this TV celebrity from Mexico City who would show up in Yelapa for some R&R along with his entourage, always staying at the hotel. Within his entourage was a group of three friends who always seemed to travel with him. Over time and after many return visits to Yelapa, my partner at the hotel, Sam and I became very acquainted with these four youngsters from Mexico City. My girlfriend and I even became very close with one of the young lads. They were returning to Yelapa often enough that they were considering building a place of their own. Sam and I assisted them in arranging a lease on some property up above the hotel, which they used to immediately begin construction on an elaborate complex. Things had changed so much over the time I had resided in Yelapa, and they seemed to be changing more rapidly as time went on. When I first moved in, there was no electricity, no phones, and very limited intrusion from the outside world other than tourists. Now there was electricity, phone service, water service, paragliding, quad vehicles running up and down the beach, and a massive intrusion from the outside world. It was hard for me to recognize the place I had chosen to live, and I was becoming a bit disillusioned with its evolution. Nevertheless, I was determined to continue on the journey I had set upon just a few years earlier. I was still a bit unsettled in my relationship with Muffy. In my infinite wisdom, I figured if I could set the relationship in order with some type of standard, it might somehow magically become "well." You know, kind of like the concept that if your marriage is in trouble, the best course of action is to produce a child? All flawed logic. I asked Muffy to marry me, and at first, she (with great surprise to myself) offered resistance. I could not conceive of how she would not readily answer yes, so I continued to press. Unfortunately, she caved to my advances and agreed to be my wife. We both dove in and set about making this come to pass. Even though there were a good number of folks who weren't really convinced that our joining was the best idea, most everyone kept their opinions to themselves and threw in a hand to assist us in making a special day.

It actually happened; we were wed. The day itself is a good memory: a good party, good friends, and good people. As I mentioned before, early in the day while I was at the hotel setting up for one part of the day-long festivities I, of course being barefoot, stepped on a scorpion. Surprisingly enough, it was not a bad sting painful yes, but I was able, after a short "time out," to continue on with my duties. I remember the hotel's security guard was helping me with the setup when I got stung. As I yelped and pulled the little sucker from the bottom of my foot, he glared at me with a bit of an accusatory look, as if to say, "Pay attention, the universe is trying to tell you something." Obviously, I paid no attention. Early the next morning after all the festivities, Herardo whisked us away to a small exclusive resort just up the coast, where I knew the owners. We were treated like royalty. It was here that something really odd happened. My new bride and I were swimming out in the surf in front of the resort. As I looked around, at first, I thought it was deja vu, but soon I realized I was remembering a dream I'd had a few months prior. The details of the dream are pretty unimportant it was the feelings it evoked: uncomfortable, uneasy, unsettled simply put, just wrong. This was quite disturbing to me, and in sharing it with my new bride, it didn't do much for her either. It put a bit of a damper on the afternoon, but as with most everything else, we both just said "what the hell" and charged forward. If I might interject a wee bit of wisdom here? No matter how much fun you think you're having, if you're stung by a nasty beast and you're remembering a bad dream you had about the future that you happen to be experiencing now, it might not be a bad idea to pay attention to whatever vibes the universe is desperately trying to forward to your wee gray matter.

A short time after the wedding, I began to notice subtle changes in how I viewed my world, which would later become much less subtle. The obvious change was that I now had to consider two folks instead of just one in all life decisions. I was also considering the future much more than before, and even though I was indulging in much more "play," I was being forced to evaluate any and all of the ramifications of my indulgences. I began to look at and think about my artwork in a much broader sense. I was considering expanding the Art Asylum to a recognizable business. I was paying a bit more attention to the financial operations at the hotel. All of these perceptions seemed to stem from my former life. Again, I was not so comfortable with this change, but could not seem to do much to prevent its growth.

The hotel seemed to be doing OK, but interestingly, on paper the finances were in decline. "Things that make you go *hmmm*." I'm completely convinced that my partner, Sam and one of the administrators of the hotel were involved in something slick. I could never put my finger on it, but knew it was damaging to my funds and advantageous to theirs. All of this input was piling up like snow in a blizzard. It was beginning to look like what was once my paradise was evolving into life in the city, only in the jungle. Over time, I was becoming more and more conflicted. The Art Asylum was doing OK, but it was still sporadic, even after branching out to Puerto Vallarta in search of clientele. The problem was that now that I was married, my mindset had changed and I basically just wanted *more*. My Muffy and I had opened up the conversation about possibly leaving Yelapa nothing serious, just tossing ideas around. It was right around this time I noticed meth starting to show up around the area. I didn't quite understand the attraction. Since cocaine was local, it was not very expensive, and meth was being offered at just about the same price. This didn't make sense to me because both drugs have similar effects. Meth is just harder on the system and was usually used in the US as a cheaper substitute for cocaine. Anyhow, not long after meth made its debut, Yelapa began to change even more than it already had. Petty theft became more commonplace. An older gringo woman who had a place in Yelapa for years was robbed and beaten, there were more fights at the bailies (town dances), and just more than usual aggression. One more thing that seemed to be pushing me away from Yelapa.

Wildly, it was right around this period of time that the young aristocrats from Mexico City were finishing up construction on their exclusive compound and made it known that they might be interested in taking over the hotel. You know what they say timing is very important. I looked at this opportunity and figured it would probably not come around again in my lifetime. Therefore, if I were ever going to leave Yelapa, it would be now. Idle talk turned to serious discussions in a matter of a few months. It seemed like overnight, but there we all were myself negotiating for the sale of my part in the hotel, my wife and I seriously deciding where the hell we might go, and me offering my house up for sale. It all seemed surreal to me. The efforts became a reality sooner than I might have hoped.

Where to go? I had no wish to return to California, or for that matter truly anywhere else. Muffy was originally from Queensland, Australia, and even though she was not really excited about the thought of returning to her roots, it seemed to offer better possibilities than our other considerations like southern Mexico, South America, Canada, or New Zealand. It was also time to close down the Art Asylum, which was very hard for me, since the small business afforded me a good deal of fulfillment.

A gringo woman I knew who had been residing in Yelapa for a while expressed interest in taking over my house, which took a bit of work, but would end up being not a bad thing. The most important and most arduous task was negotiating the transfer of my holdings in the hotel to the youngsters from Mexico City. They came to the bargaining table equipped with shark attorneys from the big city, which would in the end translate to me losing the equivalent of nearly $45,000 if I wanted to make all of this come to pass. Putting this all together as a workable project was insane. With the loss of funds from the hotel transaction along with the ridiculous amount of money required to ship our belongings to Brisbane, Australia, as well as travel to Queensland, I had almost tapped out all the savings I had to that point. Nevertheless, it all came to pass, and it was now time to leave my beloved Yelapa and take flight to Brisbane. My wife was now showing signs of excitement about reconnecting, and I was so excited I could barely contain myself. We were off to find a new life on the largest island on the planet. Beyond the financial stress, one part of this journey seemed to strike a resonant chord. My favorite uncle on my mom's side hooked up with an Aussie just after World War II, spent time in Australia, and had a pretty exciting life. I was hoping for something similar.

This was in fact the start of an exciting new life, although the word "exciting" is not necessarily a positive one. It was time to go what hadn't been sold, traded, or given away was on the beach and being loaded into a panga bound for Puerto Vallarta. I had already taken a load of important papers, books, and tools packed up in two large boxes to DHL in Puerto Vallarta and set them up for shipment to Brisbane, Queensland. That in itself was an eye opener: two large boxes, nearly 250 pounds of stuff, would cost over $6,000 for shipping, taxes, and tariffs. Since we were traveling to another continent and also due to the fact my folks had not met my wife, our journey to Queensland would be via California. The trip took about five days and ended up costing nearly $5,000. So, all in all, just getting to Australia cost me over $11,000.

Morena

Please bear with me, this tale will come to point at why I left Yelapa. A few years after I arrived in Yelapa, I was offered a puppy: a little smoky grey pit bull–hound mix bundle of adventure whom I named Morena. As soon as she was old enough to realize what was going on around her, we bonded. An amazing connection; I only had to look at her to know what she was about to do, just as her with me. She would grow to be an incredible animal. She and I were pretty much inseparable, other than the times I would go to Puerto Vallarta. She somehow knew I was only going away for a bit, and when I returned, whether she was up the beach or away in the jungle, she could sense I was back and would make a beeline to greet me. I've had other dogs in my life, but the relationship we had was nothing less than cosmic. One time during the high season, she and I ventured up to the waterfall above the pueblo. This was something we did quite often, only on this particular day it was right around the time the tourists were arriving. Morena and I arrived at the restaurant below the waterfall just in front of a large group of tourists.

I greeted my friend, the owner of the restaurant, *"Buen dia, mi hermano."* Morena sat by my side as we took in the beauty of our surroundings. All at once, centered at the top of the stairs above us, a magnificent four-foot-long male iguana presented himself in all his glory. I noticed a good thirty folks standing behind me just as I looked down at my side to see the hairs on Morena's neck standing straight up. The command "NO" rang from my mouth, but it was too late. Morena charged up the steps, the poor iguana had no idea what the hell was happening. Morena grabbed it by the throat, violently thrusting back and forth until in an instant there was now centered at the top of the stairs only one really proud dog standing on top of a mangled and bloody corpse of a very large lizard. I could feel the horror of the tourists behind me as well as the look of disdain coming from the restaurant owner. I walked up the stairs and removed the mangled body, after which I was going to attempt to slip away with as little fanfare as possible. But no Morena went about with lizard blood dripping from her face and tail wagging, greeting each and every person there. I offered my apologies to the proprietor and we left, but only after Morena said goodbye to as many folks as would pay any attention to her. On the way home, Morena was the sweetest and most obedient pup one could imagine. This was our relationship. We had many adventures during our time together.

Now back to leaving Yelapa. I loved Morena and I could not conceive of her enduring the ordeal of the one-year quarantine required by Australia for incoming dogs. She was a jungle dog; she had never seen a car. She was staying put. My wife and I were leaving, everything was in the panga, and I gave Morena one last hug goodbye. We hopped in the boat and set out for PV. In the past when I would leave, Morena would fuss a bit, but as the boat moved away, she would then go about her business. Not today she knew something was up. As we moved away from the beach in the boat, she bounded into the surf. People were calling her back, I was screaming at her to stay. But she was determined. She was not putting up with the idea of me leaving. Almost half a mile out to sea, I could see her little grey head bobbing in the waves. I saw a friend of mine leave the shore in his panga heading toward Morena. Finally, he plucked her from the water, barking all the time. I was crying at the sight of this, as I am right now while I write these words. It's amazing how connected two animals can become.

Brisbane, Mt. Nebo

Obviously, I was much more excited about being in Brisbane than my counterpart. I had always wanted to visit Australia. I met the family and they were nothing like Muffy,; they were very conservative and upper middle class. Her parents, sister, and her sister's husband greeted us with open arms very nice folks. This was the first time in my life that I became aware that Californians had an accent just about every time I opened my mouth it was, "Oh, you're a yank from California." No one could ever explain the accent to me, but folks just seemed to hear it. Even though we all spoke English, when some folks talked, all I heard were alien noises.

Until we settled, we stayed with my Muffy's sister and her family in Brisbane. The transition was abrupt and a brutal awakening: once again I was stranger in a strange land. Coming from a third-world Latin environment, barefoot in the jungle, donkeys instead of cars, regular use of tequila and cocaine, painting and teaching folks how to be creative to this upscale, conservative, predominantly white metropolis was a big order of change. I hadn't thought that much about it prior to making the trip, but damn it was a shock. At least in Queensland (I can't speak to other areas in Australia), it was common practice in speaking to add an "e" sound to the end of particular words "blankie," "ciggie," etc. So immediately I was called "Lozzie," short for Lorenzo. I'd always wondered why my wife called me "Renzie."

One of the first orders of business was to change my visa status and begin the process of immigrating to Australia and becoming a naturalized citizen. It's funny, folks talk about how hard it is to obtain citizenship in the US ha! As hard as that is, try immigrating to Australia or New Zealand. It was an arduous and expensive process. All throughout this time while we were living with my wife's sister, trying to secure working papers for myself, and looking for a place to live, my wife and I were running though funds like water from a fire hose. It was amazing to me after traveling from Mexico to Australia and only being in the country for a few months, we had already gone through close to $30,000. This was alarming to me because I only had about $30,000 left. I was also amazed at the abundance of "social care." Coming from the US and Mexico, I was not familiar with the idea of living in a country that was so devoted to the welfare of its citizens. These social services seemed to be funded by heavy taxation on booze, cigarettes, and fuel a few of the things I was used to consuming on a regular basis all of a sudden increased in price beyond belief. The idea of social medicine was cool, but damn!

Example:

1 pack of Camel filters	Jalisco: $1.00	Queensland: $10.45
1 six-pack of Coors	Jalisco: $1.60	Queensland: $13.50
1 bottle of cheap tequila	Jalisco: $3.50	Queensland: $48.00
1 bottle of Jim Beam	California: $7.00	Queensland: $39.00
1 gallon of regular fuel	California: $2.00	Queensland: $7.00+ per liter
1 doctor's visit	California: $150-$250	Queensland: $0

An opportunity arose at Mt. Nebo a wooded community in the hills above Brisbane. A place where I soon found out Muffy had lived in a past life, and where she still had some contacts. It seemed my wife knew a woman who had a piece of property there that needed some construction work done. She was willing to let us live in the house rent-free in the meantime. For the work I would perform and for maintaining the property, she was willing to pay me $900 per month. Also, she was willing to pay cash, knowing I did not have my working papers yet. This was an interesting proposition, because she already had someone working on the house. I agreed mainly because I knew we would run out of funds before I was able to get my working papers. Moving to Mt. Nebo also meant getting a car I know, it doesn't sound like a big deal. But wow! The car had to be purchased under my wife's name since I was not documented yet; with fuel being expensive, travel came at a cost, and auto insurance (also in my wife's name) was expensive due to her poor driving record in the past. With a little help from my wife's parents, we were able to pick up a ten-year-old Volvo station wagon.

It seemed like everything required uphill movement. Nevertheless, we made the move to Mt. Nebo. It was beautiful! It was set amid an arid tropical forest with lots of animals. Even with all the challenges, I was still pretty close to heaven. The house was a multilevel structure set on the side of a steep hill overlooking the forest, with a large deck on three sides. Did I say the place was beautiful? There were a fair number of marsupials and snakes, but an overwhelming complement of birds. Cockatoos, kookaburras, parakeets, and so many different types of parrots. I was amazed at the sheer numbers. I immediately set up feeders two 2' × 6' flats for seeds, mounted on the handrail of the deck. The day after I installed the feeders, it started. At first it was just a few birds, then more and more! Before I knew it, there were enormous flocks visiting on a daily basis. My wife was supposedly looking for employment, so she was away from the house a lot. I was working on the house, and in my spare time, I had begun to paint once again after the few months of transition. Painting was coming hard to me; I considered that this was the effect of having just been uprooted and that it would come easier after I had settled.

Back to the birds they were intense. Every day, without fail, first thing in the morning, the lorikeets would show up possibly 100 or more. They were loud, aggressive toward one another, and did not like me to be too close to them. A little later on in the morning, the cockatoos would come in, anywhere from 20-30 of them. They weren't as chaotic as the lorikeets, and if I was very quiet and still, they would put up with me being right next to them. Next in line came the king parrots these guys were a hoot. They really knew how to party. When I stood outside on the deck, they would land on my shoulders, my head, and all around me. They let me handle and feed them we were buds. There was one rosella that would show up once a day, usually while I was working, and come into the house, where he would walk around and find his way close to me. He would not let me touch him, but I could feed him, and for some reason he was cool with being near me. He would eventually bring his mate as well as his offspring to visit. There was a female kookaburra that would hang out periodically. Eventually, once I hadn't seen her for a while, a young male kookaburra started showing up out on the handrail of the porch. I noticed he seemed to be a few bricks short of a full load. He'd just sit on the rail and wildly yack all day. After a couple of days, I noticed the female was back with another female about the same size as the little wacko sucker. Seeing them all together, I realized it was a mother with two chicks. The young damaged male that had become a permanent fixture on the handrail didn't seem to be feeding, and the mother wasn't helping him either. But she was still hanging around to keep an eye on the little guy. I decided to step in to the mix. I gathered about a bowl's worth of bugs and individually maimed each one just enough so they couldn't crawl or fly away. I then waited till the little weirdo was asleep and placed the bowl-o-bugs near him. The next morning, the little guy didn't seem to have been yapping so much, and most of the bugs were gone from the bowl. Mom was still hanging out with her little girl, who she did feed. I repeated the bug maiming act the next night, only placing the bowl a little further away, and woke up to a similar result. On this day, the little male seemed a bit perkier and the mom with the young female came down to visit him several times. As evening came around, I prepared my bowl-o-bugs one more time, placing it in the same manner as I had the night before. As I was falling asleep, I heard a wee bit of chatter from the family. The next morning when I checked outside, the bowl-o-bugs was empty and the three kookaburras were nowhere to be seen. More than likely what happened is the dumb little male fell off the porch and rolled down the hill, where he became fair game for a brown snake, with the mom and young female chowing down on the bug snacks I'd left before they made their exit. But I like to think that I simply managed to provide this mama kookaburra with the assistance her challenged offspring needed, helping make it possible for them all to fly off into the night as a happy family. Yea, I like a good fairytale.

My existence up on Mt. Nebo reminded me of hippie communal life from back in the late 60s. Even living what I considered to be a simple life, our funds were dwindling quickly and Muffy's state of well-being was deteriorating. I had settled in to a point to where I was producing paintings and researching the possibilities of how and where to offer my work in my new environment.

Another thing I was becoming aware of was the seemingly innate discrimination and bigotry toward the aboriginals coming from the European set. It was widespread and deeply rooted, especially among people my age and a little older. My Muffy and her friends were cool, though, and hung with indigenous folks. Though not so analogous to the challenges between Blacks and Whites in the US, the younger Queensland generation seemed to inherently adhere to the principles set forth by that US Baptist minister from the 60s: "Judge people not by the color of their skin but by the content of their character." The only impressions I had of these indigenous people in my youth had been gathered from books and film. In person, it was all too harsh of a reminder of how European colonizers treated (and continue to treat) the indigenous peoples of the US. Just as in the States, I could never wrap my head around how such indignity could be shoveled out to fellow human beings.

I was putting the finishing touches on the house which, I must add, had called on and challenged every bit of my experience in construction. Cement work, framing, wall boards, glazing, tilework, painting, metalwork, plumbing, electrical, roofing, engineering, general carpentry, etc. Some things I had to learn from zero. Mt. Nebo offered little or no access to groundwater, so folks there had adapted to collecting rainwater as their primary source for the household. This meant the use of elaborate drainage and gutter systems on the house as well large storage tanks that required treating and maintaining. This was a surprisingly good water system until the droughts. Then, one would have to pay for water to be trucked in. Next was framing: all house framing and wooden structural support was "hardwood." In the States, fir (softwood) 2 × 4s were the customary choice for framing. In Queensland, it was ash (hardwood) 2 x 2s. The difference in labor was significant. With fir, you cut it to size and drove a big-ass nail through to secure it. With ash, you had to use a degree of effort to cut it to size then drill screw holes in it, then use screws to bind the pieces together, which was more time and labor-intensive. Another surprising aspect of construction was that this house, like many others in the area, was surfaced with wallboard that contained asbestos. Much care was required in handling it as well as disposing of it. As I had learned in Mexico, a different country required a different way of thinking.

As I mentioned, Muffy seemed to be showing signs of "issues." This is the part where things went to hell in a handbasket, seemingly quicker that I could say, "What?" This was around the time that things appeared to be getting right for me you know, adjusting, getting used to my surroundings, creating art after a bit of a sabbatical, thinking about the future, just getting a handle on the idea that things were going to be OK. Yes, my wife was acting a little weird, but hey, she was a weirdo, so what? But her actions were becoming more unbearable on a daily basis. In a short amount of time, she had graduated from being a bit unruly at get-togethers to being nonsensical and aggressive at home. I was beside myself as to what I should do. I began to inquire with great intent to her friends and family about her past, hoping to find some sort of rationale to help sort this ugly problem out. After much in-depth conversation with the people who had shared her past, I was a little bit surprised to find that my little free-spirited, tree-hugging nymph had a long and intense history of substance abuse from an early age. Great!

It was then that she was going to hit her maximum saturation point. I must admit I was a bit pissed to hear this, because she had presented herself to me as a simple, free-spirited, tree-hugging, peace-loving nature mama, when in actuality she was a substance-abusing sociopath who just wanted to have fun. Shame on me for not being able to spot it. It pretty much came to a conclusion when she decided to go for a fanciful romp in the neighborhood dressed in not much of anything and reverted to a primal state. It had gone beyond my capacity to understand or deal with. I begged for help from her family and friends. The general consensus was "intervention." I had become familiar with this term in Yelapa due to the fact that there were a few folks worthy of the process, but I did not quite understand why it was necessary because from what I could see, my wife wasn't consuming any more alcohol than she had in Mexico and to my knowledge she didn't have access to any recreational drugs. Her family told me to really check our property thoroughly and to shake down her friends and acquaintances. I did just that, and damn in a flash, I realized why our funds seemed to be dwindling so rapidly. This made me think back to Yelapa in regards to the same subject. She was not only indulging with me, but was having a go at it on her own. Wow! She wasn't a large person, maybe 115 pounds soaking wet, and she was putting away enough alcohol to drown a sailor. The drugs were another story as far as I knew, she was only doing cocaine in Mexico, but who really knows? In Queensland, cocaine wasn't that easy to get ahold of and it was very expensive, but after checking around, I found she was doing prescription meds, ecstasy, meth, and pot. To this day, I have no idea how she could possibly function. Before I could get things under control, she wrecked the car, then wrecked the loaner car and had another romp through the forest. At my request, she had been seeing a counselor for a while; when I informed the counselor about what was really happening, she recommended that my wife enroll in a special program that treated substance abuse as well as psychological disorders. I spoke with my wife's family, and based on her years of issues, they supported the idea. Even her close friends were on board with the thought of my basically having my wife put away indefinitely. I was amazed here I was married only for a short time, finding out that the woman I married was clinically whacked-out and her friends and family, whom I had just met, were ready to assist me in having her committed. This all was well and fine, but it was a bit more complicated than I have made it sound. You see, my wife was sponsoring my efforts to become a naturalized citizen of Australia, and yes, her condition was causing issues with my status. If my wife was committed to a facility, I would lose my progress, including any and all funds put toward it to that point.

Once again, I was at a crossroads. I was losing what I knew of my wife, suffering a major setback in my Australia immigration status, and running very low on reserve funds. I had also been in contact with my parents in California and received the news of their failing health. All things considered, I was hard-pressed to find a decent direction to head, with all the choices laid out in front of me being less than desirable. With the help and support of my wife's family and friends, we decided on a course of action. One of my wife's closest friends and I convinced her to commit herself to psychiatric care. I then removed myself from the naturalization process and used my last available funds to return to California in order to assist my ailing parents. This was a sad and horrible time, as I still loved Muffy and I really did not wish to return to the US. Regardless of my notions, this seemed to be the only workable path.

Back in the USA

I returned to the US, mid-California, where my folks resided. I was broke, broken-hearted, and disillusioned with life in general (you may have heard this statement at previous points in this story). Being over fifty years old and moving back in with your parents does nothing to boost your self confidence in your life's trajectory, even though, in this case, it appeared to be the necessary evil. After so many adventures, to return to this place was devastating. I attempted to give my best to my parents, and in turn they supported me in my endeavors. I was having intense separation anxiety after leaving my wife, but was doing my best to overcome the sensation. The next bit of my life would prove to be very interesting. In the first months of my wife's convalescence, I was allowed no contact. By the time I returned to the US, limited communication was allowed. We sent some letters back and forth and emailed each other. In these communications, she seemed to be reverting back to a human being.

After helping my dad set up the house to be more manageable for both my mom and dad, helping my dad with several projects he had been unable to complete, helping them get some of their important documents in order, and, finally, helping my dad with the preliminary leg work and paperwork needed in preparation for my mom moving to a care facility, I had done whatever I could to care for and assist my parents. It was time to press out on my own. I found a studio apartment in not the best part of town and moved right in. The center of the apartment became my workspace. I had been away from painting for a while and I was basking in the idea of producing work once again. I was emotionally challenged by all that was going on, and as was apparent in my past, that in itself could be a catalyst for creating artwork. I was not the happiest of campers. I felt like I had spent half my life building a beautiful sandcastle only to see it be washed away by a wave, then reconstructing another beautiful castle only to see it get washed away by another wave. With an arrogant tenacity, I attempted to build yet another beautiful sandcastle, only to see it washed away by yet another wave. Hell! You'd think that by now, I'd stop trying to build sandcastles. No! Insanely enough, I still held hopes of possibly reconstructing my last project. As I said, I was in contact with Muffy in Australia. I was making headway with my art and at the same time creating a presence in my immediate area. Things were beginning to improve for me; along with that, it appeared that after months of treatment, Muffy was showing great improvement back in Australia. I was so alone and disturbed after what had transpired, I began to entertain the idea of rejoining her. Looking back on this time, this was the most hideous, absurdly stupid idea imaginable. Regardless, I set in motion her relocation to the States. I had involved myself in a few projects to help build my financial standing, and before I realized what I was doing, I had booked passage for my wife to America and had started the process of her naturalization. I secured a small house for us in the suburbs of Fresno and received my hopefully repaired wife with open arms. I had become involved with a few art-related nonprofits in the area that didn't do much for me but take up time and energy, other than get me a wee bit of recognition. In the process of getting my wife's papers, I had to retain an immigration attorney. Interestingly enough, I learned he was the founder and head of the board of directors of a local arts nonprofit organization. As time went on, we became better acquainted until it finally came to a conversation regarding my becoming a part of his organization.

At the time, I had an offer of an art director position with a firm in San Diego. I was still a bit iffy about my wife, who was behaving like a complete person, just not the person I was familiar with. I evaluated all the info available to me and decided to stay in the area and assume the position of executive director of the nonprofit organization led by the immigration attorney. I did this not only for the work but also to keep some stable surroundings for myself and my wife. In hindsight, this was not a good decision. The nonprofit ended up being a "boy's club," with the board of directors expressing no intention to grow. Muffy began to degrade in ways I could not have imagined, her behavior was becoming more erratic. At one moment she would be combative, the next, passive and cuddly as a baby bunny kind of like wrestling with a fur coat wrapped in barbwire. When I left the house, I truly did not know what to expect when I returned. She could not focus on anything for more than five or ten minutes, she told me that making love with me was too hard for her to cope with, so that was off the table. It became obvious that the person I was living with was not the same person I had corresponded with for some many months. I had to question myself. Was it me? Was being with me the catalyst promoting her behavior? I was very vigilant in my efforts to make sure she did not have access to drugs or alcohol, so I had to assume that was not the source of the problem. She was not what one would consider totally insane, most folks that came into casual contact with her just thought her to be a bit odd. However, anyone who spent a significant amount of time with her knew she was off with the fairies. There were no avenues open to me; it was impossible to have her committed. At the time, I was marginally working as an artist while directing the art-related nonprofit organization, she was not employed, and there were no drugs or alcohol to rehabilitate from. So, what the hell was I to do? I suffered through a year of this insanity, at the end of which I told the boys at the nonprofit organization to stuff it, and at the same time expressed to my wife that I could no longer be a part of her insane behavior, either she started to actually act like a human being or we were done. Right about this time, I received two very different offers to engage in business. One to teach, from the college in San Diego that had bought out the school I had worked for in the past; the second from a fine arts publisher located in LA that was offered to me by a person I went to high school with. Once again, holy crap! What the hell to do?

What I did first was clean house. I was near the end of the lease on the house we had been living in and was able to get out of it. I cut ties to the nonprofit, which enabled me to leave the area. My parents were doing OK, so I could move on. I told my wife I would no longer put up with her zany antics; I gave her some funds to work with and expressed that I would soon be filing for divorce. I assisted her in finding a place to live with some friends of hers in Santa Cruz, California. They came and picked her up, we said goodbye, and I never heard from her again. Later, I believe it was around 2010, I heard from a friend of hers that she was found unresponsive in her shower. I was sad for her friends and family, but it seemed to me that it was the inevitable outcome of such an indulgent life.

Back to the matter at hand: after lengthy negotiation with the school, I reluctantly said no. This was one of the toughest choices, as not only was I good at teaching, I also found it very fulfilling. I decided to take the chance and made the leap of faith to work with the fine arts publisher. Finally, after so many years of struggling to make a living via my artwork, I thought I was going to be afforded the opportunity to create art while receiving good and fair remuneration for doing so. The concept of this offering was far beyond amazing to me.

A Brave New World

I met with the publisher and was very impressed with what they had to offer our first meetings showed great promise. Then they came to the point of what needed to happen in order to move forward. Before signing me on to join their seemingly successful corral of artists, I needed to prove to them I could "cut the mustard." I was challenged to create ten works of art in one month's time, then present them to the publisher for review with no guarantee that I would receive anything for the work other than criticism. It had already been established that the work would be done on canvas and suitable for framing as well as being appropriate for their clientele. This was a big order for me at the moment, on many levels. I was without a house to live in, I had very little funds to work with, and I had no studio space. These immediate concerns, combined with the emotional trauma I was dealing with, made for an interesting challenge. I called on a lifelong friend, John for a bit of assistance. This was a person I had known since high school, a man I had always respected and held in high esteem. I presented my challenges to him, and he immediately offered solutions.

His company's offices were not in full use at the time, so the idea was that I would come and stay with him for a month and use his offices as a studio. He lived in the woods up in northern California, a good six-hour drive from where I was at the time. So, I loaded up my little hatchback with about thirteen canvas as large as would possibly fit, along with paints, brushes, work clothes, a carton of Camels, and a half gallon of Jim Beam, and took off to the great white north. I was warmly greeted, and John was ready to assist me in any way he could.

It's important that I briefly shine a light on this man as well as our friendship. From the beginning, John and I were very different from each other. Back in high school, where we first met, I was at best a loose cannon a long-haired creative, cartooning and making music in order to get through school, socially and scholastically inept, and more psychologically impaired than I would like to admit. He, on the other hand, was clean-cut, on the fast track to college, physically admired, and already at his young age commanding respect from his peers. After describing these two characters, I find it hard to believe that we developed a relationship. Regardless, it not only happened, but our bond evolved and grew over time. At this particular point, we found ourselves with over fifty years of experience in putting up with each other. Over time, we have shared good, bad, weird, wild, and insane experiences. As I put down these words, I am compelled to say that he is not only my closest friend, but an impressive individual, and yes, I buried a body for him wait backup I *would* bury a body for him.

I worked steadily for a little over three weeks, more than ten hours pretty much every day. I figured this was a bit more intense than would be required of me in the future, because I didn't have any physical models to use as reference and I was trying to narrow technique and subject matter down in order to find my niche. I ended up with eleven pieces, which seemed the best I could do under the circumstances. These works ranged in size from 20" × 20" to 36" × 48". I stuffed it all back in my little car and drove to middle California, where I hosed off and threw together an invoice. Then I made the five-plus-hour trip to southern California. I did all of this without any expectations that the publisher would contract with me. Arriving there, I was told to lean my work up against the wall in the lobby so that David, the CEO could take a look. I did as I was asked, then did a little pacing while I waited for the big kahuna. After a short time, David the CEO, with an entourage of three other folks, showed up for the kill. He moved from piece to piece, offering only positive comments. At the end of his viewing, he offered me a bit more defined direction for what he'd like to see in the next group. Hell! There was going to be a next group? He then asked for my invoice good thing I had one! Then he added that he wished to buy the entire group of paintings. Hot diggidy! With check in hand, I floated out to my car, high as a kite. Fortunately, my brother and his wife lived in Upland, just east of Los Angeles, so I could stay there the night and not have to drive all the way back to central California. My brother was hugely excited for me and we raised a glass or ten that night. Once again into the fray. I decided to stay with my parents again, and since I now had a little funding, I could rent some studio space for a month. In my price range, I could only afford a small office space, which I found in a couple of days. I covered the entire room with plastic tarps, threw in my easel and work table, and I was just about ready to fly.

Just one more challenge: my work included nudes. Securing nude models is a bit of a challenge anywhere you go, but in Fresno, California, it was simply impossible. I had to get creative eureka! There were a few topless clubs on the outskirts of town. I figured, here are women who get paid to take their clothes off, would it be too much of a stretch to model nude for the sake of art even if it was for a little less money? Apparently, it was a bigger stretch than I thought. I was completing what work I could, then I would hit the topless clubs for a while and try to hook a model. It was taking too much time and energy and it was getting expensive. I was just about to give it up when I finally found a taker. She showed up early the next morning; I photographed her from different angles in different light and different poses. I could only afford her for four hours, so I had to shoot her in mainly generic poses. My efforts helped solve some of the obstacles to my work, and I would get better at this in time.

I was able to turn out ten more works in just under a month's time, and then it was off to the publisher again. Again, the same program played out: spread out the work, David the CEO looked at it, David gave it the thumbs up, publisher cut me a check for all ten pieces, and I was charged with doing it again. This was all great, but I must say it was beginning to wear on my nerves, day after day of uncertainty. Oh well one more time, with feeling. I continued to stay with my folks, renting the office space for my studio, and in less than a month I had created twelve more works, once more delivering all of them to the publisher. This time was a bit different David the CEO and Arron the CFO wanted to talk about the possibility of signing with them. Finally, after three months of kickass work, we were talking turkey! I returned to central California where I received via email a sample of the contract. As I could not afford an attorney, I had a corporate law paralegal review the contract with me. It mainly covered the aspects of exclusivity and publishing, since it had been agreed they were only going to represent "original" work from me the publishing part of the contract was of no consequence to me at the moment. My legal counsel expressed to me that the contract in regards to myself was pretty straight forward and open-ended. Either party could end the relationship with short notice. Over the past months, David had been telling me about the strength of the company and how successful they had made their corral of artists, adding how financially successful they were going to make me, and it all seemed to add up. Prior to signing the contract, I was also informed that as long as I was under contract with them, I could receive a monthly royalty advance. It was explained to me that this was done in order to see me through the startup process, because after they had built up sales of my work it would not be necessary. In regards to this, I was told that I should not concern myself with any sales in the first two years, as they figured it would take at least that long to develop branding for my work. All of this sounded great at the age of just over fifty, for the first time in my life I could finally be a full-time artist, something I had not only desired but felt I was designed for. Prior to signing the agreement, I laid out my current situation in full. My soon-to-be publisher expressed that they thought it best if I was moved closer to their location. Based on all I had been presented with, I signed, at which point the publisher suggested I create a new name for myself to work under. No problem while I was in Yelapa, most folks called me Lorenzo Spanish for Larry and then some of the kids there began calling me Renzo. I liked the name and the publisher did too, so within that short conversation, I became the painter known as Renzo.

I began to search for a home/studio space in southern California. This was 2006, and rents in California, especially Los Angeles, were insane. Under contract, I was still required to produce a minimum of ten works a month, but instead of having access to a royalty advance equal to that, I was informed it would be much less. This was not only immediately disturbing, but also pointed to the inevitability of this project's failure due to the fact I could not afford my existence. David floated an idea to me: David had a piece of property with a house on it, and he offered to let me stay there rent free, indefinitely, if I would agree to take care of the property. Sounded good, but wait! It was a long shot at best: a ten-acre parcel that belonged to the David's parents. It did have a house on it that was nearly functional (if we're being kind). I agreed to look at it. Leading up to the house was over a quarter mile of dirt road I wouldn't waste on a mule with a broken leg if I'm not being clear, it was a really bad road. The house itself was in total disrepair. A bad roof, the exterior was partial old stucco and the rest bare plywood, broken windows, most exterior doors missing, no electrical service, no water service, no phone service, no kitchen cabinets or appliances, two bathrooms with one not hooked up to plumbing and the other simply nonfunctioning, floors a combination of old damaged wood and partially finished damaged ceramic tile, old exposed pipes sticking up through the floor, a really old bad septic tank that I would soon find to be highly problematic, garbage/debris covering most of the interior, plus much more. No one in their right mind would consider this heap to be a residence. But wait there I was, so determined to make things work; I suggested a plan of action. I offered that I would come to the area and stay off-site. I would use my abilities in construction to transform the house to a livable residence. In turn, my publisher would supply funding for all materials and extra labor as required, and I would occupy the residence rent-free indefinitely. This idea got thrown around a bit and eventually was agreed upon in person. This whole process took a fair bit of time; meanwhile, my publisher was anxious for me to get to work. I expressed the cost, time, and energy involved in my relocating myself, and received an interesting response. He asked me how attached I was to my furnishings, then he said he used to do show houses and he had a warehouse full of furniture. He suggested I dump my furniture and just get my butt to southern California, and then he would provide me with furniture on loan to me indefinitely. I was a bit wary of the idea, but I agreed. Again, I was willing to do just about anything the make this project work.

Perris, CA

I sold or gave away most everything I had except for my tools, paints, and clothes, reducing my belongs down to what I was able to fit into my little car. I headed south and moved into a hotel a few miles away from the house for two weeks. I believed that if I put all my energy into the house, I could make it at least livable in that time period high hopes. I arranged for some people to provide the massive labor needed, and when I wasn't working, I was on the horn attempting to gain some order of utilities for my new residence. What a miserable time it was early October and the area was enduring a late summer. We were working without air conditioning, and temps during the day were rising above 117 °F with 70 percent humidity. After about a week, I was wondering what the hell was I doing. There was trouble at every turn.

- There was a huge hive of bees that had set up home in the walls of the house.

- The electrical company refused to connect service because the house's system was so antiquated and required a full inspection.

- There were major issues in obtaining water service.

- The septic tank was overflowing and so toxic no one would pump it out.

- The road to the house was killing my car.

- It was taking more money than my publisher wanted to spend to complete the project.

The house was located in a rural area outside of Perris, California. With my immediate neighbors being goat herders, horse ranches, salvage yards, one regular family, a totally dysfunctional poor white trash family, and a meth lab (plus distribution center), I could not believe what I had agreed to step in. But I achieved what I had set out to do: Relocate myself and bring the house in which I was going to reside into some shape of livability within a little over two weeks. I had already been occupying the house for a few days while I set up my studio; it was now time to change gears from construction to the real work at hand.

I was filled with a raw energy and determination; with little distraction, I was ready to set to my task. At that time, my publisher had agreed to provide me with stretched canvases (which I was overcharged for, of course). Over the last three months, I had been zeroing in on the content of my work, which had always been driven by concept as well as content. I began to solidify the conceptual foundations I was going to be addressing.

My Methodology

Texture: I applied heavy texture to the canvas, even digging and scraping the surface with my fingers to represent the random and impetuous nature of humankind.

Stones/Rocks: I chose stone and rocks because I perceived them to be a most basic element unpretentious, solid, hard, heavy, of the earth, foundational. I used them as metaphors for thought, memory, and emotion. This way, I could offer a physical presence to the intangible.

Symbols: Petroglyphs, pictographs, icons, symbols a few of the most fundamental means of communication. Humans have been using them since the beginning of recorded history. I used them in my work as a secondary means of expressing message. Some of the symbols I used were created by myself, and others were composites devised by combining symbols from different cultures, both ancient and contemporary. I also used mathematical symbols.

Bindings: Wrapped around stones, binding stones together, wrapped around the wrists and ankles of my figures, figures bound together. This represents my belief that everything is connected. All things in our universe have a common bond, interconnected as a network. In my work, I attempt to bring this to light by physically binding elements, or binding elements together.

Nudity: Clothing can depict a specific period in time; it also represents one's social standing or a specific culture. I wished to present to the viewer an environment not relative to a time period nor any single culture. I attempted to address "human qualities" with my work not just one group of people, but humankind as one tribe. I believe this effort is best served by offering the representation of my figures without the restraints of these signifiers: no clothes.

Masks: In my life experience, I've found that everyone I have come in contact with at some point in time has had to put forth a façade or wear a mask, either to protect themself, protect someone else, offer an idea, etc. I have observed this as a human trait and portrayed it as simply as that: everybody wears a mask of some type.

In establishing these conceptual foundations, I had no idea what it might mean in the years to come. I was totally immersed in the idea of creating work, to the point that I was not paying the necessary attention to the rest of my life eating, sleeping, paying bills, and buying groceries. It took me a bit over a month to settle into my new reality. In a very short time, my publisher was already selling my work, contrary to what I was told about it taking a couple of years to "brand" me. I was also getting pressure from the publisher to create works similar to what had already sold. I understood the rationale for the request, but damn! I was so eager to please that I agreed, but only to a matter of degrees. At the time I was still producing work in a similar size parameter as before. Very soon, David began asking for larger works. I didn't even think about the ramifications of the request, I simply said OK. Soon, the size of my work was ranging from 36" × 36" to 48" × 72.

If I might add here, in painting, size matters. When you increase the exterior measurements of a work, yes, you increase the area of the canvas.

But that's where the math stops. To maintain consistency in applying ground, pigment, and finishing, it almost always requires more time and material than one might think. Regarding labor, working larger is never relative to the increase in size it's just more.

In my experience with my technique, to make a painting that measures, for example, 24" × 36", it will require a specific amount of materials, and for the purpose of illustration, I'll say approximately fourteen hours to complete. Making the same painting larger, say 48" × 72", could take more than four times the quantity of materials to complete. More importantly, it could take, more like sixty-five to eighty hours to complete. I had already agreed to a formula for pricing with my publisher. I did this with the understanding that the largest work I would be doing was around 48" x 48". Unfortunately, the formula was not based on price per square inch. Then, I was all of a sudden being called upon for larger works. I think, due to the increasing speed at which things were happening, I will admit I did not address this particular issue in a timely matter, but it would become more prominent in the future.

At this stage in the game, I considered my publisher to be pretty much the incarnation of omnipotence. I saw from our first few meetings that David was a gifted salesperson and that he knew in no uncertain terms how to put on a show. The company had a grand presence, with artwork seeming to fly from its source. I was completely convinced that I had died and gone to heaven. I guess I didn't care if this whole experience was bad, good, or indifferent as long as things continued to play out to be all I had ever dreamed of.

In the first year of my life in Perris, I would produce over 130 paintings. This was not an easy or kind existence for me. I was living in a house that by most folks' standards would be considered trash, I was alone and attempting to repair past emotional trauma, I was demanding way too much of my own physical machinery, and I was trying to maintain ten acres of shite property. Even though I was so intent on keeping the mechanism alive, I was finding myself hard-pressed to meet all the demands. Within the first couple of years I spent producing work for my publisher, I actually documented on the wall of my studio having booked 110 hours of work in a single week. This was far and above the time demanded even of workers at the turn of the twentieth century and ended up bringing about the need to address labor reform in my personal life.

I was out of control, pushing myself to unreasonable standards. In my infinite wisdom, I looked to artificial enhancement for assistance. "Crank" was readily accessible and affordable hell, it was right next door. Stepping into this world, I perceived it to be a calculated risk. It was handy, cheap, and considering I was working in the middle of nowhere, by some strange rationale it somehow made sense. I figured, if I was going take this path, I was going to have to set some ground rules for myself I would never carry or use outside the studio, and I would keep a strict schedule (once when I got up around 4:30 or 5:00 a.m., next around 10:30, then another in the afternoon, and none after 2:00 p.m. to ensure that by midnight, I would have a decent chance to get some sleep). I did my best to abide by this, although they don't call it "abusing drugs" for nothing.

I was obsessed with my work, and my life was revolving around it. When one opens themselves honestly to the brush, it's easy for demons to slip in.

After some months, I was told of an upcoming exhibit for my work that my publisher had arranged with a gallery in southern California. "Cool," I thought to myself. Here was an opportunity to get some feedback on my work from my newly developed clientele. I must interject that after spending hours, days, weeks, and months alone in my studio jamming out work in a surreal environment where the sum of my interactions with the world was defined by said work, the idea of presenting myself and my paintings in public was at the least a little frightening. However, I was up to the challenge. I cleaned myself up, hopped in my little vehicle, and headed off to the posh new gallery in La Jolla, California. Bright lights, expensive cars, self-proclaimed sophisticated folks, the media, and more. It was difficult for me to maintain a level of composure, but I somehow managed to make it through the night.

At one point during the evening, a wonderfully striking young woman was talking to me about my work. I knew she was somehow connected with the gallery, but other than noticing how attractive she was, I didn't pay too much attention at the moment. Toward the end of the evening's festivities, she approached me again, at which time we engaged in an intimate and in-depth exchange about my work and myself. Several times during the conversation, I was thinking to myself, "What the hell is happening here?" It was inconceivable to me, but if I wasn't mistaken, this gorgeous and intelligent young woman was coming on to me? We talked for a very long time, and when it was time to go, she walked with me to my car to bid me goodnight. After a kiss, I left in utter confusion. It was apparent this lovely young lady had some sort of interest in me beyond my work. Holy crap I was so comfortable wallowing in my life as the tortured artist, and now this. We made contact soon after, which was a bit cryptic, but she did make it clear that she had interest in me. Not long after the exhibition, I was asked to attend a dinner that involved the gallery. There she was again, Melanie. We exchanged engaging glances across the table all night. At the end of the evening, when we found a second to be alone, we shared a kiss and an embrace that impacted me as if I had just hugged a nuclear bomb at the point of its detonation. Wow! I had been struck directly in the heart with the full content of the "I am yours" arsenal. Besides the fact that I could not see any reason why this young woman would have anything to do with me, I was completely and totally smitten. Upon returning to my studio, I found myself feeling twitchy through the endless hours of work. I so much wanted to share time with this person, but we were limited to sporadic phone calls.

But there was a political side to this bizarre pseudo-relationship. Not only did Melanie work with the gallery, she was also involved with someone very close to its owner. This made for a professional and ethical disaster waiting to happen. I was so concerned that I even broached the subject with my publisher, who warned me to "run away." Which I did kind of.

I was told by David that I was going to be included in the upcoming New York ArtExpo show, and because it marked a significant anniversary, they were going to bring all their artists along for the ride. This was big news for me, as I had never been afforded the opportunity to show my work in New York before. I busted my hump to prepare for the show, and before I knew it, there I was in the big city. It was incredible; I caught a plane to New York, was picked up at the airport by a stretch limousine, taken to the Marriot in the middle of Manhattan, and deposited into a plush hotel room overlooking the city. That's what I'm talkin' about! Once again, I thought I had arrived.

The experience was incredible. Of course, my publisher had one of the largest and most lavish exhibits there. As I explored the show, exhibiting artists would take a look at my nametag and see who I was affiliated with, then stop me to inquire how they might be accepted by my publisher. This helped solidify my thoughts that I had chosen wisely. Four days of dinners, drinks with gallery owners, meetings with collectors, hours of talking to prospective clients it was a lot to take in.

The first night of the expo, at a VIP engagement that my publisher was hosting, I was shocked when early on in the evening I looked up to see the lovely young woman who had a hold on me, Melanie. Awkward! We both did our best to conduct ourselves in a professional manor. This in itself added a whole new dynamic to the proceedings. Later that evening, we were afforded a little alone time to share some of our intimate thoughts with each other, which lead to a late night of highly charged intimate exchange. After being up all night, I was called early the next morning to meet for breakfast with a couple who owned a gallery in the UK prior to their signing on to represent me through my publisher. Although I was a bit of a wreck, I think the meeting went well, and they did sign.

The excitement continued. During the show, my publisher was launching an exclusive book for one of the other artists obviously a big deal. I recall David taking me aside to offer, "This is you next year." I was overly excited by this notion. All of this elaborate expression made my head spin.

I returned to my seclusion in California with a grand energy, both professional and emotional. I really was not equipped emotionally to deal with all the immediate input, but as always, I trudged forward. I set about painting with great ferocity. After I returned from New York, I attempted to nurture a relationship with the young woman. I began to notice she was becoming even more cryptic and elusive during our phone conversations. At the time, I desired a bit more than just noncommittal talks on the phone. I was looking for a little more defined response and began to move away from her.

One thing my short involvement with this young woman reminded me of was that I am actually "more" when I am in a relationship with a woman. Let me clarify that a *good* relationship. After I sadly broke it off with Melanie, I decided to set myself to task finding a more appropriate woman to be with. At the same time, I was painting up a storm I did not have the time or the funding required to hit the streets looking for romance. Besides, my immediate geographic area was very limiting. So, I hit the internet! Connecting myself with several different sites seemed to be the most efficient means of reaching my goal. Not having done this before, I had no idea what to expect. Employing my knowledge in marketing, I tried to generate the online profile that would attract the person I was looking for. Kind of like fishing without good bait, no good fish.

The response was immediate everything from women who were just looking for a sex toy to women who wouldn't bother if I wasn't guaranteeing a ring and a car. I was amazed at the diversity of the contacts. I had an extended conversation with a twenty-eight-year-old Ukrainian woman living in Florida, who I believe was looking for naturalization, not a relationship. Another woman was living in Santa Monica, California. We got off on such a sweet note that we decided to meet. We met for lunch, and after talking about the future a little bit, we concluded that she was happy living in Los Angeles and I was unwilling to relocate. This was presenting a whole new dynamic to me for the dating process.

Also, while I was painting and attempting to find a relationship, I was also experiencing winter at my home and studio. Although I had done my best to familiarize myself with the ten acres of "bliss," there was still much to learn. The first time the temperature dropped and things froze something I hadn't considered too much since I had lived most of my life in warm climates all at once, I was without water. I went searching about the grounds to find where this disturbance originated. Unfortunately, I found there were exposed pipes everywhere. I did what I needed to do to thaw them out as well as to protect them from future problems. I was finding out that from just about every angle, I was destined to be challenged with something if I was going to be living on this property. During the summer, it reached 118 °F; during the winter, it dropped to 18 °F. There were black widows, scorpions, and centipedes large enough to name. There were meth heads and coyotes (you know, wily four-legged critters, not to be confused with the two-legged creatures of Yelapa) so tenacious that if you left the front door cracked, they'd come on in and make themselves at home. The area was a drop-off spot for unwanted livestock dead horses, sheep, and goats were common. There were two packs of feral dogs that ruled the valley and were not to be taken lightly. Because it was a rural area, the locals would periodically dump their unwanted trash along the road. My mailbox, being over a quarter-mile away from the house where the pavement ended, was a target and was attacked several times, with my mail stolen at least four times. The gas for heating and cooking was propane, so I had to keep watch on my storage tank. In the winter months, when the road to the house would become nearly impassable, there were times when the delivery truck could not deliver my propane. Several times while I lived there, vagrants moved onto outlying areas of the property, at which time I would have to confront them. Both the water and sewage systems were old and required almost constant attention, and more. This place was one constant task.

I had made contact (via the internet) with a woman in the desert northeast of Los Angeles, and we began to communicate on a regular basis. This happened at a time when I was stabilizing my surroundings. Other than being alone and lonely, considering all that was happening, my life was progressing pretty well. The communication between myself and Ruby in the desert was intensifying and we began to email and call each other on a regular basis. There was a little personnel shakeup at my publishing house. When I began working with them, the company consisted of the CEO, CFO, executive secretary, marketing director, director of accounting, head of sales, a graphics engineer, a staff of six sales folks and four warehouse workers. They got rid of the marketing director, changed the title of the executive secretary, and offed two sales folks and one warehouse worker. I guess I should have said downsizing. It seemed all was OK, just normal business stuff. At this point, Ruby and I agreed we had talked enough; it was time to meet face to face. Remembering this, I probably should have paid more attention to how this was playing out in real time. It was an exhausting ordeal to select a time and place to meet. After much conversation, it was agreed upon that I would visit her house, then we would go out for dinner. It was a bit over an hour drive to her location. I hosed off and tried to put on my best, showing up at her doorstep with flowers all bright-eyed and bushy-tailed. When Ruby greeted me at her door, she looked like the photo she had posted online, which was a relief, although she was dressed in a baggy sweatsuit, which left me questioning her choice of dining attire.

We shared a cocktail, and after talking for a while, she mentioned she would rather dine in. One thing led to another, and we didn't end up eating dinner, but I did end up staying the night. This was the start of a bizarre relationship.

Things seemed to progress in a somewhat normal manner, I guess. I continued to work like crazy, now emotionally charged and uplifted at the idea I might have found a partner. My energy was immeasurable I was painting fifty to sixty hours a week while carrying on and driving a few times a week back and forth to visit my newfound interest in the desert. After a while, this became at best insane.

We seemed to get along really well, although she could get a bit tricky now and then. She had expressed to me that she was manic-depressive, also telling me she was a highly jealous person. I hadn't really seen her display any of these tendencies, but it was still pretty early in our relationship. The driving back and forth was starting to get old, and we thought that since we were getting on so well, it might be a good idea to move in together. I closed up the house in Perris and moved to Hesperia. It was great to be playing house again Ruby went off to work five days a week, teaching, and I stayed at home painting in the garage. Life was good for a short time. As

I said, she could get a bit tricky and tricky stared becoming commonplace. She began sleeping 12-13 hours a night, her mania manifested itself as gambling, so we started hitting the casinos a lot. She was missing a lot of work, and finally her jealousy started to show. I couldn't believe how wonderful was turning to not wonderful so quickly.

I remembered telling her when we first got together, "As long as we are able to love, nurture one another, and treat each other with respect, I'm here for good. But I have zero tolerance for chronically troubled relationships I'll be gone in a flash." I don't think she really believed me, because her actions were pushing me right out the door.

During the time I lived with Ruby, I had a couple of exhibitions. My "desert lady" did not fare well at these events. Customarily at exhibitions, I would spend the evening talking with people of course, some of those people were women. Just the fact that I was having a social conversation with a woman other than herself would make Ruby crazy. I had a show in Reno that was not far from where my closest friend, John lives, so I invited him and his girlfriend to attend. The owners of the casino that housed the gallery I was exhibiting in graciously put on a dinner for all of us to celebrate the opening. The evening started out just fine; I was seated in between my girlfriend and John's girlfriend. It just so happened that John's lady friend imbibed a wee bit too much, thus becoming a little feisty. This pushed my girlfriend off the planet and ensured that the rest of my time there was ruined. I might add that this experience combined with all the other destructive behavior convinced me it was time to go. Not long after that, I sat down with Rudy to share my perception of what was transpiring between us and that we were not good for each other. I could not put up with her insanity any longer. I also asked her if she thought she had the capacity to alter her destructive behaviors. Her response was that she did not want to lose me, but she did not believe she could change. I sadly said goodbye and headed back to pick up the pieces in Perris. Once again, not being in the best emotional state, I continued to paint.

After (kind of) surviving my recent interlude, I immersed myself in my work yet again. It became apparent that my publishing house was experiencing more change. First, they let go the marketing director, then a couple more salespeople, and then they replaced their digital graphics person. I not only noticed the organizational change, I also saw a drop in sales. My publisher assured me it was only growing pains and that they were simply adjusting to the changing market. Right around this time, my publisher joined forces with another publishing house, which had the capacity to greatly expand the offerings of my work.

Of course, this also meant increased production requirements for me. My publisher was also putting pressure on me to sculpt. I still maintained the definition of a sculpture as "something you back into while you're looking at a painting." Why were they bothering me to make sculptures? I'm a painter! By now, it was near the end of 2007. You may remember 2008 as the year criminals managing obscene profits in the stock market, banking, and in DC forced an inflated economy to crumble. The consequences of these reprehensible actions were felt by the totality of the country.

The fine art industry was hit hard. Fine art publishers as well as art galleries began falling like well-placed dominos. Prior to this debacle, there were numerous art publishers across the nation. After the fallout, there remained only a handful. Galleries were hit in a similar manner. Due to these closures, my publisher's corral of galleries shrunk in accordance. Fortunately, my publisher had maintained a strong presence in the industry and was thus able to survive. This might be an argument toward Darwin's "survival of the fittest." This occurrence combined with the presence of other issues in the company offered me nothing less than reduced sales. Damn! I was just getting started. It was amazing to me: once again, through no fault of my own, my journey was being dismantled before my eyes. Like so many other folks, I put my head down and pushed forward.

Right around this time, I began communicating with a young woman, Ruth near Los Angeles. The contact was good, but she was a good distance away and it appeared we might be heading in different directions. Ruth expressed to me that the physical distance between us might be an issue, and we broke off communications. I continued on with my work, looking forward to the upcoming ArtExpo in New York.

A Bright Moment

Changing the subject. As I said before, I lived in a rural area. My neighbors up the road (the only normal folks in the general vicinity) had three dogs that roamed the countryside; all three were friendly and would visit my house daily. I knew they belonged to the neighbors, so I did not feed them, although I did put out water for them when it was really hot. There was a sweet-hearted female, an overenergetic male golden retriever, and a goofy smaller female black Labrador. All three of them together were a circus of laughs, and their daily visits brought me a great amount of joy. The little black lab did not have the brains she was born with, but she seemed to enjoy my affection. She became pregnant, and even though my neighbor went to great lengths to provide her with a suitable birthing place, she with her limited brain capacity opted to have her litter in a nearby tick-infested dry creek bed. After a time, I saw a couple of the pups they were completely feral and did not look well. Only one out of eight survived. The surviving pup, cute as he was, unfortunately inherited his mom's brain functions or lack thereof. One sunny afternoon, Mama Lab came for a visit with her last little pup in tail. I went out and sat on the steps of the studio to greet her. She ran to me with great excitement as always, leaving her pup hunkered down in the bush about ten yards away. I got up to get closer to the pup, but both she and the pup moved away. I returned to sit on the steps and Mama Lab returned with her pup hunkering down a wee bit closer to me. I tried to be patient, calling the pup to come not a chance. I sat there for a good thirty minutes in the hope of meeting her new offspring. I was just getting ready to go back inside to work when Mama Lab went over and grabbed the pup by the neck, carrying the frightened youngster to where she dropped him about two feet from me. The poor thing was shaking and curled up in a ball. I didn't say a word, just sat really still. Soon Mama Lab positioned herself on the opposite side of the pup and began to nudge the pup with her snout toward me. I was in complete awe. Finally, once Mama pushed the pup close enough for me to reach, I gently stretched out and caressed the little thing, repeating "it's OK." The pup accepted my embrace and perked up a little; Mama Lab danced around as if she could not contain herself. We all shared a little time together, after which I went back inside to work. The two of them spent the next few hours sleeping on the steps of the studio. This was a magical experience I will always hold in great esteem. Mama Lab and her pup returned off and on for about a week, after which I was never able to get near the pup again.

Ruth

Like I said, I had earlier made contact with a woman online who for some reason didn't wish to continue our correspondence. I would find out later that it was under the advisement of her mother, whom she was living with at the time, suggesting that I lived too far away. Interestingly enough, after a time, we began corresponding once again. I saw Ruth as a possible prospect for my future. Our online communication was good, and after a short time, we graduated to phone conversations, which also went well. This went on for a while, until we both agreed it was time for the ominous face-to-face meeting. Choosing to meet in a "demilitarized zone," we opted for lunch at a restaurant located about halfway between where each of us lived.

The day arrived, and I immediately reviewed my "run for your life" list. Was she on time, did she look like the photo she had presented online (attractive), did she have her own wheels, was she a good communicator, did she present herself well, was she easy to be around, did she display any peculiar behavioral traits? All in all, a pretty nice package. She more than met my requirements. After lunch, we kissed goodbye and agreed to continue forward with our exploration. When I returned home, I realized I was not swept off my feet, nor smitten with love or lust I just felt good inside. We continued communicating and saw each other again; it was during this time I began to discover that this unassuming woman was a real treasure: she was attractive, intelligent, fun to talk to, kind, compassionate, giving, considerate, playful, a hard worker, and more. Wow, could I have stumbled onto something here? Continuing our correspondence, little by little I was introduced to her complexities; she was a damn fine woman. Soon after, she agreed to a "sleepover" at my place; by this time, I was pretty much hooked. I met her mom and that went well; shortly after, she met my folks, which also went well. Damn, other than us moving along so quickly, this was looking like textbook "we should be together."

Yet again, I was demanding a lot from myself. I was spending a great number of hours and energy painting; at the same time, I was expending energy and time nurturing this new relationship. Just as before, trying to juggle all of this began to wear on me. It was also becoming apparent that the relationship between Ruth and myself was evolving into something serious. I knew I was in love with this woman. She offered something to me that I had not been exposed to on a regular basis in a great while joy. No matter how tough things were, how complex the confrontations, or even the fact that sometimes stuff was just weird, Ruth would not only carry on but she would do so with a smile and kindness in her heart. I was a bit unfamiliar with this type of behavior, considering recent encounters. I was becoming ever more aware of the importance of Ruth in my life. I was becoming highly focused on winning her affections to a definite end so much so that I recall a time when I was driving on the freeway to visit Ruth and was daydreaming about her when suddenly I realized I had blown by the exit to her house times two. I had to call her to let her know I was going to be late, but also to share with her why. This small instance would become a mark in our relationship. My heart belonged to Ruth. Being afforded the opportunity to possibly share my life with a woman of such quality was beyond my comprehension. One of my life choices that screamed Yes!

One time, we met to enjoy a dinner out. Dinner was good, and after dinner, we decided to go for a walk. During our little journey, we stopped walking and talking to take a break for a kiss ok, maybe a bit more than a kiss we were standing in the middle of the sidewalk, making out. Anyone witnessing these displays of affection I am certain was thinking to themselves, "Get a room!"

It was time for the next step. I asked Ruth to move in with me. I figured if she was OK with living in the house in Perris, she would be up for anything. To my surprise, the little trooper said yes, and before either one of us could find a good reason not to, we were playing house together out in the badlands of southern California. She was working as a purchaser for an industrial lubricants firm, and I was working my butt off painting, anxiously awaiting the financial rewards promised by my publisher.

211

With Ruth moving in, I thought it might be a good time to clean up my act a bit. I decided to stop with the artificial enhancements (crank). She was aware of what I had been doing, but she had agreed to sign on anyway, and that was the end of my bad behavior, at least that particular bad behavior.

Right around this time, I spoke with my publisher only to receive discouraging news: I was not going to be premiered at the upcoming ArtExpo in New York, as I had been promised earlier. I was told that for political reasons, they were showcasing an artist who had been with them longer than I had. This was a harsh reality to accept. I had not only been busting my hump producing work for the event, I had also offered it to my new partner as a grand experience we were both about to partake in. This was one of many challenges that would be instrumental in shaping my new existence with Ruth

It's hard to describe how important this new relationship was to me. Financially we were doing OK, and it seemed like there might be new things on the horizon for us. Ruth was one of the sweetest things to happen to me in a long time. Here's a woman I actually could visualize spending the rest of my life with. So, what's a guy do when he meets a girl that he wants to grow old with? Ta da, you get ten points if you said, "You ask her to marry you." Fourth time's a charm. Filled with anticipation, I booked a cottage at Big Bear Lake (just east of Los Angeles in the San Bernardino Forest). We had gone there fishing a couple of times, so I hoped she would not suspect anything. I was giving my best clandestine performance. We arrived at the lake and drove around scoping out where to fish. Of course, we were looking for fishing spots near where I had secretly secured the cottage. It was getting late in the afternoon as we drove by the cottages. "This looks really cute," I said, suggesting we stop and check out what the prices were like; heck we might want to come back and spend a weekend. I picked up the keys from the office while Ruth waited in the car. I returned holding up the keys to the cottage. Happily, I offered, "Hey, we're in no hurry, let's take a look. If we like it, I'll book us a reservation." Ruth and I meandered through the little gnome dwellings till we arrived at the one I had previously selected. Prior to our arrival, I had made arrangements with the folks that managed the place to ready the interior with one dozen roses on any surface large enough to hold them (trust me, it was a small place, not that many surfaces large enough for a good size bouquet), a table in the middle of the room with, of course, more roses, a bottle of Dom Perignon on ice with two champagne flutes, and two chairs artfully displayed beside the table. Oh! Don't forget the rose petals, carefully placed on the floor and the bed. Hey! I wanted my best chance at her saying, yes. I opened the door; Ruth walked in. I don't recall what she said, but her eyes were as big as quarters. She turned around and gave me a great big hug. I won't bore you with all the mushy stuff that followed; the point of the story is that she said yes. Neither of us wanted a big wedding. We set a date a couple of months out. June 13th we were married in a courtroom in Los Angeles, with a few friends and relatives attending. After the ceremony we all went to dinner at a wonderful Mexican restaurant; fun was had by all. After dinner, Ruth and I said our good byes and headed south to San Diego for the honeymoon. Since we were already living together, we both just carried on.

Not long after this, David, my publisher finally wore me down. I agreed to take a stab at sculpting.

This was a big step on my part, knowing very little about the discipline of sculpture. Sure, in my forty-plus years of experience in design, display, and exhibit design, I'd had some practice with creating the human form in 3D, but nothing really to prepare me for the journey I was about to embark on. This besides the fact I had never had much interest in the discipline. It was obvious I had some challenges ahead, with the immediate issue being "where the hell to start?"

I grabbed a couple of books on working with clay; from there, I went to the internet to research current techniques and locate material sources. I felt like I was lost in the woods without a compass. All the information was overwhelming. Without someone to instruct me, I was left to trial and error in order to sort things out. After a couple of meager attempts at bossing around the clay with no desired outcome in mind, I figured, "you need to do and practice the thing you are intending." I did and failed on just about as many levels as I found success. Going through this process helped remind me of how I began to be involved in the arts in the first place.

Sometimes, one's vision can be as important, possibly more important, than the sum of knowledge gathered and synthesized in regards to that specific discipline.

At any rate, I began to move forward in my practical application to produce a concept figure of my own in clay, ready and worthy to be cast for a limited-edition bronze. If you're wondering, yes, I was still being pushed to create paintings alongside the sculptures. Of course, the first work I chose to create, due to my ignorance of working with clay, was a squatting figure. When I was becoming very frustrated in attempting its completion, I joined in conversation with other sculptors via online chat rooms, only to find out squatting or kneeling figures posed challenges even to seasoned sculptors. After massive amounts of hours devoted to learning this new discipline, I was able to bring to completion three works in clay that would be ready for casting in around three months. Hell, even I was impressed. Over the next few years, I would create well over twenty-five sculptures in clay set to be foundered in bronze for limited editions.

It was now 2008, and this last bit of time I think offered as much adventure as the preceding years. I was now juggling my craft at painting as well as nurturing my sculpting, a newly acquired discipline, while adapting to a new relationship. All of this proved to be a lot. Sound familiar? Ruth and I attended an event put on by my publisher where we were seated at a table with various clientele, one of whom was an HR person responsible for recruiting people for possible employment at a rare earth mine near the border of California and Nevada. Ruth immediately struck a chord with this person. There was much conversation to follow, and within weeks we were exploring the possibility of Ruth being employed as an executive assistant for the corporate part of a mining operation. This was a lot to consider, as the closest city to the mine was Las Vegas, Nevada. To translate, this would mean moving to a new state.

The task proved to be as difficult as it seemed. Ruth needed to begin her employment prior to the time we could relocate. This created all sorts of trouble we were living apart, keeping two households, and somehow, on my own, I was required to secure a new domicile in a different state and to transport all of our stuff to that place at a time not particularly of my choosing. Also, I was still required to maintain a steady flow of paintings and sculptures. Oh, and yes, all of this was being done in between folding paper bags and studying to be a nuclear physicist (that last comment was a joke, just a little comic relief). Damn, it was a lot to ask of one's self.

Driving a forty-two-foot moving van with a twenty-four-foot vehicle trailer attached basically made me the length of a medium-sized semi. Unless you have actually experienced something like this, you may not understand the gravity of the situation. OK, so it got done.

A note: When I met my angel of a partner, Ruth, I was still fully engaged with the promises and future vision of my publisher. Over the course of time, this would become apparently unfounded. Oh crap! I met a wonderful individual, courted her with an incredible future, and within a short amount of time, had to face her with my failure to recognize the deceit of my publisher and its effect on my existence. This is one of the few things I regret in my life.

So, there I was, new to Las Vegas. If you're not aware, Las Vegas as a whole is a good size. Top to bottom, about twenty-five miles; side to side, about twenty-two miles. Approximately 550 square miles, a bit over 2,651,000 people, a lot of flash, commerce, development, crazy stuff, international influx, small-town politics, and a whole lot more. Relocating to Las Vegas was not just relocating to a new area. The entity of Las Vegas asked much more. I located a place where we could live and I could work score. Survived all the moving in and setting in. All of a sudden, Ruth and I were existing and moving forward in our new domicile and life experience. For a while we reveled in our accomplishment and moved forward. At this point, I was still going pretty strong with my publisher new paintings to do and new sculptures to be made ready.

After a time, things began to slow, mainly in the art arena. After doing a few exhibitions nationwide, sales as well as communication began to drop. All of a sudden, I not only did not have revenue coming in for what I had already produced, but I was not in regular contact with the folks who were responsible for promoting my product. As time passed, I was not being called on by my publisher to produce more paintings, only sculptures. Also, during this period, I produced my first life-size sculpture quite an undertaking.

My wife was also dealing with many changes in her work environment. Being the trooper that she was, she met them head-on and for the most part seemed to be advancing rapidly. All in all, things were not too bad. We were both becoming more and more acclimated to our new environment. And exploring our new world, we found new outdoor adventures to involve ourselves in at Red Rock state park, Valley of Fire state park, Mt. Charleston, and various other locations. Las Vegas was not just an entertainment and casino-based destination.

Over time, things did not improve with my publisher. A little over a year earlier, David had called and told me that at the request of the board of directors, all artist royalty advances were to be cut by one third. Since sales were diminished, royalty advances were what I was surviving on at that time. To that point, the day after Christmas, David called to say that due to the downturn of the market, I was not going to receive any more royalty advances. With a single phone call, my work was shut down. I inquired why he waited until after Christmas to inform me of this; the response was that he did not want to ruin my Christmas. Holy crap! I just approached a major holiday knowing funding was in place, and the day after I was told it was not, because they did not wish to screw with my holiday. What kind of screwed up mind thinks that. In the next couple of days, my publisher reinstated my royalty advance, adding that it was at his personal expense (although I have my doubts).

Things were dissipating. My publisher was building a new presence in China Beijing, Shanghai, Macau, Hong Kong. I was told I would be represented prominently in this new arena. Of course, as time progressed,

I would find this not to be the case. As I learned of more exhibitions promoted by my publisher in China and more artists represented by my publisher traveling to the area for exhibition, I began to ask, "What about me?" I was offered positive information and told to be patient. Later, I would realize this was merely placation.

I was slowly becoming disenchanted with these folks whom I had so eagerly signed up with seven years earlier. I had become so attached to this process over the course of years, it was hard to let go. So much had transpired, just not enough to move me forward in the art industry.

I continued to work, and so did Ruth. I had not had a price increase in several years, so I alerted my publisher I would be increasing my rates by 20%. The response was immediate and direct. At my next exhibit, the price per piece was raised exponentially, and I was informed that the maximum percentage taken by my publisher would be enforced. Damn I increased my artist price by 20%, but the publisher's response was to double the current price plus 50 percent, making their take 250 percent of what it had been. This may not make much sense to most folks: simply put, a painting that was before being offered at $10,000 was now being offered at over $25,000. Overnight, the retail value of my work had more than doubled, having little or nothing to do with the marketplace. This was at least a bit alarming. In just a few years, I had gone from looking at a promising future, to what the hell. I was still producing a fair amount of work. My wife and I were fully embedded in Las Vegas. Ruth was working at the mine, and I was working fiercely out of my studio.

Around this time, I did a little research into the purchasing trends of folks with similar demographics as my clientele regarding what type of art was selling best. You know: classical, traditional, modern, contemporary, conceptual, abstract, abstract expressionist, figurative, portraits, etc. One thing stood out almost immediately: contemporary, abstract, and abstract expressionism was selling much better than classical figurative work. Equipped with the information I had just dug up, I immediately prepared a presentation to share with my publisher, intending to alter my style to a more contemporary approach. At first, they were strongly opposed to the idea, but after some talk back and forth, I convinced them it was a good idea. Once again, I set about the task of recreating my style as well as my technique. The change was not overly difficult, and almost overnight, I found myself producing, in my opinion, conceptually based contemporary paintings. I must add, they began to sell immediately.

The art market in Las Vegas was and remains a bit tricky at best. There were seemingly only two arenas. One: high-end, very commercial art sold out of casinos and resorts or very limited individual gallery space. Two: emerging artists, often just out of school, working in the "Arts District." I did not fit into either of these scenes, and there was no apparent middle ground in the environment for an internationally established, functioning artist to turn for local representation.

I hope you're still with me. Writing this, I find it might be a bit laborious for folks to sort through, but in order to grasp the reality of what was transpiring, it seems reasonable to fill in at least most of the blanks. I tell this story not so much to record my history but to offer insight into the life of an artist which might be a little different than you imagined.

For a while, even with all the stuff that was happening, things seemed to move forward. Both my wife and I worked hard and tried at every moment possible to entertain ourselves and embrace our newfound environment.

Medical Issues

Being covered by medical insurance was new to me I had not had health insurance since back when I was at the school in San Diego (1999) and I thought it might be a good thing to take advantage of the opportunity. As most people in the US know, the first step is to connect with a primary care physician. I did so, approaching the physician with my back pain and tremors. What took place in the short time after was a bit insane. The doctor completely ignored what I initially came in for, only focusing on the fact that I smoked that was the inherent problem to address. I went through a myriad of tests and procedures regarding my lung functions. I was tested for COPD, and when the test results returned negative (meaning I did not have COPD or any other problems with my lungs), I saw that the doctor was physically disturbed. To my amazement, the doctor continued to obsess over my lack of lung and heart symptoms while remaining passive in regard to what I actually came to see her about. Meanwhile, she did manage to prescribe to me copious amounts of narcotics to help manage my back issues. This would prove to be a very difficult period of time. Sorry to bore you with all of this, but these events not only had a defining effect on my life, but also a consequential effect on my art.

Now I was taking large amounts of narcotics for pain management accompanied by procedures for the same. At the same time, I was informed that, according to one of the many lung images I had done, I had a blood clot in my right lung. I had no symptoms, but according to medical practice, it was there. What happened next was again insane. I was immediately locked down from any travel and began a regiment of blood thinner shots I had to administer myself several times a day into my abdomen. This was by no means fun, and continued for several months. For a short time, I had pretty much shut down producing artwork, but as I eased out of the presumed crisis, I started to work again. At this time, I thought back to earlier times, remembering music from the Allman Brothers. I had always wondered how this group of musicians could make such incredible music while strung out on heroin I found myself on a similar journey. While taking a good deal of morphine, Percocet, and other narcotic pain meds, I too was attempting to create good art while under their influence. Looking back, I see it was a messy time. Not so much the artwork, but I found trying to navigate the business end of making art was offering much more of a challenge. Phone communications, emails, letter correspondence all seemed to be disconnected and somewhat blurry. As I remember this time, I felt as if I were like looking on while someone else did the deeds. I offer my apologies to whomever I communicated with at that time. What a train wreck! After all of this craziness, I was finally referred to a back surgeon, and within a short time, I found myself scheduled for surgery. I went through the process and made it out of the other end of the tunnel, and after several months of recovery again propped up with a lot more pain meds I was ready to embrace the universe as a somewhat functioning human being. During this time, I dove into my work and produced a fair amount of art. I was now moving away from the pain meds, seemingly going back to what I considered normal.

My relationship with my publisher was becoming a bit strained so much had changed. Communication had dropped off dramatically (I found myself calling them much more than they contacted me), sales had dropped again, and I had been promised things that weren't coming to fruition, noticing that their other artists were being promoted in arenas where I could function well. All of this was compounded by the publisher now marking my work up 250 percent plus framing and handling. I was very frustrated that things had deteriorated to such a state. Things became so intense that I chose to take a leap of faith and negotiated to set up terms for me to work out of my contract. Over the next months, we negotiated a settlement. Of course, this negotiation favored the publisher. It was astonishing nearly ten years of representation down the drain in one pull of the handle.

Now without representation, I sought other venues. I made contact with a gallery I had worked with before, and they readily took me on. Amazingly, sales were brisk and offered great prospects in the first year once things got rolling. As in the earlier days, I was so excited, and suddenly no longer under the thumb of an overseer. Possibly, I had made a good choice here.

Unfortunately, this perceived wellness and seemingly good fortune did not last for long. A bit more than two years after my first surgery, things began to go south with my back. I was experiencing more symptoms and requiring more medical attention just to maintain some sort of normality. Again, after many more pain meds and procedures, I found myself before a surgeon. Things had become so bad at this point that I had virtually stopped doing art again. I was informed I had to stop smoking and drinking alcohol for one month prior to surgery damn, two out of my three favorite indulgences. Once again, I found myself prepped and waiting in a hospital bed, not so eager but somewhat ready to go under the knife. Then, here we go I remember being instructed to count from one hundred backward: one hundred, ninety-nine, ninety-eight, ninety-seven, ninety? And I was off with the fairies. About twelve hours later, I awoke to a war zone. The first thing I saw was a large group of folks adorned in surgical scrubs hovering over me. The next thing I remember is excruciating pain; as I began to thrash about, I recall someone yelling for more of something the actual name I do not recall, but I presume it was some type of anesthesia. I don't recall much about this time, but I was told that I came out of surgery and was placed in a hospital room for a day. The next day, I went back into surgery another eight hours of cutting. This time when I awoke, I was not really awake. As I was informed later by my wife, I was in and out for three days.

I think I have already bored you with too much medical information, although I believe it relevant to the whole story. Although I do not quite remember, I believe I was in the hospital for about a week, then I was taken to a rehab facility. This time is really fuzzy, as I was on massive amounts of pain meds. I will not regale you with all of the laborious details. I miraculously somehow came out the other side as something resembling a human being. After twenty hours of surgery, I could walk again, sort of whoopie!

Recovering from this ordeal was a big task. I must state that without the tenacious, unflinching care and unconditional love bestowed on me by my wife during this time, I know I would not be here today. I do not know where she found the strength and energy to carry on. My goddess.

After about three months, I was moving about the cabin without too much trouble. I began to slowly get back to work, though not without problems. Even though I could walk, I was still suffering the effects of the brutal physical assault on the operating table. I had been on the pain meds for over a year at this point, and doing business proved to be interesting. Needless to say, I wasn't quite myself.

Also, during this time, as I was attempting to recover from surgery, I noticed my tremors were worsening. Addressing the universe, damn, can you cut me just a wee bit of slack? I cannot quite remember how many times in my past I had adjusted not only the way I approached my art, but my technique as well. Where was it going to end? At this time, I was only using alcohol to ease the tremors. Just a reminder, in the past, alcohol had actually been prescribed by physicians as a last resort to addressing tremors when nothing else worked; also, when prescribed, alcohol was intended in small doses and for a specific period of time, not forever and with ever increasing quantities.

I was informed via the gallery I was working with that I had a commission available if I wanted it. It was a good-sized project; I was quite willing to take it on even though I'd had issues with the client in the past. This was a person from abroad whom I did not particularly trust. The commission required multiple large works to be done in a short amount of time, and in the end both myself and the gallery ended up being short-changed. Overall, this project was uncomfortable for both myself and the gallery. Over the next year or so, sales flattened out. I continued producing work, it just did not seem to be the right mix for the clientele I was being offered by the folks representing me. This story goes on, much like other stories about people's lives. No, I'm not dead yet. I am still working and looking for new arenas to promote my work. Living here in Vegas, sharing life with my wife, Ruth.

For my next trick, I volunteered for brain surgery, a deep brain stimulator implant my last resort to address the blasted tremors that have been such a damn nuisance for so long. Attempting to orchestrate this in the middle of the COVID-19 pandemic was quite the trick, almost as tricky as the procedure itself. For those of you who might be curious, here is the shortened version of the procedure: Two holes are cut in the skull, right and left side, top front of the head. Once the brain is exposed, two four-inch rods (the stimulators) are pushed into the brain. You recover for a few days, then a small incision (about three inches) is made just under the collar bone on the right side of the chest, where the sending unit and battery are inserted in between the skin and muscle; at the same time, two connecting wires are run just under the skin, up over the shoulder, up the neck, and along the right side of the head to connect the sending unit/battery with the stimulators. After about three weeks of recovery from all this, you pay a visit to your local neurologist, at which time the system is turned on and they begin the process of dialing you in, or making adjustments. The system's battery is rechargeable and lasts for over ten years. I even get my own personal remote control. After going through this process, I'll say it was necessary and somewhat successful, but not the miracle I was hoping for.

Okay. It's time to put this puppy to bed. As with many other things in my life I never imagined myself doing, I never thought I would invite the public to share in my life experiences as a person and as an artist via the written word. I am hopeful that after reading through this mass of words, you might gain a bit of insight into what it means to be a person who is considered by themselves as well as others to be an "artist," whatever that may mean. If not, I hope you were at least entertained.

Merriam-Webster

Definition of Art

The conscious use of skill and creative imagination especially in the production of aesthetic objects

Oxford English Dictionary

Definition of Art

The expression or application of human creative skill and imagination, typically in a visual form such as painting or sculpture, producing works to be appreciated primarily for their beauty or emotional power.

My Personal Definition of "Visual Art":

As a fundamental descriptor, I subscribe to the premodern, pseudo classical description of "visual art" as being one of the humanities and therefore requiring the application of a discipline. Without the discipline, there's no "art"; without the application of discipline, it's just one's personal expression, nothing more.

Yeah, enough deep thought. I have survived much longer than I thought I might, and in doing so, after listening to scores of folks tell me "you're an artist" as well as "your life is interesting," I figured I might put a few words down to document it, just in case it might be so.

Exhibitions and Gallery Representation

USA: Washington State, California, Massachusetts, Nevada, Colorado, New Mexico, Arizona, Texas, Louisiana, Arkansas, New York, Indiana, Kentucky, Florida.

China:

Shanghai, Hong Kong, Beijing, Macau

Other Countries

Canada, Germany, UK, Russia, Mexico

Museum Affiliations

The DeYoung Museum of Art, California (slides of my work accepted into the museum's archives in 1975)

The Crocker Museum of Art, California (purchased my work in1976)

The Hot Springs Museum of Contemporary Art, Arkansas (one-person exhibition, collected work of mine in 2012)

The Dolan Museum of Modern Art, Shanghai (collected one work of mine in 2013)

The Coral Springs Museum of Fine Art, Florida (one-person exhibition, collected two works of mine in 2014)

The Evansville Museum of Art, Indiana (one-person exhibition, collected one work of mine in 2015)

Current Representation
Simard Bilodeau Contemporary

1923 South Santa Fe Ave. Los Angeles, CA, 90021

The Peninsula, 14th Floor, The Bund, Shanghai, China 200002

Metropolitan Gallery Las Vegas Art Museum

450 Fremont St. Las Vegas, NV, 89101

Larry Lewis

(AKA Renzo)

Painter, Sculptor, Author